MEDIA

PAST, PRESENT AND FUTURE

MEDIA

PAST, PRESENT AND FUTURE

W. Lambert Gardiner

Academica Press
Bethesda

Library of Congress Cataloging-in-Publication Data

Gardiner, W. Lambert.
  Media : past, present, and future / W. Lambert Gardiner.
    Includes bibliographical references and index.
    ISBN 1-933146-00-1
  1. Mass media—History. I. Title

P90.G354 2005
302.23—dc22   2004022397

British Cataloguing data are available

Editorial Inquiries:
Academica Press, LLC
7831 Woodmont Avenue, #381
Bethesda, MD 20814
Website: www.academicapress.com
To order: (650) 329-0685 phone and fax

TABLE OF CONTENTS

LIST OF FIGURES

ACKNOWLEDGMENTS

The solitary nature of writing a book as opposed to creating a film is discussed in Section 4.4. That's why there is not a long list of credits at the beginning and end of a book. Writing a book is, however, only *relatively* solitary. I had more than "*a little help from my friends*".

Colleagues helped. Dr. Ira Nayman, and Dr. Edgar Zurif (with Dr. Françoise Zurif reading over his shoulder) all read various parts of various drafts of this book and made many helpful suggestions for its improvement. Dr. Ray A. McKenzie who works in Silicon Valley for Fujitsu – wrote a 100-page critique of the history section of the book in which he convinced me that it was the back story for his hi-tech industry. Thank you, Ray, now here is the front story! Their precise contributions are acknowledged in context in the text. Dr. Gail Valaskakis and her colleagues in the Department of Communication Studies at Concordia University in Montreal also helped by inviting me back into the academy after a fifteen-year "sabbatical". This offered me the rare opportunity of focusing on one discipline from the point of view of another. This book could only have been written by someone educated in psychology and then immersed for 20 years in Media Studies.

Publishers helped. Stan Wakefield found a home for my book at Academica Press where it was warmly welcomed by Ginger McNally and Dr. Robert West.

Neighbors helped. Dr. Ray Charron read the whole manuscript. He tore it apart in the evening and helped me put it together again, in much better shape, over breakfast. Dr. Maben Poirier didn't read the manuscript - he didn't have to since I "talked" the book to him on the train to our classes on the Loyola Campus of Concordia University. He made many useful suggestions. Trisha Santa helped me upload my messy mind to an elegant web site (www.siliclone.com) and to transform my messy manuscript into a camera-ready book. In the process, she taught me a lot about the fourth generation of media.

Students helped. They are mentioned here and there throughout the text but are, as is the academic tradition, rarely identified. Someone should erect a monument to The Unknown Student. Playing professor is a wonderful way to get an education. They teach us as much as we teach them. This is especially true in fast-moving times like now when the old can no longer say (with a straight face) that they can guide the young into the future since they have been there. My students, who are more at home on the other side of the "digital divide" with video- and computer-based media, kindly help *me* feel more at home there. This book is thus dedicated to my students. May it help them move into the future with less fear and more hope.

CHAPTER 1
PRE-HISTORY AS PROLOGUE

1.1   WHY PRE-HISTORY?

1.2   THEORY OF EVOLUTION

1.3   CO-EVOLUTION OF PERSON AND MEDIA

1.4   COMMUNICATION VERSUS CONFLICT

The further backward you look, the further forward you can see.
Winston Churchill

All humans do it. Gossip, schmooze, chitchat, gab, talk, tattle, rap, banter, discuss, debate, and chew the fat. Why? To exchange information, share knowledge, criticize, manipulate, encourage, teach, lie, and self-promote.
Marc T. Hauser, 2000

(Our) ways of knowing and core intuitions are suitable for the lifestyle of small groups of illiterate, stateless people, who live off the land, survive by their wits, and depend on what they can carry. Our ancestors left this lifestyle for a settled existence only a few millennia ago too recently for evolution to have done much, or anything, to our brains. Conspicuous by their absence are faculties suited to the stunning new understanding of the world wrought by science and technology.
Steven Pinker, 2002

We've arranged a global civilization in which most crucial elements - transportation, communications, and all other industries; agriculture, medicine, education, entertainment, protecting the environment; and even the key democratic institution of voting - profoundly depend on science and technology. We have also arranged things so that almost no one understands science and technology. This is a prescription for disaster. We might get away with it for a while but sooner or later this combustible mixture of ignorance and power is going to blow up in our faces.
Carl Sagan, 1996

What's Past is Prologue.
William Shakespeare, THE TEMPEST, Act 2, Scene 1

1.1   WHY PRE-HISTORY?

HISTORY is mostly STORY - the HI is just to get your attention. So HI - now here's the STORY.

But when does the story of media begin? Who made the Big Bang? Who heard it? There is merit in going far back to the beginning, but perhaps not that far back. That was way before our time. We appeared only during the Pleistocene Era of the Quaternary Period in geological time (1,800,000 to 10,000 years ago). That is, we appeared on the global stage only in the fourth act. During that era, there was a more-recent but less-familiar Big Bang - not of the universe but of the brain. There was a sudden explosion of human creativity - cave paintings, ornaments buried with the dead, musical instruments - about 35,000 years ago. There are differences of opinion about the date, about the "suddenness" of the event, and about its cause. William Calvin attributes it to the shift from protolanguage (using only simple subject-verb-object sentences) to true language (using complex sentences) [CALVIN].[1]   Stephen Mithen attributes it to some genetic change in the brain which permitted three brain modules, specialized in social intelligence, mechanical intelligence, and natural history, to communicate more effectively [MITHEN].

For us, it is important only to note that the breakthrough involved language. During that Pleistocene Era, two candidates were competing to be our ancestors - Cro-Magnon and Neanderthal. The former survived and evolved into us, whereas the latter became extinct. Neanderthal was bigger, faster, and stronger than Cro-Magnon but Cro-Magnon had a vocal apparatus which could emit a wider range of sounds, and thus a more sophisticated language. The Big Bang thus occurred in the Cro-Magnon brain but not in the Neanderthal brain.

---

[1]   References appear in the text in upper case within square brackets. The full reference appears in the alphabetical Reference section at the back of the book.

Communication was an important factor right from the beginning. This book focuses on the Holocene Era (10,000 to the present) - that is, since the beginning of the agricultural society, when the hunter-gatherer settled down. It argues that during this Holocene Era, our species has extended itself by piggy-backing media on to language, acquired during the Pleistocene Era.

The traditional theory has been that the original function of language was to enable us to cooperate to hunt large animals. We will consider later (Section 2.1) more recent arguments that language evolved not so much because we hunted large animals but because large animals hunted us. As relatively small, slow, and puny animals, we banded together for mutual protection. We are social animals and thus heavily dependent on communication. The fact that communication continues to be very important today was driven home to me by an empirical study I conducted on myself (see Section 16.1). I kept a record of the time I spent communication and found that I consistently spend over 70 hours a week - that is, more than 10 hours a day - communicating.

Traditionally, the collective biography of our species - history - starts with our invention of writing. However, our pre-history has had a profound impact on our history. Here are five advantages of starting our story with pre-history rather than with history.[2]

• A HAPPY BEGINNING Life does not have a happy ending.[3] However, it has a happy beginning. Each of us receives the conception-day gift of all the wisdom our species has accumulated over thousands of years of survival

---

[2] Some of my students have asked why my lectures tended to cover FIVE points. It's because I write my notes on my fingers and I have five fingers. There was a cocktail party before a lecture I gave to the Canadian Association of Secretaries in Toronto. The glass of Scotch on the rocks thickened my Scottish accent and wiped out my notes. When I started to enumerate my five points, I discovered that my notes were gone and had to come clean. Now that my dirty little secret is out, you might as well know that this is part of my operating manual.

[3] Later, in Chapter 12, we will consider attempts at eternal life, by people who aspire to prevent the unhappy ending.

in a harsh environment. You were born wise. Social science has been dominated, till recently, by the **Standard Social Science Model (SSSM)**.[4] This model assumes that the mind at birth is a blank slate (**tabula rasa**) on which culture writes. Your tabula was far from rasa. Your mind is a medium shaped by the past experience of our species and it in turn shapes the content assimilated from your culture. Steven Pinker documents this process in detail in his recent book *The Blank Slate: The Modern Denial of Human Nature* [PINKER 2002].

• A FIRM FOUNDATION   In another book - modestly entitled *How the Mind Works* [PINKER 1997] - Steven Pinker argues that the theory of evolution is the basic theory of psychology. This places psychology within the firm foundation of biology. Pinker argues further that the function of the nervous system is the processing of information to enable the organism to survive. My previous book - *A History of Media* [GARDINER 2002] - placed media studies in turn within this firm framework of psychology, by arguing that media are best considered as extensions of our nervous system.

• A COHERENT STORY   What we know of the history of media tends to be a miscellaneous collection of facts and theories, anecdotes and opinions. The pre-historical context provides a coherent story. The Big Story of historical time is the co-evolution of the person and media as extensions of the nervous system. We are born with a means of storing information (memory) and a means of transmitting information (speech). This first generation of media was adequate for a hunter-gatherer society. However, our inventions of an agricultural society, an industrial society, and now an information society, required correlated inventions of media to extend our nervous systems. We had to store information outside our bodies (Print and Film - second generation), transmit information outside our bodies (Telephone and Television - third generation) and both store

---

[4]   Technical terms appear in bold. Definitions can be found in the Glossary at the back of the book.

and transmit information outside our bodies (Multimedia and Internet - fourth generation).

• A CONSISTENT THEORY   Media studies is a pre-paradigmatic discipline.[5]   That is, there is no broad framework, widely accepted by the scholars in the discipline, within which they work. This book aspires to provide such a broad framework by fitting media studies into perhaps the most widely-accepted paradigm of all - the theory of evolution. There is no generally accepted theory of history. There is, however, a theory of pre-history - the theory of evolution. Our species has co-invented social and media systems to survive in our changing cultural environment - agricultural society and the second generation of Print and Film, industrial society and the third generation of Telephone and Television, information society and the fourth generation of Multimedia and Internet. We have witnessed over the last ten thousand years of our evolution the unfolding of the human potential.[6]

• A LONG PROJECTION   It's not possible to move confidently into the future from a standing start (the present). It's necessary to go back into the past to take a long run at the future. Historian Arnold Toynbee uses the metaphor of trying to see yourself in a mirror with your nose pressed against it. You have to stand back to see clearly. Chapters 2 to 8 describe the long run in the past; Chapters 10 to 18 describe various jumps into the future, with a pause in the present (Chapter 9) to consider where to jump. I hope that this book enables you to move into the future with more hope and less fear.

---

[5]   Actually, it's NON-paradigmatic. There seems to be little movement towards creating a paradigm, which may help explain the low status of the discipline within the university (see Section 3.2). Part of the motivation behind this book is to fit Media Studies within the evolutionary paradigm and thus establish its central role within the university.

[6]   This implies that psychology is the central discipline. ALL professors argue that their discipline is central. The other professors are wrong!

1.2   THEORY OF EVOLUTION

Our story opens then in a quiet country home in an English village. The first character in our cast is seen puttering about in his greenhouse and muttering about in his library. It was in this place and in this manner - apart from a famous voyage around the world aboard the H. M. S. Beagle - that Charles Darwin (1809 - 1882) [7] spent most of his life. Yet this uneventful life of this unassuming man in this unspectacular setting has had a greater impact on our world than the lives of the more flamboyant figures - the Caesars, the Napoleons, the Hitlers - who have stomped around our globe.

Darwin created a revolution. Not that shoddy shift in political personnel that typically passes for a revolution, but a real revolution - a change in our view of ourselves. After carefully collecting and collating evidence for 17 years, Darwin gently but firmly told us that we are not a special creation of God with an exclusive soul but an animal on the same scale as our dogs and our cows [DARWIN].   After the inevitable violent reaction - Scopes v. State of Tennessee, Professor Huxley v. Bishop Wilberforce - we swallowed this bitter pill. Indeed, we now find it not only palatable but sweet.   Most of us feel better as raised apes than as fallen angels.[8]

We are all familiar with the basic principles of the **theory of evolution.** Here, however, is a Rip Van Winkle special by way of reminder. There are differences among individuals within any species. Because of certain

---

[7]   Names with dates in the text indicate that this is one of the major characters in our story. This person is included in the Cast of Characters (see Appendix A) so that you can see him/her in temporal perspective.

[8]   Or, at least, most of us scholars. Members of the religious right prefer to be "fallen angels" and can still persuade school boards to eliminate the theory of evolution from school curricula. Even some scholars consider the theory if not wrong at least irrelevant, since they claim that human behavior is determined by culture.

environmental conditions, the individuals at one end of a particular scale have some advantage over the others; because of this advantage, they are more likely to survive; because they are more likely to survive, they are more likely to reproduce;   because traits are inherited, the next generation of this species will be, on the average, further along toward the desirable end of this scale. This generation, in turn, breeds another generation even further along, and so on and so on.

Let's take a concrete example.   Giraffes differ in the length of their necks. The longer-necked giraffes are better able to feed off the leaves in high trees and are thus more likely to survive and reproduce. Since long-necked giraffes tend to have long-necked babies, the next generation will have, on the average, longer necks, and the next generation even longer necks, and so on. Note that no giraffe grows a longer neck during its lifetime by stretching it to reach leaves and then passes its longer neck on to its progeny. This is Jean Baptiste Lamarck's erroneous concept of the **inheritance of acquired characteristics.**

Whereas most of us are familiar with the initial reaction to the theory of evolution, we may not be as familiar with its subsequent history. It suffered a decline, because many malicious or simply silly people mis-used the theory as a rationalization for an extreme interpretation of capitalism as a survival-of-the-fittest principle applied to the social sphere and as an argument for eugenics - the "improvement" of the species by pruning out the unfit [DEGLER]. As stated above, this decline permitted the Standard Social Science Model (SSSM) to dominate the social sciences, including media studies. The SSSM assumes that the mind is a "tabula rasa", a blank slate on which culture writes.

The debunking of those false arguments has resulted in a revival of the principle of natural selection as a basic principle for the psychological and social sciences.   Evolutionary psychologists argue that the human mind, which has evolved over thousands of years to enable us to survive in the harsh arena of our environment, is a medium which determines how the message of culture is received and interpreted [see, for example, BARKOW ET AL, WILSON]. This "tabula" is far from "rasa". Much has been written on this slate over evolutionary times. They argue therefore that we need to ground our sociology in psychology and our psychology in turn in biology. This inevitably leads to **natural selection** and the *natural selection* of Charles Darwin, superficially an unlikely candidate, as the first member of our cast in a history of media.

Darwin did not understand the mechanism underlying natural selection. However, Gregor Mendel did. He had conducted a series of brilliant experiments which demonstrated the basic principles of genetics. This cloistered monk had published his results in an obscure journal in 1866 (ironically there was an uncut copy of this journal in Darwin's library). The profound implications of his findings were not explored until they were re-discovered at the end of the century, and the detailed synthesis of Darwin's theory of evolution and Mendel's theory of genetics was not completed until the 1930s when a group of distinguished biologists - Ernst Mayr, Theodosius Dobzhansky, and others - created the evolutionary synthesis [MAYR].

The big breakthrough in biology was, of course, the breaking of the genetic code by James Watson and Francis Crick in 1953 [WATSON].[9] They told us that we are written in four letters - ACGT - arranged in pairs around a double helix. This discovery triggered the **Human Genome Project** to write the sequence of those pairs. This project was completed in record time - partly because of the improvement in technology in the interval, and partly because of the race between public and private teams. The Human Genome Project to write

---

[9]   This is the official story. However, it has subsequently been revealed that Rosalind Franklin deserved to have shared the resultant Nobel Prize. Two recent books present a strong argument for her case [MADDOX, SAYRE].

our code was touted like the project to land one of us on the moon as a *"great leap for mankind"*. It seems perhaps to the lay-person - hyped up by the media to have unrealistic expectations - to be a great anti-climax.

However, as we will learn in Section 2.2, in every language there is a hierarchy underlying the sequence. The language in which we are written is no exception. As we go beyond the sequence of the genes to the hierarchical structure of their function, we will tease out the relative contributions of nature and nurture in the various aspects of human behavior. In his book *Genome: The Autobiography of a Species in 23 Chapters*, Matt Ridley claims that *"Being able to read the genome will tell us more about our origins, our evolution, our nature and our minds than all the efforts of science to date. It will revolutionalize anthropology, psychology, medicine, palaeontology and virtually every other science."* [RIDLEY].

The revolution in linguistics - the discipline most relevant to media studies - was started by Noam Chomsky in the 1950s. He challenged the prevailing behavioristic concept of language based on the "tabula rasa" by arguing that we have a language-acquisition device (LAD) built into our biology. The device does not, of course, work in a vacuum - it needs a language-acquisition support system (LASS). As the language in which we are written is decoded, we will learn the precise interaction between this biological device and the environment in which it unfolds, the relationship between the LAD and the LASS.

We tend to think of the theory of evolution as a biological rather than a psychological theory - as concerned with the development of structure rather than of function. Perhaps the emphasis has been on structure because , with the death of an organism, structure survives but function fades. Much evidence for evolution is therefore based on structure (skeletons) or the imprint of structure (fossils). However, modern evolutionary theory is beginning to swing to an emphasis on function. The giraffe survives not only because it has a long neck but also because it can *use* it. The structure-function relationship is a chicken-and-egg problem. Is the egg the chicken's way of producing another chicken or is the chicken, as Samuel Butler suggested, an egg's way of producing another egg? Do birds have wings because they fly or do birds fly because they have wings?

Modern evolutionary psychology is exploring the evolution of the mind as well as of the body. Steven Pinker recently published a book with the title *How The Mind Works* [PINKER 1997].   Such a title may be premature and presumptuous but it is no longer preposterous. Evolutionary psychologists, like Pinker, are transforming many mysteries of mind into mere problems. As a child, I was addicted to jig-saw puzzles. I would start with the outer edge and work inward frame by frame. According to Pinker, the outer border of the jig-saw puzzle of mind is the principle of natural selection and the next border is the concept of the nervous system as a tool for processing information to enable us to survive. This book could be considered as my attempt to fill in the third border (Figure 1-1).

Edmund Hillary, the first European to climb Mount Everest, (or was it George Mallory, who earlier got lost near its summit?) explained his motivation by saying *"because it was there"*. Evolutionary psychologists if pressed for a motive may answer *"because we are here"*. Our species is here and we would like to know how we got here. Natural selection helps explain. Nervous system as information-processing tool helps explain. However, those two principles, expounded by Steven Pinker, explain only how we got to a hunter-gatherer society.

The recent shifts from a hunter-gatherer society to an agricultural society to an industrial society to an information society have taken place in too short a time to be explained by the theory of evolution. Historical time is too short for the mechanisms of evolution to have much effect. Barbara Parker points out that it takes 500-1,000 generations for a survival-enhancing adaptation to become genetically encoded and we have had only about 100 generations since the birth of Jesus Christ [PARKER].   It is unlikely then that there is much genetic difference between our hunter-gatherer ancestors and you and I.

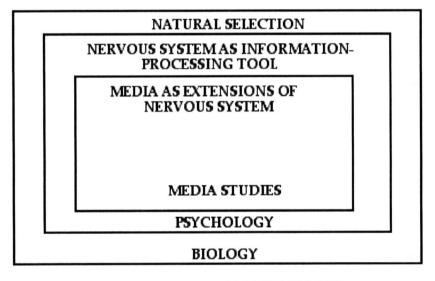

FIGURE 1- 1   HOW THE MIND WORKS
(with thanks and apologies to Steven Pinker)

Alfred Russel Wallace (1823-1913) had discovered the principle of natural selection at the same time as Darwin. Indeed, he published the same theory in the same issue of the same journal [DESMOND & MOORE, Pages 466-471]. Most people assumed, as did I, that he does not get as much credit as Darwin, because he did not spend 17 years accumulating empirical evidence for the theory. However, modern evolutionary theorists argue that he had done his homework. The main reason he does not get as much credit is because he subsequently abandoned the theory. He could see no way in which adaptation to a hunter-gatherer society could explain the sophisticated modern mind. How could a species, which evolved by adapting to a hunter-gatherer society, deal with the dramatic shifts to an agricultural society, then to an industrial society, and now to an information society?

This book suggests that at least part of the answer to this **Wallace Paradox** is that, during historical time, we have extended our nervous systems by developing tools for storing and transmitting information outside our bodies.[10] The story of how we acquired those extrasomatic tools is the history of media. This history of media could thus be considered as an attempt to solve the Wallace Paradox, or, returning to the jigsaw metaphor above, to fill in the third border in the emerging picture of the human mind (see Figure 1-1).

1.3   CO-EVOLUTION OF PERSON AND MEDIA

The story told here is a sequel to the Darwin-Mendel-Watson&Crick-Chomsky story told in the previous section. That previous story takes us only to speech and the hunter-gatherer society in which it evolved. Here the story continues into the Holocene era, that is, since our species settled down about

---

[10]   Ever since I discovered that one of my ancestors was Alexander Selkirk, the shipwrecked sailor who was the original for Robinson Crusoe, I have often imagined myself on a deserted island. (Many people have shared this experience since seeing Tom Hanks in *Cast Away*.) Without all my extrasomatic tools (books, videos, and CD-ROMs) I imagine that my mind would soon become considerably less "sophisticated" . Man Friday's arrival would have some civilizing effect (though without a common language, our conversations would have been very elementary). Our time and conversations would, no doubt, be devoted largely to hunting and gathering.

10,000 years ago. That period is too short for biological evolution to have much effect. I will argue that cultural evolution has piggy-backed on biological evolution, as we acquired communication tools to extends our nervous systems.

As we noted above, we find it convenient to start the collective biography of our species - history - with print, since we have records then. However, as argued above, it is important to embed history in pre-history (if only to credit oral cultures with a history of their own - even if it has boiled down to myth - as opposed to the truncated, biased history retroactively assigned oral cultures by print cultures). We also find it convenient to start our individual biographies with birth, since that date is easier to pin-point than the date of conception. However, the latter date is much more important.

At the moment the sperm of our fathers met the ova of our mothers to create the zygote, the single cell which became us, Zog and Anu (our hunter-gatherer ancestors) and you and I were all given the conception-day gift of all the wisdom our species has accumulated over millions of years of survival in a harsh arena plus *three score and ten years* to add our footnote to this wisdom. An important part of the conception-day gift is a means of storing information (memory) and a means of transmitting information (speech). Since a medium can be considered as any means of storing and transmitting information, Memory and Speech could thus be considered as a first generation of media.

This first generation of media is adequate for a hunter-gatherer society. How did we manage the transitions to an agricultural society, an industrial society, and now an information society? I will argue that, over historical time, we have supplemented this first generation of media with three further generations of media. We have developed means of storing and transmitting information outside our bodies. We learned to store information outside our bodies in print and on film (second generation), to transmit information outside our bodies with telephone and television (third generation), and to both store and transmit information outside our bodies in multimedia and internet (fourth generation).

Carl Sagan distinguishes between **extragenetic information** (not included in the genetic code but still inside the body) and **extrasomatic information** (outside the body) [SAGAN].   Since we can store and transmit extragenetic and extrasomatic information, we can represent those four generations of media in the 2x2 matrix depicted in Figure 1-2.

Those four generations of media are discussed, respectively, in Chapter 2 (Generation 1 - Memory and Speech), Chapter 4 (Generation 2 - Print and Film), Chapter 6 (Generation 3 - Telephone and Television), and Chapter 8 (Generation 4 - Multimedia and Internet).

This is a history of media - not a history of media studies. A fine history of media studies has already been written - *A History of Communication Theory : A Biographical Approach* [ROGERS]. Principle characters in that story would not merit a mention in the history of media, whereas such giants in the history of media as Bell, Marconi, etc. may appear only as footnotes in a history of media studies. Media Studies is an academic discipline, which tends to be highly critical of media - as attested by some titles of books by communication theorists – *Bread and Circuses: Theories of Mass Culture as Social Decay* [BRANTLINGER], *The End of Conversation: The Impact of Mass Media on Modern Society* [FERARROTI], *Killing the Messenger: 100 Years of Media Criticism* [GOLDSTEIN], *Technopoly: The Surrender of Culture to Technology* [POSTMAN 1993].

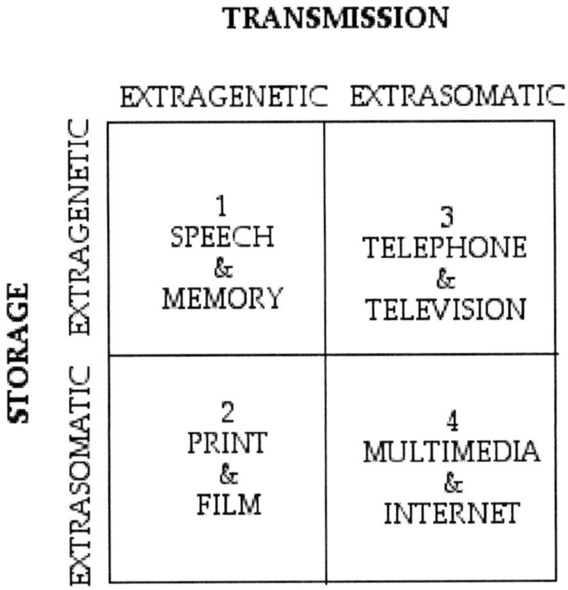

TRANSMISSION

EXTRAGENETIC EXTRASOMATIC

1 SPEECH & MEMORY	3 TELEPHONE & TELEVISION
2 PRINT & FILM	4 MULTIMEDIA & INTERNET

(Left margin labels: **STORAGE**, EXTRAGENETIC, EXTRASOMATIC)

FIGURE 1-2   FOUR GENERATIONS OF MEDIA

However, the Toronto School of Media Studies is used here to help provide a context for this history of media. This school seeks to understand what's happening rather than to pronounce on whether it should be happening. The history of media, presented in terms of four generations in Chapters 2, 4, 6, 8, will thus be augmented by descriptions of each shift as we assimilate each generation of media in the interspersed Chapters 3, 5, 7 from the point of view of the Toronto School.

We are currently experiencing a structural shift in media with the introduction of the fourth generation. Some perspective on this shift can be gained by examining the first and second shifts with the introduction of the second and third generations of media. Those three shifts are discussed, respectively in Chapter 3 (Shift 1 - Assimilation of Second Generation), Chapter 5

(Shift 2 - Assimilation of Third Generation), and Chapter 7 (Shift 3 - Assimilation of Fourth Generation).   We are too close to this current shift to see it clearly. The ubiquitous is paradoxically elusive. The fish will be the last to discover water. Perhaps by stepping back and looking at the big picture, we can see this third shift more clearly by analogy with the first and second shifts. This long view will help us not only to better understand the present but to better project into the future.

1.4   COMMUNICATION VERSUS CONFLICT

History is usually the story of conflict as told by the winners.[11]   During a war between two groups in Egypt, the Library of Alexandria was destroyed. Because of the outcome of a war in Turkey, scholars were forced to flee to Europe and thus trigger the Renaissance. Those two events are presented in traditional history as incidental by-products of the wars. In the history presented here, those events are viewed as the important events.

Who remembers or cares that this gang of thugs captured that piece of land? The important effect on civilization was that a certain subset of the knowledge of the Greeks was preserved, which determined our view of them and the subsequent history based on their wisdom. The important issue between those two events is not which gangs gained which territories but who preserved this wisdom during the interval and how it was stored and transmitted to future generations.[12] Cleopatra had lent 30,000 volumes of the books in the Alexandria Library to her lover, Mark Anthony, who had them copied and preserved in the

---

[11]   Mark Russell, the political satirist, covered 1000 years of history in 10 minutes during his millennium presentation. How is this possible? He leaves out the wars.

[12]   Thomas Cahill has added a fascinating contribution to this discussion in his recent book *How the Irish Saved Civilization* [CAHILL].

Pergamon Library in Turkey. (That's partly why the scholars were there.) By the way, fortunately for us, Mark Anthony kept the originals and sent back the error-ridden copies. Such little-recorded facts are much more important than the well-documented wars that bracketed the destruction of the library in Alexandria and the flight of scholars from Istanbul.

Much current conflict is a continuation of ancient battles. The Battle of the Boyne on 12 July 1690 continues in Ireland today. Growing up in Scotland, I knew many people who continued to rerun in their minds the Battle of Bannockburn in 1314 (the last major battle we won) or the Battle of Culloden in 1745 (the last battle we lost, if we don't include a certain recent soccer match at Wembley Stadium). Here in Quebec, we're still fighting a short skirmish on the Plains of Abraham on 13 September 1759.[13]

The newspaper, being the first draft of history, is also the story of conflict told by the winners. Thus the front page news is about wars or politics (war by other means) or economics (what they are squabbling about).

During the 1970s, I stopped reading the morning newspaper. It occurred to me that I was reading it simply to get the latest installment on various current soap operas - for example, the Patty Hearst story in which the newspaper heiress was kidnapped and subsequently re-emerged as Tanya aiding her kidnappers in a bank robbery was unfolding in my *San Francisco Chronicle*. The Vietnam War (1965-1975) story, the current installment in the saga of the Third World War (the

---

[13]   Some Scottish soldiers escaped to France with Bonnie Prince Charlie after the Battle of Culloden and signed up as mercenaries with General Montcalm. Some of the few Scottish soldiers who survived the Battle of Culloden signed up as mercenaries with General Wolfe. The Battle of Quebec was fought largely between the French Scots and the English Scots. Since both Montcalm and Wolfe were killed, the treaty was signed by their second-in-commands, who were both Scots. It was written in Gaelic, the common language of both sides. The two Scots happened to be cousins and ancestors of the two Johnsons who subsequently became Premiers of Quebec.

War in the Third World), was also being told.[14]   It was instant history in serial form with my instant coffee and cereals. I decided not to waste prime time - the first hour of the day when my mind was fresh - on such trivia. I shifted to reading *Newsweek* , which filled me in on the news weekly rather than daily, and then to reading the *Encyclopedia Britannica Book of the Year*, which filled me in on the news yearly.

So why am I back to reading the newspaper every morning? There is something happening now in that important story of the history of media which I will tell in this book. We are in the throes of the assimilation of the fourth generation of media - multimedia and internet - and the accommodation of the media system to its impact. During the 70s, our story was in a latent stage. The telephone and the television set had penetrated to a limit of over 90% in industrialized countries. Excitement over the shift from rotary to push-button dialing or from black-and-white to color TV screens during this period demonstrated how little of significance was happening. Now, however, every day, my morning newspaper has information about the profound impact of multimedia and internet. I'm keeping abreast of those day-by-day innovations in the hope of understanding what is going on. Writing this book is an attempt to step back to get the big picture in which those changes are put into a larger perspective.[15]   Section 1 - THE PAST (Chapters 2 through 8) could be considered as the "back story" for our current assimilation of multimedia and the internet, that is, of the hi-tech industry.

---

[14]   Of course, the Vietnam War was very important to those whose lives were disrupted or even terminated by it. However, in the larger scheme of things, one cannot help thinking in retrospect: *What was that all about?*

[15]   When I stated above that the fish will be last to discover water, I was tempted to describe this book as an introduction to water for fish. (I usually take the advice of Oscar Wilde that the best way to deal with temptation is to succumb to it.) Let me succumb to this temptation now by extending the metaphor. As a child growing up in a Scottish village, I enjoyed the culinary delight of fish and chips wrapped in newspaper. Perhaps a better metaphor is that this book unwraps the newspaper to introduce the fish to the chips.

H. G. Wells describes human history as *"a race between education and catastrophe"* [WELLS]. Traditional history focuses on "catastrophe" with "education" as footnote; this history focuses on "education" with "catastrophe" as footnote. Well's metaphor of the race has been brilliantly rephrased in modern and empirical terms as an *"ingenuity gap"* between our problems and our capacity to solve them [HOMER-DIXON]. This book is my small contribution to closing that ingenuity gap.

Despite the argument that *"the pen is mightier than the sword"*, history continues to tell the story of the sword. This is the story of the pen, penned in the hope that it will not be used to encourage conflict. It argues that the history of media is the Big Story of historical time. It tells how our species has dealt with the dramatic shifts from a hunter-gatherer to an agricultural to an industrial to an information society by developing extrasomatic tools to store and transmit information outside our bodies.

Many people, to whom I described my plan to put history within a pre-historical context, recommended I read *Guns, Germs, and Steel: The Fate of Human Societies* [DIAMOND]. When I finally read the book, I realized that they were telling me gently that it had already been done! Jared Diamond answered a question posed by his New Guinea friend, Yali: *Why is it that you white people developed so much cargo and brought it to New Guinea, but we black people had little cargo of our own?* by going back to pre-history to explore a complex of factors including food production, domestication of large animals, germs acquired from those animals, large population, and central organization. It has indeed been done for traditional history based on conflict. Here it is done again for an alternative history based on communication.

CHAPTER 2
FIRST GENERATION -
MEMORY AND SPEECH

2.1   FROM ANIMAL TO HUMAN

2.2   FROM CHILD TO ADULT

2.3   THE SEARCH FOR MEMORY

-- so much more language sophistication comes out of a child than goes in, that you have to conclude that they were born with blueprints, plans, software - whatever you want to call it - that enables them to learn as fast as they do.

Jay Ingram, TALK, TALK, TALK, Pages 185-186

There is no step more uplifting, more momentous in the history of mind design, than the invention of language. When Homo sapiens became the beneficiary of this invention, the species stepped into a slingshot that has launched it far beyond all other earthly creatures in the power to look ahead and reflect.

Daniel C. Dennett, 1996

The brain is born not as a blank slate but as an exposed negative waiting to be slipped into a developer fluid.

Edward O. Wilson
(Quoted in Tom Wolfe, HOOKING UP, Page 80)

2.1   FROM ANIMAL TO HUMAN

We can walk more confidently into the future when we better understand the present. We can better understand the present by stepping back and looking at our past. How far back? Who made the Big Bang? Who heard it? Not that far back. The answer to both questions is: nobody or nothing that we can identify with. It only begins to get interesting from our point of view during the Pleistocene Era of the Quaternary Period of geological time (1,800,000 to 10,000 years ago). Our species only stepped on to our planetary stage towards the end of the fourth act.

Two species co-existed during this period, as candidates for our ancestors. Homo sapiens sapiens (Cro-Magnon) survived, whereas homo sapiens neanderthalensis (Neanderthal) perished.[1]   Cro-Magnon won the battle for survival over Neanderthal, not because they were bigger and stronger, but because they had better vocal equipment to sustain language [INGRAM 1992]. Language was the basis of the Big Bang of the Brain which ushered us, but not Neanderthal, into the Holocene Era (10,000 years ago till now) [CALVIN]. Cave paintings, musical instruments, ritual burials, dated from this time, indicated a dramatic shift in the history of the mind.

There is much speculation about what happened at that date (which shifts back and forth with each account), One breakthrough in ontogenetic development (from child to adult) may serve as a clue. Helen Keller, blind and deaf, reports in her autobiography that her teacher, Anne Sullivan, poured water in one of her hands and wrote "water" on the other hand. Suddenly, she realized that the word

---

[1]   One of my students disputed this. She said she had met two Neanderthals the night before in a bar. I suggested that she read *The Clan of the Cave Bear* [AUEL]. In this wonderful fact-based but fictionalized account of this period, a group of Neanderthals adopt a Cro-Magnon girl who had lost her family in an earthquake. The novel helps counter the bad press of Neanderthals.

"water" represented water. That is, that something can be a symbol for something else. She rushed around, demanding the symbols for familiar objects. From then on, her cognitive development progressed rapidly. Perhaps, there was a similar moment in phylogenetic development (from animal to human). For the sake of simplicity, let us consider **symbolization** as the breakthrough which distinguished our species from all the others.

Thus communication was an important factor right from the beginning. Its importance is traditionally linked to the need for cooperation in hunting large animals. However, the fact that large animals hunt *us* also plays a role. To defend ourselves we clustered in groups so that we have many eyes and many ears to warn us of their approach. Since social animals need to trust one another, we established trust through mutual grooming. In his book, *Grooming, Gossip, and the Evolution of Language*, Robin Dunbar argues that language evolved as a sort of grooming-at-a-distance mechanism when the social group got too large for direct grooming [DUNBAR]. Gossip too serves an evolutionary function because it leads to a bad reputation and thus ostracizing of members of the group who can't be trusted. Thus, whether for attack or for defense, communication played a role right from the beginning, and, as I will argue in this book, will continue to be the major factor in the subsequent story of our species.

Despite such attempts by evolutionary psychologists like Dunbar, the origin of language in our species is still shrouded in mystery. It happened very long ago and it has left no physical record. The absence of evidence does not, however, prevent us from having theories about it. Indeed, it seems that the fewer the facts, the more the theories. Speech evolved as imitation of sounds heard in nature (ding-dong theory), as imitation of sounds made by animals (bow-wow theory), out of interjections (oof-ouch theory), to accompany strenuous group activity (yo-he-ho theory) are a few of the candidates. Speculation about the origin of language was so rife and viewed as so futile that, in 1866, *Société*

Linguistique de Paris banned any further discussion in their journals [DEACON, Page 14].

An alternative approach is to identify the design features of language and determine which features distinguish human from animal communication. Charles Hockett lists three such design features of human language - displacement, productivity, and duality of patterning [HOCKETT]. While I was a graduate student at Cornell University, a campus debate developed between Charles Hockett and Karl von Frisch.   Von Frisch had conducted extensive research on the "language" of bees [VON FRISCH 1950]. He had discovered that a bee could communicate the source of pollen to other bees in the hive by doing a dance in a figure-eight, in which the angle of orientation of the 8 indicated the direction and the number of wiggles in performing the figure-eight indicated distance from the hive.   That is, it passed on the polar coordinates of the pollen source.   Von Frisch argued that this *"language of the bees"* had the design feature of displacement - the bee could *"talk"* about things which are not here and now - and productivity - the bee could *"say"* things which have never been said before, when it gives precise polar coordinates never before used by its species.

Hockett argued that such communication between bees should not be described as "language" (hence the inverted commas around language in his title). It was pre-wired into the genetic code of bees - that is, it was genetic not *extra*genetic.   This argument was vindicated by later work by von Frisch himself on dialects in bees.   When North American bees were mated with European bees with a different "dialect", the sons of bees could not communicate with either parent, since their "language" was some compromise between the two dialects [VON FRISCH 1967].

In my introductory psychology textbook, I included a footnote to the third distinguishing design feature of human language - duality of patterning - which stated that I didn't understand this feature [GARDINER 1970].[2]   In the second edition, I added a footnote to this footnote, in which I stated that I had talked to Charles Hockett about this feature and I still didn't understand it. You'll be happy to know that I now finally understand it.

Language is a hierarchy of units plus rules for combining units at one level to create meaningful units at the next level. More precisely, language consists of **phonemes** (roughly equivalent to the letters of the alphabet), **morphemes** (roughly equivalent to the words in the dictionary), sentences, and discourses, plus the rules of vocabulary to combine phonemes into morphemes, of grammar to combine morphemes into sentences, and of logic to combine sentences into discourses (Figure 2-1).[3]

The foundation of language - the sounds which we utter and hear - are converted by our auditory system from an analog to a digital code - the language which we understand. "Duality of patterning" refers to this analog-to-digital feature of language. Our auditory system, like all our sensory systems, is an analog-to-digital convertor.[4]   At the upper level of language - the level of logic - it is digital in a more global sense. Since a sentence can be considered as a statement about the objective world, it can be said to be either true or false. The rules of logic enable us to determine what follows from certain assumptions about

---

[2]   My editor was initially horrified. Textbook writers are supposed to know everything about their subject. However, he kindly permitted me to include the footnote, on the grounds that *this* textbook writer was an exception.

[3]   I say "roughly" because there is not perfect phoneme-grapheme correspondence and there are some morphemes - the smallest linguistic unit which has meaning of its own - which are not words. For example "-ed" at the end of a verb means past tense.

[4]   During an argument in a bar between two of my students about the relative merits of analog and digital media, I suddenly realized that the argument was familiar. It was an argument I had had with myself. After fifteen years of concentrated study and teaching, I spent a decade in California to get "*out of my mind and back to my senses*". I had become too digital and needed to restore my analog-digital balance.

the objective world. Thus, for example, if we assume that *"the shortest distance between two points is a straight line"* and the other axioms of Euclidian geometry, we can deduce that *"the square on the hypotenuse of a triangle is equal to the sum of the squares on the other two sides".*[5]

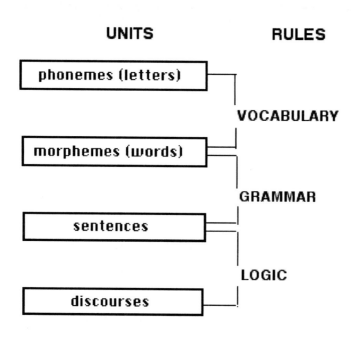

FIGURE 2-1 HIERARCHICAL STRUCTURE OF LANGUAGE

---

[5]   I flunked mathematics all the way through High School. My first teaching assignment was to teach math to all the High School grades in a small school. In desperation, I sat down and read the preface to Euclid's *Geometry* . Euclid said, lets pretend the following statements are true and listed his axioms - *The shortest distance between two points is a straight line* , etc. Now, he said, lets see what follows and proceeded to build up his system of theories on this foundation. I learned Euclidian Geometry in an evening. In four years of High School, I couldn't learn it because no one told me that it was a game of let's pretend and let's see what happens. The Pythagorean Society considered those theorems sacred and killed anyone who divulged them to outsiders. This secret society is still alive and well with cells in High School common rooms!

In school, we learn the rules for combining phonemes into morphemes (vocabulary) and for combining morphemes into sentences (grammar) but not usually the rules for combining sentences into discourses (logic). Here's a short course in logic to help fill that gap in your education.

Let us imagine an empty universe and let us introduce into it the proposition. In the beginning, was the proposition. A proposition may take many forms - *today in Tuesday* , *Now is the time for all good men to come to the aid of Jennifer* , *Kafka is a kvetch* , *E equals M times C squared* - but they all have in common the fact that they can be said to be true or false. Our proposition - let us call it P - looks lonely in an empty universe, let us introduce another proposition - say Q - which , like all propositions, can be said to be true or false. In an empty universe containing two propositions, there are thus four possible states of affairs - they are both true, the first is true and the second is false, the first is false and the second is true, or they are both false (Figure 2-2). There exists within the English language, the means of eliminating each subset of this exhaustive set of alternatives. "Not both P & Q" eliminates the first alternative, "If P, then Q" eliminates the second alternative, and so on.

The four logic problems set for you in Figure 2-2 focus on "if P, then Q". Check your answers as follows. The premises (the propositions after "*Suppose you know that* ") eliminate some subset of the alternatives in a universe containing two propositions, and the conclusion (the proposition after "*Then would this be true?* ") is evaluated in terms of the remaining alternatives. If it is contained in all the remaining alternatives, the answer is "yes"; if it is contained in some of the alternatives, the answer is "maybe"; if it is contained in none of the alternatives, the answer is "no".

A certain subset of propositions (e.g. *I am a Scotsman* , *this is a pipe* , etc.) states that a particular element is a member of a particular set. Because such propositions occur so often, the cumbersome "*If x is a member of set A, then x is a*

QUESTIONS

1   Suppose you know that
**If I have a marble in my right hand,
then I have a marble in my left hand
I have a marble in my right hand**

Then would this be true?
I have a marble in my left hand

YES   NO   MAYBE

2   Suppose you know that
**If I have a marble in my right hand,
then I have a marble in my left hand
I have a marble in my left hand**

Then would this be true?
I have a marble in my right hand

YES   NO   MAYBE

3   Suppose you know that
**If I have a marble in my right hand,
then I have a marble in my left hand
I do not have a marble in my right hand**

Then would this be true?
I have a marble in my left hand

YES   NO   MAYBE

4   Suppose you know that
**If I have a marble in my right hand,
then I have a marble in my left hand
I do not have a marble in my left hand**

Then would this be true?
I have a marble in my right hand

YES   NO   MAYBE

ANSWERS

	p.q	p p or notp or p.notq	q q or not q or notp.q	or notp.notq
1 if p, then q			x	
p			x	x
Therefore q	YES			
2 if p, then q			x	
q				x
Therefore p	MAYBE			
3 if p, then q			x	
notp		x		
Therefore q	MAYBE			
4 if p, then q			x	
notq		x		x
Therefore p	NO			

FIGURE 2-2   A COURSE IN LOGIC

member of set B " is condensed to *"All As are Bs"* The statements *"Some As are Bs"* and *"No A's are Bs"* can be generated in the same way. Class reasoning, involving those relations of All, Some and No, permits us to place the objects in our world into categories and consider the relationships between them within those categories. In the same way, the propositions stating the position of an element with respect to a dimension generates the relations "is greater than", "is equal to", and "is less than". Ordinal reasoning, involving those relations, permits us to place the objects in our environment along dimensions and consider the relationships between them along those dimensions.

Having placed objects along dimensions, we can conclude that, if A is greater than B and B is greater than C, then A is greater than C. In order to be more precise - to say how much greater A is than C, we have to invent the natural numbers. Thus, if A is 8 units, B is 6 units, and C is 3 units, then A is 5 units greater than C.

Within this system, you can always add and get an answer. However, if you reverse this operation and subtract you can't always get an answer. You have to invent 0 to provide an answer when you subtract a number from itself and negative numbers when you subtract a number from a smaller number. Within this system, you can always multiply and get an answer. However, if you reverse this operation and divide, you don't always get an answer. You have to invent fractions or decimals to provide an answer when the division is not even. Within this system, you can always square and get an answer. However, when you reverse this operation and take the square root, you don't always get an answer. You have to invent irrational numbers to provide an answer when the number is not a perfect square.

Thus the entire superstructure of mathematics is erected in order to permit closure under various mathematical operations (Figure 2-3). No matter how sophisticated it gets however, it is still based on class and ordinal reasoning, which are special cases of propositional reasoning, which is an aspect of everyday language.

This "nutshell" history of mathematics is, of course, grossly oversimplified. Two recent books [KAPLAN, SIEFE] describe the long, complex, and arduous process of discovering only one element in this system - zero. The important point is that those elements are discoveries rather than inventions. They are all implied in the conception-day gift. It just takes us a long time to unwrap it. My Ph. D. thesis was a study of the development of understanding of the meanings of such "logical operators". John Roberts, an anthropologist on my thesis committee, replicated my study with Indian children. He assured me that every North American Indian language he knew also contained a full set of such logical operators. All languages are equally complex. They all contain the means of logic and thus of mathematics. The conception-day gift is a gift to all members of our species.

Thus, logic is the link between everyday English (or Ethiopian or Estonian or whatever) and mathematics. In school, we learn English in English class and mathematics in mathematics class. Because of the missing link of logic, we seldom realize that they are different aspects of the same thing. Thus, a wedge is driven between the artists, who excel in English class, and the scientists, who excel in maths class. Thus, we create the two solitudes of the two cultures as bemoaned by C. P. Snow [SNOW]. Everyday language and mathematics are part of the conception-day gift of the wisdom of our species. This gift culminates in the magnificent invention of speech. Using language, we can share our experience of the world. Mathematics simply allows us to talk more precisely. It also allows us to talk to people who are not part of our linguistic community. Cosmonauts and astronauts both got into the same orbit around the same planet, despite the fact they spoke different languages, because they shared the common language of mathematics.

CLASS LOGIC (All, some, no)
Puts things into categories and considers
relationships among those categories

All men are mortal
Socrates is a man
Therefore, Socrates is mortal

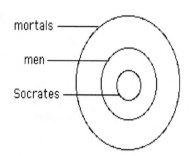

ORDINAL LOGIC (greater than, equal to, less than)
Puts things along dimensions and considers
relationships along dimensions

A is greater than B
B is greater than C
Therefore, A is greater than C

A

B

C

NATURAL NUMBERS (1, 2, 3, ----)
To permit more precise propositions about differences
along dimensions
A is 5 units greater than B
B is 2 units greater than C
Therefore, A is 7 units greater than C

ZERO (0)
To provide an answer when a number is subtracted from itself

NEGATIVE NUMBERS (-1, -2, -3, ---)
To provide an answer when a large number is subtracted from
a small number

FRACTIONS and DECIMALS (1.1, 1.11, 1.111, ---)
To provide an answer when one number is divided by another
and it doesn't go in even

IRRATIONAL NUMBERS (2 ,3 ,5, ---)
To provide an answer when the square root of a number is not
a natural number

9
8
7
6
5
4
3
2
1
0
-1
-2
-3
-4
-5
-6
-7
-8
-9

FIGURE 2-3   LOGIC AS "MISSING LINK"

2.2   FROM CHILD TO ADULT

The origin of language in individual members of our species is more accessible to study than the origin of language in our species as a whole. We can see language emerge here and now as we watch our children acquiring language.

Burrhus Frederick Skinner (1904-1990) attempted to explain the acquisition of language by children in terms of his behavioristic principles of instrumental conditioning. Finding himself sitting beside the distinguished philosopher, Alfred North Whitehead, at a banquet, Skinner launched into an enthusiastic exposition of his project to explain all human behavior in terms of conditioning. The calm old philosopher listened benignly to the brash young scientist, conceded that he could perhaps explain all non-verbal behavior within his model, but could not explain verbal behavior. *"How could you explain that I choose to say at this moment 'No black scorpion is falling on this table'? "* Skinner began his book *Verbal Behavior* next morning and published it several decades later [SKINNER]. In that book, he presented the following argument in response to Whitehead's challenge.

Verbal behavior is behavior reinforced through the mediation of other people. At that famous dinner, Skinner could have got the salt either by non-verbal behavior (reaching for it himself) or by verbal behavior (asking Whitehead to pass the salt). We use language, then, to gain reinforcement through the mediation of other people. But how do we acquire language in the first place? Skinner proposed three mechanisms:

- A child utters at imitation of a word in the presence of the word, and an adult voices approval (**echoic response**);
- a child utters the name of an object in the presence of the object, and an adult hands over the object (**tact** - short for con*tact*);

•   a child utters the name of a satisfier of a need while experiencing the need, and an adult provides the satisfier of the need (**mand** - short for de*mand*).

This argument would seem to fall far short of meeting Whitehead's challenge. However, Skinner argues that the scientist is not required to explain each specific event but only the general principles underlying specific events. The physicist is required not to explain the order in which leaves will fall off a tree and the pattern they will form on the ground but only the general principles underlying falling bodies.

In a review of *Verbal Behavior*, Noam Chomsky (1928-   ) argued that the acquisition of language by children can not be explained in terms of instrumental conditioning [CHOMSKY 1959].   He argued that biological research demonstrated that there simply was not enough time for feedback from each response to get back in time to be linked to the next response. We speak much too fast for that to be possible. Skinner's theory was therefore inconsistent with the facts at the lower level of analysis and was thus incorrect [CHOMSKY 1966]. We need, as argued in Chapter 1, to anchor sociology in psychology and psychology, in turn, in biology. This does not mean that sociology is reduced to biology. It merely means that theories must be consistent with the facts at the next level down.

Grammatical mistakes by children provide further evidence against Skinner's theory.   The fact that children initially use "goed" as the past tense of "go" and "foots" as the plural of "foot" could not be explained in terms of imitating adults.   Such mistakes are better explained as an inappropriate application of rules that children have learned. They have learned to add "ed" for past tense and to add "s" for plural. Later they learn that crazy adults have weird exceptions to those rules, and agree to go along with this craziness.

Steven Pinker devotes most of his book, *Words and Rules*, to a discussion of regular and irregular verbs [PINKER 1999]. Learning a language involves learning words which are arbitrary and learning rules which are not. Words and rules are processed by different areas of the brain. The child begins to process irregular verbs as rules but learns that they should be processed as words. In English, we have arbitrarily decided to use "went" for past tense of "go" and "feet" for the plural of "foot".

Chomsky proposes an alternative theory for the acquisition of language. All children learn those grammatical rules so easily because they have a **language-acquisition device (LAD)** built into the genetic code. It is part of the conception-day gift mentioned above. However, it comes in a package, along with teeth and breasts, labeled *"do not open until -- some appropriate date"*. It works only if fueled by input from the linguistic community to which the child belongs. Thus, the child will acquire the particular language of the community which will contribute to its survival. The LAD is genetically determined but it depends on input from the environment.[6]   Jerome Bruner calls this necessary input the **Language Acquisition Support System (LASS)** [BRUNER]. Every lad needs a lass.

Natural selection arranges that this LAD works best during a certain sensitive period in the development of the child, to enable the child to acquire the language of the community to which it belongs.   Thus the acquisition of language is easy during this sensitive period. This sensitive period is also the best time to learn a second language.

Wallace Lambert distinguishes between coordinate bilingualism, in which one acquires two separate language structures during this period, and piggy-back

---

[6]   The LAD is, of course, not a discovery but an invention. No physical structure has yet been found which can be clearly identified as the LAD. It is a hypothetical construct invented by Chomsky to explain the facts of the acquisition of language by children. It's the best explanation so far. However, just as Skinner's explanation was superseded by that of Chomsky, so another explanation may displace Chomsky's. Beautiful big theories are always vulnerable to ugly little facts.

bilingualism in which we later acquire a second language by linking it word-by-word to our first language [LAMBERT]. Contrary to the simple-minded assumption that a second language takes up mind space which could better be used to improve the first language, he finds that coordinate bilinguals are clearer thinkers than monolinguals, because they learn very early that language is arbitrary. There's one label for a thing in one language and another label in the other language. Their thought is thus less determined by language. They use language as a tool.   René Lésvesque and Pierre Trudeau are two brilliant examples of clear-thinking coordinate bilinguals.[7]   Perhaps this helps explain why some of the great stylists in the English language are people, like Joseph Conrad and Vladimir Nabokov, who acquired this tool as a second or third language.[8]

Darwin did not understand the mechanism underlying evolution.[9] However, modern genetics has since demonstrated that information is passed from generation to generation in genes. As the genetic code is being decoded by thousands of scholars working together on the human genome project, we are beginning to understand the language in which we are written. One important feature of that language is that gaps are left in the genetic codes of various species to be filled in by the environment. Konrad Lorenz demonstrated the phenomenon

---

[7]   When acquiring two languages, it helps to keep them in separate contexts. When we mentioned this to Pierre Trudeau at a GAMMA meeting, he said: *"That's good. The boys speak English when they're with Margaret in Ottawa and French when they're with me here in Montreal"*.

[8]   It does not necessarily follow that three and more languages are better than two. We all know language junkies who keep adding more and more languages to their repertoire, rejoicing in the fact that each new language is progressively easier to acquire. They tend to emphasize media over message. I once met a man who spoke ten languages but had nothing to say.

[9]   Ironically, there was an uncut version of the book describing the principles of genetics by an obscure monk called Gregor Mendel in Charles Darwin's library.

of **imprinting** by arranging that the first large moving object baby ducklings saw when emerging from the egg is not mother duck but Konrad Lorenz [LORENZ]. By interfering with nature's plans, the useful-for-survival function of following mother duck is replaced by the useless function of following Lorenz.[10]

Nature's magnificent invention of speech is based on leaving a larger gap to be filled in by the language community. This permits our species to benefit from experience through learning to learn and, more important, to benefit from the experience of *other* people through teaching.[11]   It is speech which has enabled our relatively weak and slow species to dominate, for better or worse, other animals which are stronger and faster.

My neighbors in the Gatineau Hills, footnoted above, adopted an Inuit baby girl called Karina. She, of course, learned English, since that was the language she was exposed to by her adoptive parents, rather than Inuktitut, the language spoken by her biological parents. The same family also "adopted" a husky dog called Pattuk, who had spent the first half of his life in an Inuit community. Pattuk should have been a bilingual dog, but he learned neither Inuktitut nor English. Alas, he lacked a LAD, which is an exclusive feature of our species. Although she comes from a culture which was hunter-gatherer (until recently when their traditional life-style was screwed up by short-sighted policies of the Federal Government), she has become a very competent member of the emerging information society. Hence my argument that the dramatic changes during historical time are changes in culture not in the person. We need to

---

[10]   When I first arrived to live in a farm in the Gatineau, I was amazed while crossing a field that two sheep within a flock ran towards me. In Scotland, for reasons I won't go into, sheep always run away from you. When I asked the farmer Diedrich about this, he said *"Ah, they're Betty and Mabel. They lost their mothers at birth and were raised in our kitchen by my wife Joan"*. They had been imprinted on people.

[11]   Uncle Lefty tells the tale around the camp fire of how he entered a dark cave and disturbed a hibernating bear - hence his name. The children who hear this story have a better chance of survival.

explain how that same person adapted to dramatically different societies.

2.3 THE SEARCH FOR MEMORY

If I tell you something today and you can recall this some time in the future, then you must have stored it somewhere in your body. Where and how is it stored? One would assume that it must be stored in the association areas of your brain. Sensory and motor functions, to receive stimuli and initiate responses, have been localized in certain parts of the brain. The association areas are the *"uncommitted cortex"*, the parts of the brain not directly linked to the environment,   But precisely where in those association areas is memory stored?

Kurt Lashley spent a lifetime trying to find out. He trained rats to run a maze, cut out parts of their association areas, and retested them on the maze. The extent of the deficiency was related not to the location of the ablation but to the extent of the ablation. The more association area removed, the greater the deficiency, regardless of where it was removed from. He concluded that, for certain functions, the association area acts as a whole. This principle of **mass action** was presented as an alternative to the principle of **localization** [LASHLEY].

Karl Pribram concluded that Lashley could not find memory anywhere because it is everywhere [PRIBRAM]. The nervous system is like a hologram, in which all the information is contained in all the nervous system. Each part of the hologram contains the whole image. The smaller the part of the hologram, the worse the resolution of the image. That is parallel to what Lashley discovered - the more association tissue he removed, the more the deficiency in maze-running.

A psychologist called James McConnell generated some evidence that memory is stored throughout the body with a series of experiments he conducted using worms. [MCCONNELL]. In one experiment, he taught worms to turn right in a T maze. When the worms regenerated after he cut them in half, he found that the new worms took significantly less time to learn to go right in the T maze than the regenerated halves of untrained worms. In an even more dramatic experiment, he ground up trained worms, fed them to untrained worms, and found that those cannibal worms took less time to learn to go right in a T maze than worms which had been fed on untrained worms. The information must thus be retained at a chemical level, since that is all that survives being minced and eaten.[12]

McConnell suspected that the information is retained in the chemical **ribonucleic acid (RNA)** which is a biological cousin to **deoxyribonucleic acid (DNA)**, which contains the instructions for the development of the organism. If phylogenetic memory is stored in DNA, it is not surprising that ontogenetic memory is stored in RNA. Phylogenetic and ontogenetic memory can dovetail at a chemical level. Mother Nature leaves gaps in our program to be filled in by our environment so that we can adapt to our particular environment. McConnell's results were so bizarre that they were simply ignored by traditional psychology. His findings were not disproved by subsequent research. They were simply ignored [INGRAM 1998]. In the light of evolutionary psychology, those findings are no longer so bizarre. Perhaps we should look at them again.

The nervous system of the worm permits it to choose between response A and response B. However, it is only with the development of an association area

---

[12]   This produced a rash of rude suggestions about what to do with retired professors who had lost their faculties.

in the brain, which mediates between the sensory and motor areas, that the organism begins to escape from the tyranny of the environment. It can then choose not only whether to make response A or response B but whether to respond or not to respond.

Thus it is no coincidence that, in the octopus, we find the beginning of an association area and also the beginning of the capacity not to respond.   The spontaneous response of the octopus to the stimulus "crab" is the response "grab".[13]   A psychologist has been able to teach octopuses to inhibit this response for a few seconds [YOUNG].   This capacity for a **delayed response** is possible only when sensory neurons are not directly linked to motor neurons. The organism can say "no" to the environment. The capacity not to respond, or, more accurately, to delay responding, is a sophisticated accomplishment of living systems.   The length of delay possible is a useful index of phylogenetic development.

The spontaneous response of the octopus on seeing a crab is to go straight to it. Young put a glass screen between the octopus and the crab and found that the octopus was capable of learning to go around the screen to get at the crab. This **detour behavior** is very significant. In turning away from the crab, the behavior of the octopus is directed not by the stimulus of the crab but by an image of the crab.   We see here the beginning of mental life. The octopus can make a sketchy subjective map of the objective world and operate within the map as well as within the world. This emancipation from the tyranny of the environment is possible only if there is a part of the nervous system (neither sensory nor motor) in which images can be stored.   The uncommitted cortex has yielded the unsolicited gift of consciousness.

Wilder Penfield found evidence that memory is localized in a particular

---

[13]   Or, more accurately, "grab, grab, grab, grab, grab, grab, grab, grab".

place within the association area of the brain [PENFIELD & ROBERTS]. He was operating on patients suffering from epilepsy by removing the area of the brain which triggered the epileptic seizure. Such an operation can be conducted while the patient is fully conscious, since there are no pain receptors in the brain. He dropped an electrode into the brain of the patient to make sure that the affected area is not part of the speech center. If it was, the cure would be worse than the disease. When he dropped the electrode into the temporal lobe of one patient she reported experiencing an event in her past. It was a rerun of a past event with all the accompanying sights, sounds, smells, tastes, and touches. When Penfield lifted the electrode and dropped it again into the same place, the relived experience continued where it had left off. It was as if the patient had a complete videotape of her past which could be played by triggering it with an electrode.

The localization of memory in a particular area would seem incompatible with the mass action of the brain as a whole. However just as the deposit and withdrawal of money in a bank differs from the storage of that money in the bank, so the deposit and retrieval of information from the memory bank may differ from its storage. When you withdraw $100 from your bank account you don't expect to get back the same five crumbled $20 bills you deposited some time before. Memory may be stored chemically throughout the brain yet deposited and retrieved neurologically in a particular area of the brain. Whatever the mechanism, the important point is that the nervous system has the means of storing information (memory) and transmitting information (speech). It is interesting that the storage and transmission areas of the brain are close to one another. No doubt, as the solution to the mystery of memory and speech unfolds we will find how this first generation of media is ingeniously designed by natural selection.

Memory (however nature designs it) is the foundation of all media (however we design them). In Greek mythology, Mnemosyne (memory) was the mother of the nine muses:

Klio	History
Melpomene	Tragedy
Phalia	Comedy
Kalliope	Heroic poems
Urania	Astronomy
Euterpe	Art of music
Polyhymnia	Song and oratory
Erato	Love and marriage
Terpsichore	Dance

Those muses were the "media" of that time. However, Mnemosyne is still the mother (or grandmother?) of Teevee, Telephono, Multimedia, Internete (or whatever we decide to call our modern muses).

CHAPTER 3
SHIFT 1 - ASSIMILATING
THE SECOND GENERATION

3.1   WHAT IS A STRUCTURAL SHIFT?

3.2   TORONTO SCHOOL - HAROLD INNIS

3.3   THREATS AND OPPORTUNITIES

The discovery of the alphabet will create forgetfulness in the learners' souls. You will give your disciples not truth but the semblance of truth: they will be heroes of many things, and will have learned nothing; they will appear to be omniscient and will generally know nothing.

Plato, PHAEDRUS

We didn't need dialogue. We had faces.

Norma Desmond in SUNSET BOULEVARD
(Commenting on shift from silent movies to talkies)

3.1   WHAT IS A STRUCTURAL SHIFT?

The four generations of media are defined formally in terms of the storage and transmission of information using extragenetic and extrasomatic tools (see Figure 1-2). They are presented respectively in Chapters 2, 4, 6, and 8. Between each of those chapters, there are chapters describing the shift resulting from the introduction of each new generation of media. Thus, Chapters 3, 5, and 7 describe the effect of the assimilation of the second, third, and fourth generations of media, respectively.

The introduction of the second generation did not simply mean that we now had first generation (memory and speech) *plus* second generation (print and film). They are no more additive than the properties of water are the sum of the properties of hydrogen and the properties of oxygen. The whole is greater than the sum of the parts. Each shift is like a vigorous shake of a kaleidoscope yielding a completely different pattern. Since this shift is structural rather than simply sectoral, it is necessary to have a broad model to understand it. That is, it is necessary to have a model of the whole society rather than simply separate models of the various sectors of which it is composed.

The need for a broad model is reflected also in the work we did at **GAMMA**, the inter-disciplinary, future-studies "think tank" to which I belonged from 1970 till 1985. We were approached by a variety of organizations seeking help in managing the structural shift as the media system accommodates to the assimilation of the fourth generation of media. They found that the sectoral models they had used to date no longer applied in those turbulent, transitional times.

Working at GAMMA, you sometimes feel like a sort of intellectual James Bond in thought-filled adventures - Mr. Think-Think, Write-Write rather than Mr. Kiss-Kiss, Bang-Bang, or like a futuristic Sherlock Holmes, dealing not with mere murders in the past but with the larger mysteries of the future. As in most James Bond and Sherlock Holmes cases, the story opens with someone with a problem. Let me describe, by way of example, the case of the missing predictions.

It all began with a call from the Ministry of Transportation and Communications of the Ontario Provincial Government. They had a problem. They had a nice neat little demographic model from which they predicted the distribution of households in Ontario and, hence, the flow of traffic, and, hence, the focus of road-building and maintenance. The model, which had worked reasonably well for many years was no longer working. They got zapped by the energy crisis. They got zapped by the OPEC decision. All sorts of such surprises from outside upset their model. Planners don't like surprises - at least, not when they are the surprisees.

They had to expand their model. The world was becoming interconnected. How much did they need to expand? The surprises were coming from - everywhere. In a very bold move, they decided to expand to include - everything! They set up a group called Futures Outlook and asked them to study the future.

After some moments of consternation (*Study the future? But we've never been there! Nor has anyone else so you can't be contradicted*), they set to work. They invited a number of consulting companies to

- Select seminal sources on the future
- Distribute them among themselves
- Squeeze out predictions from each of those sources, and their implications for the future of Ontario, within six categories - Demographic, Economic, Socio-cultural, Environmental, Resources, and Technology.

We dutifully did as we were told. So they ended up with piles of predictions and implications. Another call from the Ministry. *Help! What do we do with this pile of information. Will you synthesize it for us?* (About half the time our clients were seeking synthesis because they have too much information and half the time they were seeking analysis because they have too little information.) It happened that, when this call came in, I had just returned from Europe and Kimon Valaskakis, the President of GAMMA, was just leaving for Europe.

The following conversation ensued during the day we overlapped in Montreal:

He: *You want to take this case on?*

Me: *Synthesis? I never learned synthesis in school. Analysis, yes but synthesis no. We learned how to take the universe apart but not how to put it together again.*

He: *You publish textbooks in psychology, don't you. That is synthesis. You must have learned it somewhere.*

Me: *I guess so, now that you mention it. I must have learned it after school by accident. Okay.*

Thus began the Summer of the Synthesis. My first attempt at climbing this mountain of data was to develop a cross-impact matrix which listed the predicted impacts of variables within each of the six categories on variables within each of the other five. Hence, I spent the first part of the Summer staring - my little mind boggling - at this six-by-six matrix pasted to my wall.

The second attempt involved collapsing the six categories into three - to be more manageable by my mind. Thus, demographic, economic, and socio-cultural became sociosphere (the social world), environmental, and resources became ecosphere (the natural world), and technology became technosphere (the artificial world). Now I had to deal only with the more manageable three-by-three matrix.

It was still stretching my cognitive capacities. Suddenly something snapped. There was something missing. Surely a psychologist should have noticed sooner that there was no person in the model. The great spheres were all moving in their interdependent ways as if there was no person present. Where was the person? The person, it seemed, should be in all three spheres - the person is the most complex system in the natural world, the person is the element of the social world, and the person is the source of the artificial world. Then it clicked. The model should not be a square three-by-three matrix but three overlapping circles, with the person in the center. This progression from a six-by-six matrix to a three-by-three matrix to three overlapping circles is illustrated in Figure 3-1.

The model can be called, somewhat whimsically, *The Three Interfaces of Adam*, because it can be described in terms of the Christian cosmology.[1] Imagine Adam all alone on our planet before it got so complicated. He had to deal only with the natural world - let us call it the **ecosphere**. Along came Eve and they prospered and multiplied, introducing another great sphere to Adam's environment, consisting of other people - let us call it the **sociosphere**. As Adam and Eve and their progeny made discoveries about and inventions from their environment, they built up a third great sphere, consisting of person-made things - let us call it the **technosphere**.

So here we have Adam or Eve, or you or me, in an environment represented by three spheres (Figure 3-2). The person, the only system within the universe which belongs to all three spheres, is in the center - the triple overlap of the three spheres. Our environment is differentiated into those three spheres because the person has a different logical relationship to each sphere. The ecosphere conforms to the laws of the natural sciences; the sociosphere to the laws of the social sciences; and the technosphere to the laws of what Herbert Simon calls *The Sciences of the Artificial* [SIMON].

---

[1] Feminists in my class complained that I was perpetuating the male bias of the Christian cosmology. I protested feebly that I was simply playing with the analogy with *The Three Faces of Eve*. However, they are right. So, after exploiting the heuristic value of the analogy, let us call it simply the **Triad Model**.

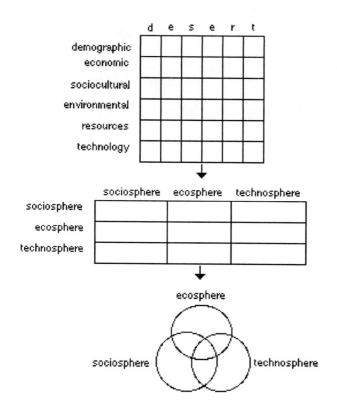

FIGURE 3-1
FROM 6x6 MATRIX TO 3x3 MATRIX TO TRIAD

You may reasonably say that this model is too broad. Indeed, it is. How broad is it? It is so broad that it contains not only everything I am going to write but everything anyone has ever written in the past or everything anyone will ever write in the future. However, we academics tend to be too narrow. If the person in the center is a natural scientist (physicist, biologist, etc.), s/he tends to look out over the ecosphere; if the person in the center is a social scientist (economist, political scientist, etc.), s/he tends to look out over the sociosphere; if the person in the center is an expert in the sciences of the artificial (architect, engineer, etc.), s/he tends to look out over the technosphere.

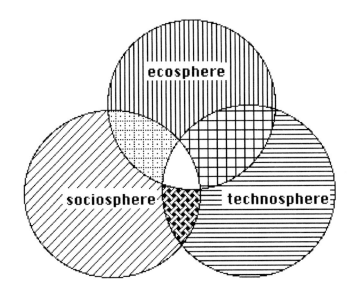

FIGURE 3-2   TRIAD MODEL

They are like the three blind men, touching respectively the trunk, the tusk, and the tail of the elephant, and thus getting a false view of the whole elephant. One encouraging sign of the recent times is that we are beginning to step back and look at more of the elephant. Some people are looking at the overlap of ecosphere and sociosphere - for example, studies of legislation about conservation on our natural environment; some people are looking at the overlap of sociosphere and technosphere - for example, social assessment studies of the human impact of technology; some people are looking at the overlap of the ecosphere and the technosphere - for example, technology assessment studies of the environmental impact of technology. We need to stand even further back and look also at the triple overlap of all three spheres - the person in the center. We will do so in Chapter 9.

You may reasonably say that this model is too simple. Indeed, it is. However, we academics tend to under-simplify things. It is a useful first slice of reality. It is like a first introduction to Montreal. It is an island with a mountain in the middle. Downtown is between the river and the mountain. There are four major East-West streets - Sherbrooke, de Maisonneuve, St. Catherine, and René Lésvesque. The other major downtown streets - Atwater, Guy, Peel, University, Park, St. Laurent, St. Denis - cut those four streets at right angles. Within that general framework, the details can be fitted in.

Indeed the model has an optimal level of complexity. It consists of seven categories (represented by the seven different patterns in Figure 3-2). George Miller, in his classical paper *The magical number seven, plus or minus two: Some limits on our capacity for processing information* argued that we are capable of handling simultaneously only seven categories (give or take a couple, to allow for individual differences) [MILLER]. Being average people, then, seven categories are just about right for us.

Did it work as a synthesis? Indeed, we think, it did. Our future will be determined, as has our past, by the complex interaction among those three vast spheres. Futurists differ, however, in the relative emphasis on those three spheres.

Some argue that the ecosphere will become more important in the future than it has been in the past. Let us call this the ecosphere-as-cause scenario. Within this camp, there are pessimists and optimists. The pessimists - for example, the Club of Rome in their book *The Limits to Growth* - argue that we are going to destroy our civilization by using up our natural non-renewable resources [MEADOWS ET AL]. The optimists - for example, the GAMMA Group, to which I belonged, in our book *The Conserver Society* -   argue that we can eke out those resources for considerably longer by conservation policies [VALASKAKIS ET AL].

Some argue that the sociosphere will be relatively more important in the future. Let us call this the sociosphere-as-cause scenario. Once again, we have the pessimists and the optimists. The pessimists, all the way from Thomas Malthus to Paul Ehrlich, argue that the primary problem is one of over-population. The optimists are the advocates of capitalism and communism and - a third option for the Third World - the New International Economic Order, who argue that those people can be organized into productive systems which will generate the wealth to sustain them [e.g. BRANDT, GALTUNG].

Some argue that the technosphere will be relatively more important in the future. Let us call this the technosphere-as-cause scenario. Once again, as always, the pessimists and the optimists. The optimists - for example, R. Buckminster Fuller in his book *Utopia or Oblivion* [FULLER] - argue that, through technology, each of us can live as kings lived in the last century. The pessimists - for example, Jacques Ellul in his book *The Technological Society* [ELLUL] - argue that technology is not only not a solution but is part of the problem.

Within each pessimist camp, there is, of course, the no-future future. The ecosphere-as-cause doomsday scenario is that we will wipe ourselves out by using up our natural resources; the sociosphere-as-cause scenario is that we will destroy ourselves by over-populating our planet; the technosphere-as-cause scenario is that we will blow our planet up with nuclear weapons. In *The Hollow Men* , T. S. Eliot predicts

This is the way the world ends

Not with a bang but a whimper.

Doom-sayers offer us a choice between two whimpers and a bang.

Returning to our history of media, the four generations of media represent changes within the technosphere. That's where much of the current action is. Let us for now consider this book as falling within the technosphere-as-cause scenario. More precisely, the book falls into the optimistic sub-category of the technosphere-as-cause scenario. You should read the work of the European Schools (Frankfurt School, Sussex School, etc.) to balance this book with those in the pessimistic sub-category. In Chapter 9, we will argue for a person-as-cause scenario, not considered in this original research.

The structural shifts as we assimilate each generation of media may best be described using the language of Jean Piaget, who does for ontogenetic development (from child to adult) what Charles Darwin does for phylogenetic development (from animal to human). Both describe development as a process of continuous discontinuity. It is continuous with respect to function and discontinuous with respect to structure. The function in both cases is adaptation to the environment. Different organisms developed different structures to adapt to different environments. The child acquires different cognitive structures as s/he develops. Piaget describes the process of adaptation as alternations between the process of **assimilation** and the process of **accommodation**. That is, the child assimilates information from the environment and, if necessary, adjusts the cognitive structure to accommodate it [PIAGET]. By analogy, society assimilates each generation of media and adjusts to accommodate it.

3.2   TORONTO SCHOOL - HAROLD INNIS

We need not only a broad model, as argued above, but also people who can deal with broad models - that is, generalists. Traditional education has trained specialists. We learn more and more about less and less until, as the cynics say, we know everything about nothing. We are able to speak to fewer and fewer fellow specialists until, as the cynics say, we can speak only to ourselves. When

R. Buckminster Fuller sought training as a generalist, he had to join the U. S. Navy. In those days before tele-communications, a lowly lieutenant in command of a mine-sweeper at sea had a mini-universe to control and, therefore, had to be a generalist. Now tele-communications ensures that wars are waged between admirals on shore and thus even this limited means of training generalists was cut off.

There is a danger that the centralization of control due to further proliferating tele-communications and the apprehension about increasing information overload will further increase the trend to specialization. It is in turbulent transitional times such as those that we need people who can have a broad (albeit admittedly shallow) view of things as well as those who have a narrow and deep view.

The rest of this book will zero in on categories within this broad model. It is important, however, that we retain the bird's-eye view provided in this chapter to supplement the various worm's-eye views which follow. We have to be like artists working on a large canvas, alternating between moving in close to work on details and standing back to see the whole picture. The *whole picture* of the current transition from an industrial to an information society can be seen only by stepping back and seeing things in one "eye gulp", by means of a general model such as provided in this chapter.

The four generations of media (see Figure 1-2) could be considered as an inset within the technosphere in the Triad Model (see Figure 3-2). Note that the four generations of media and the three transitions between them constitute seven categories. Once again, this is the optimal level of complexity as advocated by George Miller (see Section 3.1 above).

Future studies, the domain of my work at GAMMA, and communication studies, the domain of my work at Concordia University, are among the very few disciplines which permit the training of generalists. They do so because their subject is not a system but an aspect of all systems. Future studies focuses on the future dimension of all systems and communication studies on the communication aspect of all systems. It is to those disciplines that we may look for the introduction of training of generalists in the university system.

Whereas future studies has not been accepted at all, communication studies has established a toe-hold within the academy. A few universities have departments of communication studies, which tend to have lower status that the more established disciplines.[2] Within communication studies, the **Toronto School** best exemplifies the generalist position advocated here. By considering media as extensions of the person, this school places the person firmly in the center, as in the model presented above. The school was founded by Harold Innis, whose work was continued by Marshall McLuhan, whose work is being in turn continued by a group of scholars considered by their supporters as new McLuhans. Since Innis died in 1952, before the assimilation of the third generation of telephone and television, his work will be used to describe the first shift; since McLuhan died in 1980, before the assimilation of the fourth generation of multimedia and internet, his work will be used to describe the second shift; since the new McLuhans are still with us, their work will be used to describe the third shift we are currently all experiencing.

Harold Innis (1894-1952) began his career as a political economist.[3] His main focus was on the **staples theory** of the Canadian economy. Canada began largely as a rentier nation exporting its abundant natural resources and buying

---

[2]   Indeed, the discipline is very precariously perched on the periphery of the academy. The Communication Studies department at McGill University had to merge recently with the Department of Art History to survive and the Center for Technology and Culture founded by Marshall McLuhan at the University of Toronto is perpetually threatened with closure.

[3]   For this section, I'm indebted to my colleague, Dr. Ray Charron, who made the presentation on which it is based to my graduate class. He also read much of the manuscript and made many valuable suggestions for its improvement.

back the finished goods.[4]   He conducted careful studies of the fur industry, the cod industry, and the pulp and paper industry.

However, he came under the influence of Thorstein Veblen, an eccentric economist at the University of Chicago, who argued that one should look at economics within the larger framework of ecology. In his most famous work - *The Theory of the Leisure Class* - he introduced the concept of conspicuous consumption [VEBLEN].   Innis realized that an economy based on the consumption of non-renewable resources was disastrous for our ecology and doomed as a economic policy. If we sit back on our assets, we would become a Third World country in a post-colonial world in which the developed countries transform our raw materials into finished goods and skim off the profit. Looking at the larger picture, Innis realized that what was printed on the paper was as important as the paper itself.

Thus began his studies of various civilizations in terms of the surfaces on which they chose to write their words and draw their images. If a civilization chose to use stone tablets, then they would conquer time (note that much Egyptian writing is still with us); whereas if a civilization chose to use parchment (the skin of animals), then they would conquer space. It is easier to carry around parchment than stone tablets. Note that the Romans were able to administer most of the known world using parchment. His final two books were wide-ranging explorations of civilizations, in terms of their relative emphasis on the conquest of time and space as a function of the media they used, in contrast to his careful detailed studies of staples [INNIS 1950, 1951]. However, since he had come from a study of paper to a study of what was written on the paper, he never lost

---

[4]   Some have even described Canada as a company country. It was initially largely owned by the Hudson Bay Company. This was not so long ago. I came to Canada because of an ad for young Scotsmen to work in the Canadian North trading for furs from the indigenous peoples. One was offered free transportation and Canadian immigration status in exchange for signing up for a two-year term.

sight of the importance of the medium.

His most famous student, Marshall McLuhan, who continued this Toronto School he had started, encapsulated this insight into his famous aphorism: *The Medium is the Message.* McLuhan considers his work as a footnote to that of Innis. Part of that "footnote" is a metaphor for the structural shift as we assimilated the second generation of print and film. We traded an ear for an eye.

The major difference between the ear and the eye is that we have much more control over the eye than over the ear. We can choose not to see by closing our eyes. We have no earlids.[5]   We can train our eyes to focus on a point in space to see more clearly, but we can't train our ears to focus on a point in time to hear more clearly. What we see remains, what we hear is gone as soon as we hear it.   We can train our eyes to move more precisely along lines and to jump from the end of one line to the beginning of the next line.   When information is presented simultaneously to the eye and the ear as in television, the video dominates the audio channel in the famous **vampire effect**.[6]

One of McLuhan's students, Paul Levinson, adds in turn a footnote to McLuhan's footnote. He argues that the ear is preferred over the eye under certain circumstances [LEVINSON 1997]. Why, he asks, did the talkies wipe out silent films within a couple of years, whereas television did not wipe out radio? It would seem that the two situations were parallel. In both cases you have a single channel challenged by a double channel. Silent movie is seeing-without-hearing and talkies is seeing-*and*-hearing; radio is hearing-without-seeing and television is

---

[5]   J. J. Gibson often turned down his hearing aid and went to sleep during colloquia. This was a cue to we graduate students that the presentation was not worthwhile. This was the bright side of his deafness - he had, as he said, volume control.

[6]   Michael Deaver, a spin-master who worked for Ronald Reagan, admitted that he didn't care what the voice-over was saying about his client or even what his client was saying, he just wanted to get his smiling face on the screen.

hearing-*and*-seeing.

The obvious answer is that while listening to radio you can do other things which you can't do while watching television - driving, housework, making love.[7] However, Levinson provides a more profound answer - seeing-without-hearing is not part of our human experience. Since we have no earlids, whenever there is video there is also audio. On the other hand, hearing-without-seeing is part of our human experience. Over millions of years, we have experienced hearing-without-seeing, not just because we have eyelids and can choose not to see but because the planet is dark on average half the time.

This is part of the evidence Levinson assembles for his **anthropotropic principle:** media must respect human nature, and satisfy human needs. This principle suggests why stereophonic sound is twice as good as mono but quadraphonic sound is not twice as good as stereo. We have two ears. It also suggests why the much-heralded videophone has not yet penetrated the market. We tend to think of privacy in visual rather than auditory terms. Being overheard is okay but not being overseen.[8]

One familiar violation of the anthropotropic principle is the use of the keyboard and the mouse as input devices for the computer. You have to take one hand off the keyboard every time you use the mouse, prompting many people to complain that "*if God meant you to use a mouse, he would have given you three*

---

[7]   One of my ruder students pointed out that you can make love while watching television but are limited in positions. He attributes certain Canadian sexual practices to the need for both partners to watch *Saturday Night Hockey*.

[8]   My thanks to Dr. Ira Nayman for introduction to and enlightening discussion of the work of Paul Levinson., the Director of his Master's Thesis (They never met since the thesis was directed by mail, over the phone and the internet!).

In the early days of electronic extensions to the telephone, I surprised a women friend when she called by addressed her right away by name before she had spoken. How did you know it was me?   I have call display. Ah! I better put on some clothes. It's call display not caller display I assured her. Her moment of panic confirmed for me that caller display will not be a service of Bell Canada for some time, despite the exhibit of the videophone they were presenting at Expo 1967 - that is, almost 40 years ago.

hands". Douglas Engelbart (1925 -   ), who invented the mouse, advocated the **chord keyset** for the other hand [BARDINI]. This was a one-handed keyboard consisting of 5 keys, one for each finger, which translated numbers and letters into a binary code. Tests demonstrated that one could type much faster on this device than on the traditional qwerty keyboard. It also respected the fact that we have two hands. Alas, the traditional keyboard was too well established to be dislodged by an alternative, no matter how reasonable.

3.3   THREATS AND OPPORTUNITIES

GAMMA, the think-tank to which I belonged, submitted the ETA Report to their clients. This report, emerged from our Environmental Tracking Analysis (ETA) procedure, provided them with a sort of state-of-the-universe message. It described the major processes of change currently taking place in their environment - whether ecosphere, sociosphere, or technosphere. Some of our clients asked us to go beyond describing the changes in their environment to describing the implications of those changes for their organization. Thus, to the **ETA Report**, which answered the question *What's happening?* , we added the **TAO Report**, which answered the question *So what?*.

TAO, the Chinese symbol for *challenge*, is a combination of the symbols for threat and for opportunity. It is often represented by the image depicted in Figure 3-3. The black and white parts of the circle indicate that a challenge can be considered as both a threat and an opportunity. The white circle within the black part and the black circle within the white part indicate that there is opportunity within threat and there is threat within opportunity. The Threats And Opportunities (TAO) Report thus described the threats to and the opportunities for our clients presented by the changes described in the ETA Report. It also described the opportunities within the threats and the threats within the opportunities.

Let us consider the person in the center of the Triad Model (see Figure 3-2) as our client. What are the threats and opportunities to the person as the second generation of Print and Film is assimilated?

The work of Harold Innis described above captures the major opportunity. This second generation contributes to our conquest of time and space. The process of development, whether from animal to human or from child to adult, was described above as the progressive emancipation of the organism from the tyranny of the environment. This emancipation process continues as we assimilate the second generation of Print and Film. Apart from some ingenious line-of-sight communication systems - smoke signals, semaphore, etc. - the first generation of media was constrained by the limitations of the human voice. To communicate, we had to be within eye-sight and ear-shot of one another. Print and film enable us to transcend this limitation. I wrote a book thirty years ago that you can read now. You can take a photograph in London and I can look at it here in Montreal. With the second generation of media, we can further escape the tyranny of the environment. We don't have to live in the here and now.

Socrates pointed out the threat-within-opportunity. He viewed writing as a threat because extrasomatic storage will replace extragenetic storage. That is, we will lose our memories (see quote at beginning of this chapter). He was right. Few people today could memorize *The Iliad* and *The Odyssey* as could many of his contemporaries.

FIGURE 3-3   THREATS AND OPPORTUNITIES (TAO)

Plato defied his teacher by writing down the lecture notes he had taken as *The Dialogues*. He wrote them as dialogues to preserve the flavor of the oral tradition. However, the damage was done. The live words from the mouth of Socrates were captured as dead words on a page. Those of us for whom Socrates is a hero are pleased that his memory has been preserved for us by this defiant act of Plato. Since Socrates, true to his principles, never wrote anything himself, we would not even have known of his existence and would not have been able to benefit from his wisdom.

Most great teachers, like Socrates, did not write. Jesus, Confucius, Mohammed, Buddha were all in the oral tradition. They spoke. But they had disciples, students who wrote down what they said. Every Johnson has his Boswell, who believes their mentor has something important to say and records it. Otherwise their wisdom would be lost to us. Perhaps it is still lost. Perhaps you had to be there.

The Galilean Quartet (like the Alexandrian Quartet, the same story is told from four different points of view) was written by Matthew, Mark, Luke, John many years after the events in the life of Jesus which they recorded. The disciples were eye-witnesses. However, eye-witnesses get it wrong sometimes, especially when they write some time later. Every media innovation involves a trade-off. The second generation of print preserves the wisdom of the great thinkers who used the first generation of media. However, something is inevitably lost in translation. Words lined up on a page can not fully capture the liveliness of listening to a charismatic speaker.

Some argue that there are certain skills, which can not be passed on from generation to generation using our extrasomatic tools. **Craft literacy**, for example, can only be learned by each individual from the inside out. It's like riding a bicycle - one can not learn it by reading a book. The following parable makes this point:[9]

> Duke Huan of Ch'i was reading a book at the upper end of the Hall; the wheelwright was making a wheel at the lower end. Putting aside his mallet and chisel, he called to the duke and asked him what book he was reading.
> *"One that records the words of the sages "*, answered the Duke.

---

[9]   I'm indebted to my colleague, Dr. Maben Poirier, for drawing my attention to this parable and for lengthy enlightening discussions of its implications. The distinction between craft and traditional literacy was clarified for me by the following experience. During a personal energy crisis, I bought a bike. Though I had not ridden a bike for 20 years, I hopped on it immediately and rode off. Returning from a trip, however, I found I could no longer ride my bike. I had forgotten the combination for its lock. My body had "remembered" how to ride a bike for 20 years but my mind couldn't remember the combination for a few days.

"Are those sages alive?" asked the wheelwright.

"Oh, no", said the Duke, *"they are dead."*

"In that case" said the wheelwright, *"what you are reading can be nothing but the lees and scum of bygone men."*

"How dare you, a wheelwright, find fault with the book I am reading? If you can explain your statement, I'll let it pass. If not, you shall die."

"Speaking as a wheelwright," he replied, *"I look at the matter in this way; when I am making a wheel, if my stroke is too slow, then it bites deep but is not steady; if my stroke is too fast, then it is steady, but does not go deep. The right pace, neither slow nor fast, cannot get into the hand unless it comes from the heart. It is a thing that cannot be put into words; there is an art in it that I cannot explain to my son. This is why it is impossible for me to let him take over my work, and here I am at the age of seventy, still making wheels. In my opinion it must be the same with the men of old. All that was worth handing on, died with them; the rest, they put into their books. That is why I said that what you are reading was the lees and scum of bygone men."*

Attributed to Chuang Tzu [WALEY]

The major threat, as we assimilated the second generation of media, is to democracy. The first generation of media is essentially democratic. All members of our species are issued with essentially the same equipment for Speech and Memory. Natural selection has built the capacity to speak and listen into our genetic program, though it leaves a large gap in the program to be filled in by the environment, since there is no survival value to acquiring a language which is not spoken by the language community in which a child is immersed. As we learned above, there is no such thing as a primitive language. Every language had equivalents for every logical operator and thus the basis of logic and thus, in turn, of mathematics (see Section 2.2). Every member of our species receives the same conception-day gift.

The second generation of media - since it is designed by people rather than by nature - is less democratic. Learning to read and write is a more arduous process than learning to speak and listen. There is no genetic program for learning to write and read as there is for learning to speak and listen. Writing is a human invention, which piggy-backs on the evolutionary invention of speaking. We can all learn to speak, even in poverty-stricken conditions, because the means of doing so are provided by nature. However, we can not all learn to write as easily, because writing is an arbitrary social invention of our species. Children, who do not have access to instruction in reading and the leisure to take advantage of this instruction, will not become literate.

The potential for freedom described above is only realized by those who have the means to take advantage of it. Much of the power of the Roman Catholic Church was based on the fact that priests had the means of becoming literate, whereas most of their parishioners had not. Many priests resented and resisted the democratization of print made possible by the printing press because it reduced their power as middle-men, reading and interpreting the Bible to their illiterate parishioners.[10]   They could read the Bible themselves. Much of the "protest" of Protestants was about cutting out the middle-man. When Martin Luther tacked his protest on the church door, the medium was at least part of the message.

Victor Hugo had his priest character - Frodo in The *Hunchback of Notre Dame* - say this (a printed pamphlet in his hand) will replace that (Notre Dame Cathedral). It did and it didn't. Last time I looked the Cathedral was still there but its function has changed. The parishioners do not need to depend on the medium of the stained-glass windows and the priest to get the message, but they are attracted to the immersive environment of a mass with ceremony and ceilings, chanting and music creating a sense of awe not possible by reading a book, however holy. The Gestalt principle that the whole is greater than the sum of its parts, described above, mitigates against any simple this-will-replace-that prediction. Old media are not so much replaced by new media as edged into a new niche.

---

[10]   They were the conservatives of their time. Conservatives tend to view change as threatening. This is not a surprise. Conservatives are those who have something to conserve. This is why we tend to become more conservative as we get older - we have acquired more vested interest in the status quo.

The Roman Catholic Church can claim much credit for the preservation of the wisdom contained in more secular books since monks were responsible for copying the texts of early Greek philosophers. Its initial resistance to the democratization of print, facilitated by the invention of the printing press, was subsequently reduced. The Church welcomed printing with cheap, printed versions of the Holy Bible becoming an important element in the spreading of the Gospel. A faith which seeks converts has a vested interest in media. My own Department of Communication Studies was founded by the Jesuits, the intellectual wing of the Roman Catholic Church.

This resistance to universal literacy persists today. Writing piggy-backed on speaking by creating a set of units (graphemes) corresponding roughly to the set of units in speaking (phonemes). George Bernard Shaw tried to make learning to write easier by designing written language with perfect **phoneme-grapheme correspondence**. His efforts were strongly resisted. A natural language is difficult by design. One must work hard to pass the initiation rite to join the literate club. If it was made easy, anyone could join. There would therefore be no one left to brand as illiterate and thus condemn to the lower-status and lower-paid jobs.

There is the same resistance to artificial languages like, for example, Esperanto. Some people have recently whimsically argued for Europanto, a common language for the Common Market to match the Euro, their common currency [RICHLER]. Fifteen member countries require 15 x 14 translations of all their "common" documents. Such an incredible expense could be saved by a common language. Ironically some have suggested English as such a common language, even though England has chosen not to use the common currency. My neighbor, Trisha Santa, recommends Latin, the "common language" from which most European languages were derived. The obvious necessity for such a common language encounters the excessive attachment each language group has to its own language. After passing the initiation rite, they are extremely reluctant to give it up.

The opportunity within the threat is that individuals, as well as institutions, could gain power by acquiring literacy. Egyptians could avoid back-breaking work by becoming scribes. Scribes had more status. It was a step towards upward mobility. It was the beginning of a meritocracy. However, it confronts us with the issue of elitism versus egalitarianism. Your opinion has more weight because of your expertise. Postmodern thinkers, in arguing that all opinions are equally valid, are attempting to counter this threat to democracy.

CHAPTER 4
SECOND GENERATION
- PRINT AND FILM

4.1   PERCEPTUAL AND CONCEPTUAL MAPS

4.2   A SHORT HISTORY OF PRINT

4.3   A SHORT HISTORY OF FILM

4.4   FROM PRINT TO FILM

Really we create nothing. We merely plagiarize nature.
Jean Baudrillard, SIMULATIONS

I've just had a brain scan.
In my left hemisphere, there's nothing right.
In my right hemisphere, there's nothing left.
Anonymous

4.1   PERCEPTUAL AND CONCEPTUAL MAPS

The second generation is defined as the use of extrasomatic tools to store information outside our bodies. We store information outside our bodies in words (Print) and in images (Film). Capturing this distinction between word and image requires a more sophisticated model than the Triad Model, presented above in Figure 3-2. By depicting the person as the triple overlap of ecosphere (natural world), sociosphere (social world) and technosphere (artificial world), the Triad Model focuses on the **objective world** of behavior with respect to those three aspects of the environment. However, each person at the center has a **subjective map** of this objective world which partially determines this behavior. That is, our behavior is determined by the world-as-we-see-it rather than by the world-as-it-is. It is necessary then to add an inset to our model, depicting this subjective map (see Figure 4-1). This is the level of experience.

The nervous system is unique among all systems in the universe, because it can be viewed from the inside (experience) as well as from the outside (behavior). A full description of the function of the nervous system must explain both behavior and experience. The view from the inside and the view from the outside overlap. However, there can be aspects of behavior which are not aspects of experience, and aspects of experience which are not aspects of behavior.[1]

---

[1]   A student once pointed out that I tend to touch the top of my fly from time to time while lecturing. This reminded me of the time when another student had told me *after* I had delivered a two-hour lecture to 700 students that my fly was open. My unconscious gesture was a part of my behavior which was not a part of my experience. That is what we mean by "unconscious". From time to time, when I am lecturing, I am reminded of my mother. She never understood why I continued going to school after I was allowed to leave. When people in the village asked what I was doing, she had to admit that I was still going to school. The next obvious question was how I supported myself and her not-so-obvious answer was "*he lives by his wits* " Here I go again, I often think while lecturing, living by my wits and I'm on half-salary. Unless I choose to pass on those thoughts to the class, they are a part of experience which is not a part of behavior. Such unconscious behavior and unexpressed experience demonstrate the need to explain *both* behavior and experience.

The subjective map could be considered as composed of a **perceptual map** based on things in the objective world and a **conceptual map** based on words in the objective world. Since the speech center is in the left hemisphere of the brain, it is a useful heuristic to associate the conceptual map with the left hemisphere.

Despite the fact that I attended the university most famed for its research on perception, I still was taught that this left hemisphere was the "dominant" hemisphere. Since motor functions cross over, the left hemisphere controls the right side of the body. Most people are right-handed, right-footed, and right-eyed.[2]   The right hemisphere was viewed as a sort of spare in case there was damage to the dominant left hemisphere (based on the evidence that indeed if there was damage to the speech center in early childhood, it could switch to the "submissive" right hemisphere). Now, it is clear that the right hemisphere is best considered as creating a perceptual map of the objective world.

Because of my traditional training, I strongly emphasize the conceptual over the perceptual map. An example of this is that I write directions when given them over the telephone (left side of Figure 4-2). When driving to visit my friend Sally, I had to stop a couple of times to reread my directions. In the interval between this first and a second visit, I had been thinking about my neglected right hemisphere. Hence, the next time she invited me, I drew a map as she was giving me directions (right side of Figure 4-2). This time I drove straight there, since I had a map in my mind. It is obvious to me now that nature would not create the most complex system in the world simply as a spare part and that the drawing of

---

[2]   We all know whether we are right- or left-handed. In Scotland, everyone - or at least all boys - knew whether they were right- or left-footed, because of soccer. Few of us, however, know whether we are right- or left-eyed. With both eyes open, line up your thumb with some object. Close your right eye. If your thumb is no longer lined up with the object, you are right-eyed. With both eyes open, your dominant eye does the lining up.

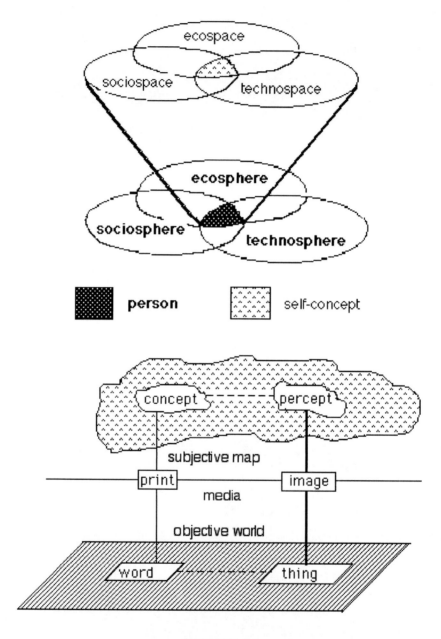

FIGURE 4-1

TRIAD MODEL - TWO-STORY VERSION

A map while getting directions clearly calls for the use of the right hemisphere.

When Barry Lucky gave me directions to his sound studio in the basement of his farm in Alexandria so that I could come to have my Siliclone pressed into a CD-ROM, I drew a map.[3]   Halfway there, I realized that I had left the map at home. My first reaction was to go back for it, but I discovered that I had the map in my head right down to the address of his farm and followed it right there.

My use of diagrams in this book - Four Generations of Media (see Figure 1-2), Triad Model (see Figure 3-2), and so on - further illustrates my attempt to learn to use my right hemisphere. Sometimes it is better to show than to tell. We have to learn to use our whole brain and not just the left side of its upper crust. A picture is indeed sometimes worth a thousand words.

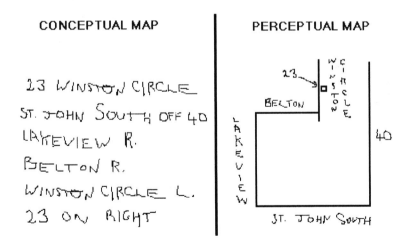

FIGURE 4-2   CONCEPTUAL AND PERCEPTUAL MAPS

---

[3]   Preview of coming attractions: The Siliclone is a silicon clone of myself. It will be discussed in detail in Section 11.2.

Another exercise to activate my dormant right hemisphere is to carry a small camera at all times. I have always carried a notebook for fishing in the stream-of-consciousness. That is, as the stream of consciousness is rushing past (or trickling past on bad days), I write down anything which is deemed interesting. My experience has been that we tend to forget even if it seems so unforgettable at the time. I'll always remember whatshername. From time to time, those notes are thrown into shoe boxes for each of the projects I'm working on. When it comes time to write that paper or give that lecture, more ideas emerge from that box than went into it. They've been breeding. Any new idea is a combination of old ideas. Now, I carry a small camera to do the same for the perceptual map. It alerts me to interesting stills in the mind movie.

The small camera embodies the Advanced Photo System. This system has a number of features distinguishing it from the traditional 35 mm camera which has been essentially unchanged for decades. It is more compact. It uses cartridges which can be easily popped in and out of the camera. There are three optional aspect ratios - classical, hdtv, and panoramic. The photographs are returned with a colored contact sheet. You can receive the images on floppy disks or on CD-ROM disks as well as hard copies. Electronic messages keep you informed about the mode the camera is in, the number of shots remaining, and so on.

Those improvements in the design of the analog camera are another illustration of the **sailboat effect**. The design of sailboats improved dramatically when the sailboat was challenged by the steamboat. Now the design of analog photography is improving because of the challenge from digital photography. While digital photography can not match the resolution of analog photography yet, it is enough of a challenge to force the manufacturers of analog cameras to finally improve them.

Despite those efforts to activate my right hemisphere, I still emphasize the left hemisphere (print) over the right hemisphere (film). To compensate somewhat for my leftish leanings, I have included, as Appendix B, a generation-by-generation list of relevant films.

4.2   A SHORT HISTORY OF PRINT

The origin of writing is easier to discover than the origin of speaking. It did not happen so long ago and it leaves a trace. In a brilliant piece of detective work, Denise Schmandt-Besserat, followed that trace to the origin of writing in small, clay tokens used in the Middle East from 8000 to 3000 b.c. [SCHMANDT-BESSERAT]. At that time and place, there were dramatic changes within both the technosphere and the sociosphere. Instead of wandering around from place to place, hunting animals and gathering plants, we learned to domesticate animals and plants, so that we could settle down in one place. The domestication of plants and animals enabled agricultural societies to accumulate more food than was immediately required. This surplus food could be stored for later dry days or traded for other goods. Accounting systems had to be devised to keep track of what was stored and what had been traded.

Hunter-gatherer societies had used **tallies** - marks on bones to indicate, for example, the number of years since the last meeting of the clan - just as a prisoner may make scratches on the cell wall to indicate the number of days in captivity. However, as we moved into an agricultural society, life became more complicated, just as the prisoner's life would become more complicated when released. Tallies could not distinguish between jars of oil and bushels of wheat. Tallies evolved into **tokens** - clay figures of different shapes to represent different things. Thus, for example, spheres for jars of oil and cubes for bushels of wheat, enabling us to represent four jars of oil with four spheres.

For convenience, the four clay spheres could be put in a clay envelope to represent a transaction involving four jars of oil. For further convenience, you could make impressions from the four spheres on the surface of the envelope so that you did not need to break open the clay envelope to see what was inside. You now realize that the clay spheres in the envelope are redundant - they have been replaced by their impressions on the envelope. Since the envelope now need not contain tokens, it can be flattened into a tablet.

Now that you have the idea of representing things by impressions on a two-dimensional surface, you can extend beyond representing concrete objects to representing abstract ideas. One basic dichotomy within abstract ideas is between quantity and quality. You need a set of symbols representing numbers and a set of symbols representing things. Thus, your four jars of oil are represented not by four concrete spheres but by an abstract symbol representing "four" and another abstract symbol representing "jars of oil". Separating quantity and quality permits you to use the symbol for "four" for four jars of oil, four bushels of wheat, or four of whatever.

Those symbols, which evolved into mathematics and writing respectively, enabled us to store not only food but information.   Writing evolved through pictograms, as in Egyptian hieroglyphics, in which things are represented by images which resemble them, to a system in which the basic symbols represent the sounds of language.[4]   Thus, the progression is from representations of the

---

[4]   My friend, Don Kingsbury, disapproves of the iconic representations on buttons in the Macintosh Operating System because they are a regression to an ancient inefficient system. As those icons proliferate, I'm beginning to see his point. "Cut", "Copy", "Paste" are easier to read

objective world to representations of the subjective map. It is this shift which enables us to map the basic units of writing (graphemes) on to the basic units of speaking (phonemes) and thus piggy-back the second generation of media on the first generation of media.

The second generation of print got a huge boost in the fifteenth century with the invention of the printing press by Johann Gutenberg (1400-1468). This democratized the distribution of writing. Until then, it had been accessible only to a privileged minority of scholars. Books were precious and scarce, since laboriously copied by hand mainly by monks in monasteries, and available only to those who had laboriously learned to read. The first printed book from metal movable type - the *Gutenberg Bible* - embodied a conscious attempt to simulate the illuminated manuscripts produced by monks [VAN DOREN, Page 153]. As we will see, our story of media demonstrates time and again, the influence of old media on new, as the new media struggles to find its exclusive niche within the communication system.

Various innovations in printed books also contributed to their accessibility. Ivan Illich came to a conference on computers in education in Montreal. Since I have long been an admirer of his book *De-Schooling Society* [ILLICH], I attended his talk expecting to hear how the computer now finally enables us to de-school society. He devoted the entire talk to a forty-year period following the invention of the printing press. Books did not appear right away as we now know them. During those forty years, we learned such taken-for-granted design features as leaving spaces between words, using upper and lower case, dividing text into paragraphs, books into chapters, numbering pages (indeed dividing a document into pages in the first place), including a table of contents

---

than the various alternative iconic systems which have emerged. In newer programs, the user can find out what an obscure icon means by passing the mouse over it. Jef Raskin, the genius behind the Macintosh interface, who now argues that even this simple interface is too complex, points out that you may as well then replace the icon with its meaning [RASKIN].

and an index.[5]   Probably the "punch-line", which he never reached since his talk inspired so many questions, was that we are in the midst of a similar period with respect to the computer. It will be some time before we assimilate it into our media system.

The invention of the typewriter by Christopher Latham Scoles (1819-1890) further contributed to the democratization of writing.[6]   The printing press helped democratize the consumption of print, the typewriter helped democratize the production of print. To print your own writing, you did not need a printing press but only the much cheaper typewriter. You had essentially a personal printing press. However, there is a vast difference between being printed and being published. Once printed, it must be distributed, and the means of distribution are available only to the few with the vast resources required.

The democratization of the production of media was thus not accompanied by an equivalent democratization of the distribution of media. Freedom of the press applies only to those who own a printing press.[7] The publication of books and newspapers involves a high cost of entry. Thus, those industries evolved into a few-to-many communication system in which a few entrepreneurs produced the books and newspapers which were read by millions of readers. The history of

---

[5]   Even silent reading was an innovation during this period. St. Augustine expressed amazement that St. Ambrose could read without moving his lips [MANGUEL, Page 42]. More recently, we have acquired the art of reading erotica without moving our hips.

[6]   It also introduced an important concept into the history of technology - the **QWERTY phenomenon**. The traditional keyboard was designed to slow typists down, since the keys stuck when they typed too quickly. The keys no longer stick but we are stuck with the purposefully inefficient QWERTY keyboard since so many people have been trained on it.

[7]   I once told a friend that Conrad Black had just bought a newspaper. He said *"So what? I buy a newspaper every morning"*.   His whimsical comment nicely encapsulates the difference in power between the newspaper-buyer as source and as destination. Now, of course, the democratization of distribution is enhanced by the internet. "Publish" is just one command in one pull-down menu.

newspapers is thus the story of powerful moguls - Randolph Hearst, Robert Maxwell, Conrad Black, etc. - who gain enormous power because of their access to a huge audience.

Peter Cooney, a neighbor of mine, who is responsible for putting the Montreal Gazette on the internet, suggests that the newspaper barons will be even more powerful in the future.   He views the daily newspaper as the tip of an iceberg. The newspaper is the point of contact between people and information. Each person, depending on time and interest, can use its electronic version to explore the rest of the iceberg. Some people aspire to raise the Titanic. His project is to raise the iceberg. His metaphor makes sense of some recent developments.

Conrad Black, who has previously built his newspaper empire by buying established newspapers, created and launched a national newspaper, the *National Post*. The Thompson Corporation, his major competitor, has put all its newspapers on the market except for their national newspaper, *The Globe and Mail*. Black needed a tip for his iceberg; Thompson realized that an iceberg needs only one tip. The wealth is no longer in the tip but in the rest of the iceberg. At their web site, *The Economist* gives you free access to the latest copy on the newsstands, but charges you for access to the archives. Their new-found wealth is that huge database of information they have accumulated over their long history. This will no doubt become packaged so that anyone considering investments in a particular company or in a particular industry can quickly access the history of the company or the industry. Scholars, the only people previously interested in the archives, now find that they have to pay for access.

An alternative system using this second generation of media evolved into the Post Office. Everyone has access to this system and can be the source as well as the destination. Here the story is not of powerful moguls but of creative visionaries - Benjamin Franklin who first conceived the idea in 1732, Rowland

Hill who initiated a simple system of payment in 1837 (pay by weight rather than by the number of sheets of paper or the distance the paper was transported), Jacob Perkins who invented the postage stamp in 1840,[8] Henry Cole who invented the Christmas card in 1843, Baron Paul Julius von Reuter who thought of the pigeon post in 1849, William Hepburn Russell who started the pony express in 1860, and some unheralded genius at the British Post Office who invented the postcard in 1870.

With each generation of media, we will find that it can be used in autocratic or democratic ways. The newspaper industry and the post office are the autocratic and democratic options within the second generation, and we will see that television and telephone are the autocratic and democratic options in the third generation. We are currently witnessing the autocratic and democratic forces battling for control of multimedia and the internet.

---

[8]   If you come across his first stamp - the penny black - don't use it to mail a letter. Your letter will be returned, stamped "Insufficient postage"!

4.3   A SHORT HISTORY OF FILM

Four of my life experiences help frame the history of film for me:

- 1940s - watching movies in the theater in my Scottish village
- 1960-1965 - attending graduate school in Psychology at Cornell University
- 1975 - party in California
- 1989 - conference on three-dimensional media technology in Montreal
- FLASHBACK Growing up in Lochwinnoch, a small village in Scotland, I used to be very impressed by Johnny Manders, who ran the local cinema single-handed. Johnny would stand out in the street as a barker. *Roll up, roll up, only a few seats left!*   When he lured in some customers, he would interrupt his spiel to be ticket collector and usher. After capturing a large enough audience, he would become the film projectionist. The movie would be interrupted halfway through while he sold popcorn and soft drinks. (It always seemed to me as a child to stop at an exciting part but now I realize that there was only one projector and it was necessary to change reels.) After the audience had bought enough to bribe him to get back to being projectionist, the movie would continue.
- FAST FORWARD Twenty-five years later, I was attended a two-day graduation party for a friend. I was taking many photographs to build a souvenir album. I ran out of color film, borrowed some black-and-white film, and continued taking pictures with more abandon, since the film is cheaper (Twenty-five years later, I am still Scottish!). I ran out of black-and-white film, but continued with even more abandon with the empty camera.   (It is now the afternoon of the second day!) Since there is not any record of the shots, I decide to abandon the camera and take shots simply by blinking. Suddenly I realized that there was little point in taking stills when I had a continuous movie going and

- blinking no more - I sat back to enjoy the movie.

• REWIND In retrospect, then, running a one-man cinema is not so impressive. Every one of us is running a magnificent mobile movie studio of a mind, with wide-angle screen, stereophonic sound, Technicolor, and cast of thousands (but only one hero/heroine), in which we are producer, director, script-writer, camera person, sound engineer, stage manager and crew. This movie studio also doubles as a movie theater, in which we can simultaneously watch the show. (We are also the movie critic who reviews the performance next morning!) The only limitation is that, in the movie theater of the mind, there is only one seat. In order to show your home movies to other people, you have to learn to write, to speak, to play music, to make films. Some of us earn reputations for being good at showing our home movies, using a particular medium, and are thus recognized as artists. However, we are all artists in the sense that we all try, by some means or another, to invite other people in to see our home movies.

• FAST FORWARD AGAIN I spent four years with J. J. Gibson while a graduate student at Cornell University between 1961 and 1965 and never understood what he was talking about. Yet he was one of the most important influences in my life. He was very excited about something (whatever it was) and I wanted to share this excitement. Ten years later, at that California party, I began to understand what he had been talking about.

Our visual world is built out of this "**Mind Movie**" which we are running in the magnificent mobile mind studio and viewing in the mind theater. "Mobile" is a important feature of this studio. Now I understand why J. J. used to chuckle when the tachistoscope arrived in the department and every graduate student suddenly realized that their research required this new tool. It enabled us to fix the subject in a chin-rest staring down a tunnel where we could systematically and accurately present stimuli and measure precisely their response. A person discovers the real world by moving around in it - moving the body with respect to the environment, the head with respect to the body and the eyes with respect to the head.   By preventing the subject from moving the body, the head and the eyes, we were able to conduct a very controlled experiment but we could not learn anything about how s/he learned about the real world.   It was street-lamp research, named in honor of the drunk who dropped his key while trying to open his door and went to look for it under the street-lamp because the light was better there.   The light may be better there but it is not where the key is.

J. J's wife, Eleanor Gibson, conducted a study with Richard Walk, in which the subjects were allowed to move. Young organisms were placed on a platform with a shallow end at one side and a deep end at the other side (it only looked deep hence the experiment was called the **visual cliff**) [GIBSON E & WALK R].   Subjects, whether young children or kittens or puppies, invariably walked off the shallow end (even when mothers treacherously called the young children from the deep end).   Gibson and Walk concluded that young organisms have depth perception. Critics replied that they had demonstrated only that they had depth perception when they could walk.   The experimenters argued that that is when they need depth perception and nature kindly supplies it by providing the necessary information as they learn to walk.

The **visual field** (J. J's name for the single frame in this movie) could be very complex, if it contained many people and things, to which the person has multiple cognitive and emotional associations.   Some German researchers simplified the visual field by building a **Ganzfeld** (German for *whole field*) consisting of a six-foot translucent sphere.   A subject sitting in the center of this sphere would have the total retina equally stimulated.   Julien Hochberg, another perception theorist at Cornell University, with typical Yankee ingenuity, built the pocket Ganzfeld by cutting a ping-pong ball in half and placing the two halves over the eyes of the subject.   The first step towards making the Ganzfeld more complex was to draw a dot on the sphere or ping-pong ball. The subject recognized this as a figure on a ground. This figure-ground relationship is the basic perceptual experience. When a blind patient has cataracts removed and sees for the first time, this is what he sees. He does not immediately reach up after the bandages are removed and embrace his fiancee, as in Hollywood movies. He could not tell his fiancee from the doctor or from the bedside-table, but he could tell that there is a figure against a ground.

•   FAST FORWARD AGAIN In 1989, Christine Davet, Hal Thwaites, and I organized a conference on Three-dimensional Media Technology. In an opening speech, I said:

Since this is a conference on the third dimension, we have decided to invite only three-dimensional speakers, hold it (as you can see) in a three-dimensional room, serve drinks in three-dimensional glasses and food on three-dimensional plates.

The point is that the real world, the world we live in, is three dimensional. Look around you - check for yourself - don't take my world for it! We live in a three-dimensional world and the eye is therefore designed to perceive objects in 3D. Adding this third dimension of depth to the current two-dimensional movie is the next logical step toward a more accurate representation of the world-as-we-perceive-it in our everyday experience.[9]

The movie metaphor is apt because film is the medium which perhaps, of all the media, best captures the full quality of our personal maps of experience. Indeed, the history of film could be considered as a series of steps towards a closer approximation of the mind movie. *Movies* added movement to the still image of the photograph, the *talkies* added sound and color was added to the

---

[9]   Indeed, the third dimension is often used as a metaphor for reality. In film scripts, an unreal character is often described as being *two-dimensional.*

black-and-white image.

A camera is simply a light-tight box with a hole at the front and a light-sensitive surface at the back. You point the camera at an object, open the hole, and an image of the object appears on the surface. Each innovation is simply a device to improve the resolution and permanence of the image. Medieval artists were familiar with the **camera obscurata** (pinhole camera) as a device for providing an initial outline for a painting. Indeed, Lynn Picknett and Clive Prince have argued that the first photograph was the Turin Shroud taken in 1492 by Leonardo da Vinci [PICKNETT & PRINCE]. Pope Innocent V111 commissioned the Shroud (ostensibly the one that wrapped the body of Jesus Christ after he was taken down from the cross) as a publicity exercise. Leonardo used a composite of his own face and the body of a genuinely crucified man, a pinhole camera and a chemical sensitive to light to create the world's first photograph.[10]

There are a number of ways of adding to the accuracy of our movie of the mind. One technology is **high-definition television (HDTV)**, which provides improved picture resolution. With HDTV the aspect ratio of the TV screen is closer to that of the eye than with conventional television. The **IMAX** film format comes even closer to our mind movie by removing the artificial frame around the image. The IMAX screen is so large that it fills most of our visual field. The **OMNIMAX** screen, even bigger and curved at the edges, does this even more effectively. Though it does not remove the border, the IMAX/OMNIMAX format allows it to be replaced by the more natural oval

---

[10]   Leonardo has a reputation as a practical joker. Some have argued that his famous Mona Lisa is a self-portrait [HONORE]. X-rays reveal a beard under her cheeks and a computer aligned her features with a portrait of da Vinci. Her enigmatic smile is the result of a male smile on a female face.

border of the eye as it takes a snapshot of the world.[11]

A big step towards simulation of the mind movie was taken when we learned to capture motion on film. Edward James Muggeridge (1830 - 1904) was born in Kingston upon Thames, Surrey in 1830 and died as Eadweard Muybridge in Kingston upon Thames, Surrey in 1904. (He had adopted the latter which he presumed to be the Anglo-Saxon form of his name.) Unlike Darwin, however, he had spent most of his intervening life outside *his* English village. He traveled extensively in North and Central America pursuing his career as a photographer.

His most famous photographs were commissioned by Leland Stanford (after whom Stanford University is named) to help him win a bet. Stanford had bet $25,000 that at some moment in its gait all four feet of his famous trotting horse Occident were off the ground at the same time. Muybridge lined up a battery of 24 cameras, equipped with a shutter he had developed which gave an exposure of 2/1000th of a second. As the horse trotted past, it broke threads which triggered the cameras and made a series of 24 exposures. On some of those exposures, all four feet were off the ground, and Stanford won his bet.

Muybridge printed those 24 photographs on a circular glass disc, which projected them in rapid succession on to a screen as it was spun, creating the illusion of movement. This **zoopraxiscope**, which created a sensation at the Columbian Exposition in Chicago in 1893, was a precursor of the film projector. He had stumbled upon the perceptual phenomenon of **persistence of vision** or **phi phenomenon**. Since an image projected on the eye persists, an appropriate series of images projected at a certain rate will create the illusion of motion. This rate,

---

[11]   Despite all those innovations, the resolution is not as good as our eyes. Julien Winfield, one of my students who helped me with the edutainment section of the CD-ROM to accompany the movie Rob Roy, told me the following story. He was working long hours staring at a screen in a beach house in Santa Cruz. As his attention drifted to the view of the Santa Cruz beach in the picture window behind his screen, he was astonished at the great resolution on that "screen". When he started however to try to get his cursor on some passing cloud to edit the image, he realized that it was time to quit.

called the **critical flicker frequency (CFF)**, is about 24 frames per second. This primitive prototype of the film projector earned him the title of Father of the Motion Picture. Muybridge devoted the rest of his life, before returning to his village to retire, to compiling portfolios of photographs illustrating the movement of animals including us. Those portfolios have served as a valuable guide for scientists and artists during the intervening century [MUYBRIDGE].

The various media could be classified in terms of spatial dimensions. Thus, print and radio would be one-dimensional, photography and painting would be two-dimensional, sculpture and holography would be three-dimensional, dance and theater would be four-dimensional since they add the fourth dimension of time. Film and television would be three-dimensional, the third dimension being that of time rather than depth. This next step in the progression toward a more accurate simulation of the mind movie for film would therefore involve filling in this "missing" depth dimension.

Progression is, of course, not necessarily progress. Many will resist this next step, just as many in the past resisted the introduction of movies, talkies, and color. Many people certainly resist the retroactive introduction of color to films originally shot in black-and-white. Whatever the arguments mustered by critics of colourization (and there are many good ones), the idea that black and white is somehow more natural, is totally unfounded. There is nothing *natural* about black-and-white unless you are totally colour-blind.[12]   The same argument applies to two-dimensional images, which are as artificial as black-and-white images. 2-D representations of our 3-D world are cultural artifacts. This is demonstrated by anthropological studies in which people, who have no previous experience of photographs and paintings, have trouble interpreting them.

---

[12]   A voice-over on some early black-and-white footage in a documentary on the life of Richard Nixon earnestly informed us that of course, in those days, the world was black-and-white, people did not talk and they moved very quickly.

4.4   FROM PRINT TO FILM

The second generation of media provides us with new sets of communication tools and skills. The traditional literacy skills of writing and reading enable us to use the tool of print. Apart from taking snapshots, our interaction with the tool of film is largely passive. Only a few of us have the resources, financial and personal, to make movies.[13]   However, now that the pre-production, production, and post-production of films is increasingly becoming digital, and we can acquire a desktop video production studio for under 10 thousand dollars, more and more of us will deal with images as we have dealt with words in an active way.

A third set of skills is the translation of print into film. John Irving describes this difficult process in his book about the adventures of a novelist in the movie business [IRVING]. He has not been impressed by the adaptations of his novels - *The World According to Garp, Hotel New Hampshire* - into movies. Indeed, he was so unhappy about the adaptation of *A Prayer for Owen Meany* that it was released under another name - *Simon Birch*. Disney's movie tells a good story but it is not the story written by Irving in the book from which it was adapted. Irving therefore set out to write his own script for the movie adaptation of *Cider House Rules*. Fifteen years, six scripts, and three directors later, it finally appeared. Although he won an Oscar for best script, he has settled back into

---

[13]   The constraints are personal as well as financial because many of us do not have the personal attributes required to make films. While author-in-residence at a publishing company in Monterey, California during the 1970s, my corner bar was the Hog's Breath Inn in Carmel. Since this bar was partly owned by Clint Eastwood, many of the regulars were film people. At happy hour, a film person would ask how I spent my day. S/he would be horrified when I replied that I had sat at a typewriter all day. When I asked about their day, their replies would be all over the place: I talked to some producer about financing for a film. I was writing a script. I was visiting a site with my location manager. I was actually filming a scene. I was editing the film. This life was as horrifying to me as my life was to them. The desktop video production studio promises to make "film-making" accessible to people like me who don't mind sitting at a desk all day.

writing novels with a sigh of relief. A subsequent adaptation of his novel *A Widow for One Year – The Door in the Floor* - wisely focuses on only the first third of the book, recognizing that a whole book by John Irving is too much to condense into one movie. Alas, this opens it to the criticism that the film lacks a middle and an end!

One interesting issue about this process of crossing the corpus callosum between the two hemispheres is why people almost invariably say that they preferred the book to the film. One person sits down with simple equipment (quill, typewriter, word-processor) to write a book; whereas hundreds of people with thousands of dollars of equipment and millions of dollars budget work together to create a movie. Perhaps the hundreds of people is part of the problem. Imagine a book written by a committee. Perhaps the thousand-dollar equipment is part of the problem. There is less direct person-to-person communication when mediated by so much technology. Perhaps the million-dollar budget is part of the problem. This investment must be recovered and the movie must thus appeal to a lowest common denominator to attract a large audience.

A more subtle explanation may perhaps be implied by the Toronto School of Media Studies. If the medium is the message, then the message can not survive the transition from one medium to another. Something is always lost in translation. As the message moves from novel to script to story-board to film, it is inevitably changed. In successful transitions, some essence is preserved. Is that essence the story? Are all media just different ways to share our stories? An important aspect of human nature is what Carol Shields calls our "*narrative hunger*". Human nature has not changed over historical time - only the means of telling stories to satisfy it.

Teachers in writing classes, delight in telling students that there are only X stories and that they have all been written already. All that the student can do is update the story for a particular time and place. X varies from situation to situation. My candidate is 4, based on the Triad Model (see Figure 3-2).   Stories involve drama and drama involves conflict. There is the conflict between the person and the ecosphere (nature), the person and the sociosphere (society), the person and the technosphere (machines), and conflict within the person. Prototype stories for each category are *"Moby Dick"*, *"The Scarlet Letter"*, *"Frankenstein"*, and *"Jekyll and Hyde"*. Sigmund Freud suggests that those dramas appeal to us because they reflect conflicts within ourselves - id (ecosphere), superego (sociosphere) and ego (technosphere) battling it out within our nervous systems.

We tend to assume that the dramatic introduction of Multimedia and Internet adds new stories to our repertoire. However, the basic stories remain the same. Human nature is the constant throughout all generations of media. All that is added is new means of telling our stories. New media at most simply add new plot devices. *You've Got Mail* is a remake of *Sleepless in Seattle* with the internet replacing the telephone as a communication device to get the protagonists together, and of *The Little Shop Around the Corner* in which the communication device was the mail. It's the same story - all that changes is the medium.

The daughter in *American Beauty* discovers that her father called her friend because he used *69 whereas before she may have made this discovery by eavesdropping. In *Sneakers* the valuable object being sought is a computer disk with crucial information, whereas in *The Maltese Falcon*, it was an object containing more concrete valuables. In every cop show, the detective now always checks the telephone-answering machine of the victim for clues about recent activities, whereas before the detective got such information from diaries. In an episode of *Hamish Macbeth*, a corpse is found because his murderers buried him with his cell-phone, and someone called him. In *A Cinderella Story*, the modern Cinderella meets Prince Charming on the internet and drops her cell-phone rather than her glass slipper. *Little Black Book* is misnamed since the protagonist sneaks a peak at her boy-friend's Palm Pilot rather than the traditional little black book.

Even such a novel movie as *The Matrix* is simply a retelling of the familiar story of a protagonist finding him/herself in an unfamiliar situation. S/he is in a strange world in which the familiar rules no longer apply. The conflict is between the objective world and the subjective map of the protagonist. The two-story version of the Triad Model (Figure 4-1) adds another story to my list of basic stories. The creative people behind the movie understand this, as they make tongue-in-cheek references to *Alice in Wonderland* and *The Wizard of Oz*. Whether you get to this strange, rule-bending world by falling down a rabbit hole or clicking your heels or being fed a virtual world, you are in the same (or rather same different) place. Indeed many references are to one of our oldest stories of all - the hero is the Chosen One betrayed by one of his disciples.

CHAPTER 5

SHIFT 2 - ASSIMILATING
THE THIRD GENERATION

5.1 WHICH SHIFT IS MOST IMPORTANT?

5.2 TORONTO SCHOOL - MARSHALL MCLUHAN

5.3 THREATS AND OPPORTUNITIES

My main theme is the extension of the nervous system in the electric age and, thus, the complete break with five thousand years of mechanical technology. This I state over and over again. I do not say whether it is a good or bad thing. To do so would be meaningless and arrogant.

Letter from **Marshall McLuhan** to Robert Fulford in 1964,
[Paul Bendetti & Nancy deHart, ON AND BY MCLUHAN,
Page 147]

5.1   WHICH SHIFT IS MOST IMPORTANT?

We tend to think of the third shift - the assimilation of the fourth generation of media (Multimedia and Internet) - as the most important. However, this may simply be because we are going through it right now. It could be argued that the first shift - the assimilation of the second generation of media (Print and Film) - was perhaps more significant. It was the beginning of the use of extrasomatic tools which mediated between us and thus ended an era in which all our communication was directly between people face-to-face. Since history is defined as that which is recorded, it begins with the second generation of media. Since I'm arguing here that this history is best understood when seen in the context of pre-history, the most dramatic distinction is between the first generation of media (pre-history) and the second, third, and fourth generations (history).

Critics of television and computers refuse to concede that the rot may have set in with their beloved print. Neil Postman, for example, extols print as he questions video-based media [POSTMAN 1986] and computer-based media [POSTMAN 1993]. However, as soon as we developed extrasomatic tools for the storage and transmission of information, the extragenetic tools for storing (memory) and transmitting information (speech) are threatened. That is, in our terms, the important shift is between the first and the second generations of media rather than between the second and third generations.

Let us consider two events which suggest that the second shift - the assimilation of the third generation of media (Telephone and Television) - may be the most dramatic of all.

American troops, led by General Andrew Jackson, routed British troops at the Battle of New Orleans on 8 January 1815. Two thousand men died. None of the combatants knew that the war had ended two weeks earlier with the signing of the Treaty of Ghent [BRYSON, Page 156].   In our world of instant communication, we find it difficult to imagine how a battle could be fought in a war that was over.   However, news of the treaty signed in Europe could only have reached New Orleans by ship which took weeks (and sometimes even months, when winds were unfavorable) to cross the Atlantic.

Fast forward half a century to 27 July 1866.   On that date, we were finally able to lay the first trans-Atlantic cable to carry telegraph messages from Europe to North America.   Arthur C. Clarke describes this Herculean task in his book *How the World Was One*.   He reports that Cyrus W. Field, who had masterminded the project, sent the following message from Newfoundland to New York in 1866: Heart's Content, July 27. *We arrived here at 9 o'clock this morning. All well.   Thank God, the cable is laid and in perfect working order.*   [CLARKE, Page 78].   On that day, the time to send a message across the Atlantic Ocean shrunk from weeks to seconds.

Whereas this shift is defined in terms of the shift from the storage of information to the transmission of information outside our bodies, it may also be considered as the shift from mechanical energy (first and second generations) to electrical energy (third and fourth generations).   That is, from a world in which the infrastructure is transportation to a world in which the infrastructure is telecommunications, from a world of energy to a world of information, or, to use the terms of Nicholas Negroponte, from a world of atoms to a world of bits [NEGROPONTE].[1]

The second shift to electronic media based on electricity was a response to the challenge posed by the globalization of trade (in goods and ideas) and thus

---

[1]   The shift into the latter world involves a **transportation-telecommunications trade-off**. I made the trade a decade ago - I sold my car and bought a computer. Now, instead of using a 2000-pound car to drive a 200-pound man to pick up a 2-pound book, I sit in the Smart Room of my Electronic Cottage and pull in the information over the Internet.

the need for instantaneous communication around the globe. As we moved into an industrial society, it was necessary to have more instantaneous communication on a global scale as raw materials were collected from around the globe and finished products distributed around the globe. Telegraphy and its descendants in the third generation of media were developed as a response to this challenge.

This second shift could thus be described as crossing the "digital divide". This term has been used to distinguish the have and the have-nots in our society (that is, those who have access to computers and those who do not have access to computers). It is argued that the haves will become the knows and the have-nots will become the know-nots in an information society. At a loftier sociological level, it can be used to distinguish between societies which have a telecommunications infrastructure and societies which do not have a telecommunications infrastructure. Whole pre-industrial societies - rather than simply individuals within industrialized societies - will be at a disadvantage.

I have argued before for a leap-frog strategy for developing countries, in which they leap-frog from a pre- to a post-industrial society [GARDINER 1987]. I will make the same argument again in Section 18.3. However, I now realize that the "frog" is much bigger than I thought. The infrastructure of the third generation of media must be in place before the fourth generation of media can be accessed. Few people will be able to benefit from a computer in a society in which 90% of the population has never used a telephone.

Perhaps, then, the question *Which shift is most important?* is like asking which leg of a three-legged stool is most important. The three shifts are integral parts of the same process. As we go back to pre-history to answer Wallace's question: *How can an organism which evolved for a hunter-gatherer society manage the transition to an agricultural, industrial, and information society?*, we find that the assimilation of the second, third and fourth generations of media are stages in a larger process - the co-evolution of the person and media as extensions. The assimilation of the fourth generation, which seems so dramatic to us as we are now experiencing it, is perhaps the least dramatic of the three shifts. Once we had invented a means of transmitting information electronically, the next inevitable step is the invention of the means of storing information electronically. What we are "hearing" now is simply the dropping of the other shoe.

5.2   TORONTO SCHOOL - MARSHALL MCLUHAN

Meanwhile, back in Toronto, Marshall McLuhan (1911-1980) was writing what he called his footnote to the work of Harold Innis. Innis had focused on the impact of the second generation of print. His major books, published in 1950 and 1951, were too early to pick up on the impact of the third generation of television. McLuhan took up his theme of the profound impact of media on society, and extended it to include the impact of our third generation of media - telephone and television. He also shifted focus from the level of the institution to the level of the individual. The various media were viewed as extensions of the person, as indicated in the subtitle of his major book: *Understanding Media: The Extensions of Man* [MCLUHAN M].

The timing of a theory is very important. If it is presented too soon, it is greeted as preposterous; if it is presented too late, it is dismissed as obvious. People say *What!* when innovators first present their ideas and, then - when the passage of time reveals their ideas to be sound - the same people say *So what?* . You have to time your theory to appear between the *What!* and the *So what?*. McLuhan seems to have suffered the fate of many innovators - his theory has gone all the way from preposterous to obvious.

Why were the ideas of McLuhan once preposterous?

He was the wrong man in the wrong place at the wrong time with the wrong message and the wrong medium.

Why are the ideas of McLuhan now obvious?

There is a new medium emerging and a new science evolving.

Although McLuhan gained some credibility in the public domain, his theories have tended to be dismissed within the academy as preposterous. Indeed, his public popularity tended to tarnish his academic respectability, as nicely encapsulated by his biographer:

"How often McLuhan's colleagues dismissed his work as merely 'interesting speculation or stimulating conversation' - in a tone that suggested that they, too, could be as interesting or as stimulating were it not for some vague moral principle." [MARCHAND P, Page 268]

I will argue here that McLuhan's theories tend to be dismissed as preposterous because he is the wrong person in the wrong place at the wrong time with the wrong message in the wrong medium.

He is the wrong person. An English professor is expected to concentrate on the specifics of a particular writer in a particular time at a particular place. Thus, having studied the novels of James Joyce in graduate school, he should have settled down to a lifetime devoted to identifying the Dublin landmarks described in the novel *Ulysses* or whatever. He is not supposed to expound general theories about writing in general, far less all media, and far far less all human artifacts. If he is also a devout Catholic, then he is doubly suspect. Science is the province of the science and not the arts faculty, of agnostics and not believers. McLuhan has ignored the *trespassers will be persecuted* signs on the academic lawn.

In the wrong place. Canadians have a delightful diffidence, which can be most politely described as an excess of democracy. See Figure 5-1 for a list of self-deprecating statements by Canadians about Canadians. The downside of this diffidence is that anyone who raises their head above the masses is in danger of having it chopped off. *John Kenneth Galbraith and Marshall McLuhan*, says Anthony Burgess, *are the two greatest modern Canadians the United States has produced*. Of the reviews of *Laws of Media* [MCLUHAN M & MCLUHAN E], co-authored and published posthumously by his son Eric, the gentlest, kindest review is from the *New York Times Review of Books*. Of the Canadian reviews, the only positive one is by Bill Kuhns, who is an immigrant from the United States.

Canada has never been a melting pot; more like a tossed salad.
--- Arnold Edinborough

In any world menu, Canada must be considered the vichyssoise of nations --- it's cold, half-French, and difficult to stir. --- Stuart Keate

My generation of Canadians grew up believing that, if we were very good or very smart, or both, we would somehow graduate from Canada. --- Robert Fulford

A Canadian is someone who can make love in a canoe --- Pierre Berton

Canada is the only country in the world that knows how to live without an identity. --- Marshall McLuhan

[All those quotes, illustrating how self-deprecating Canadians are, were taken from *Peter's Quotations* by Laurence J. Peter. He is also author of *The Peter Principle* , which states that in a hierarchy, every employee tends to rise to his level of incompetence . Needless to say, Peter is a Canadian.]

FIGURE 5-1
SELF-DESCRIPTIONS OF CANADIANS BY CANADIANS

At the wrong time. His theory is preposterous partly because it is premature. Theories are not supposed to predict the future but to postdict the past. McLuhan died in 1980 - that is, just before the explosion in multimedia and internet (our fourth generation of media) - which vindicated his theories. His genius was the recognition that the next step after the *transmission* of information electronically (third generation) was the *storage* of information electronically (fourth generation). He anticipated the dropping of the other shoe. It was only when we were startled by the sound of the second shoe dropping that we were able to be amazed that McLuhan anticipated it.

With the wrong message. In a lecture at McGill University, Bill Kuhns argued that the message of McLuhan is dismissed for the same reason as were those of Copernicus, Darwin, and Freud. Each of those innovators required us to break a discontinuity which we had erected to protect ourselves from a harsh reality. Copernicus broke the discontinuity between our planet and the rest of the universe. He tore us away from the center of the universe and placed us on a broken-off fragment of a suburban star. We tried to burn him. Darwin broke the discontinuity between our species and our furrier friends further down the phylogenetic scale. We burned his books. Freud argued further that we are not the rational animal but a creature propelled by unconscious mechanisms. We simply burned. Kuhns argues that McLuhan is destroying a fourth discontinuity between the person and the machine. By arguing that our machines are extensions of ourselves, he is requiring us to take responsibility for them. There is still a whiff of burning in the air.

Using the wrong medium. If you proclaim the end of the medium, it is probably not a good strategy to use the doomed medium to do so. It is too easy to dismiss a book proclaiming the death of the book.[2] Nor is it a good strategy to

---

[2]   While author-in-residence at Wadsworth Publishing Company in Belmont, California, I once poked my head into the office of the president, Jim Leisy, and declared *"The book is dead"*.

use language in that book which is not appreciated as scientific. McLuhan's puns and probes were too playful for an academic public which is serious about science. McLuhan did not understand the importance of being earnest.

The theory of Marshall McLuhan has become obvious, because of the emergence of a new medium and the evolution of a new science.

After a lull in interest in the work of McLuhan during the 1970s and early 1980s, there was a resurgence of interest in the late 1980s, which persists till now. There has been a biography [MARCHAND P], a collection of letters by his widow Corinne and others [MOLINARO ET AL], a book which groups him with two other Canadians, Pierre Trudeau and Glenn Gould, as a solitary outlaw [POWE 1987], and a book which places him with yet two more Canadians, Harold Innis and George Grant, as an influence on the Canadian mind with respect to technology [KROKER 1984]. Perhaps, most important, there has been an updating of his most central book, *Understanding Media: The Extensions of Man* [McLUHAN M] , by his son Eric [McLUHAN M & McLUHAN E]. Judging by the reviews of this last book, he is still considered to be preposterous.

For a time, I considered using *Understanding Multimedia: Further Extensions of the Person* as a title for this book.   This title - which is (with a small adjustment for political correctness) an exact parallel to *Understanding Media: The Extensions of Man* - was designed as a homage to McLuhan. It concedes that all I am doing is updating the basic thesis of McLuhan that the media are best considered as extensions of the person, and that the best way to understand the fourth generation of media is to trace its history. (Part 1 - THE PAST (Chapters 1 through 8) is essentially the "back story" for the current information revolution).   However, the structure of the book continues the

---

This was not good news for someone who earned his living building books. *"Who said that?"*   I showed him the book by Marshall McLuhan that I was currently reading. *"Ah, but he wrote it in a book"* said Jim, clinching the argument.

McLuhan tradition. The web version will not only be about multimedia, it will be in multimedia. It will be designed so that, in its electronic version, you can click on buttons to go to the various features - footnotes, figures, references - which complement the text. It demonstrates as it describes. The medium is (at least part of) the message.

Homage to McLuhan is contained in *Mondo 2000: A User's Guide to the New Edge* [RUCKER ET AL]. Of the 51 concepts listed as characteristic of the new edge , the only name is Marshall McLuhan. Those concepts are organized within the Triad Model (see Figure 3-2) in Figure 5-2, demonstrating that the technosphere is where the current action is, and that the basic discipline is now not physics but biology. Further homage is paid by Wired magazine, which lists him in their masthead as their Patron Saint and includes a quotation which demonstrates that an obscure English professor from Toronto who died two decades ago best exemplifies the leading edge of technology and culture today.

McLuhan anticipated multimedia, which is clearly an extension of the person. Since it is integrative and interactive, it simulates the function of the corpus callosum, which integrates the left and right hemispheres and enables the interaction between the cortex and the rest of the body.[3] It enables intelligence amplification, since it is finally a positive prosthetic which fits perfectly. He also anticipated the internet - the network of computer nodes interlinked by telecommunications. This infrastructure is the nervous system of the planet and thus the foundation of the **global village**. It is the means by which each person can extend him/herself around the globe.

When I took a sabbatical in the 1970s, it seemed obvious to go to California. This was, to use William Irwin Thompson's phrase, *the edge of history* [THOMPSON]. That was where one went to see the future now, and

---

[3]   Michael Snow, a Toronto artist who integrates art and science in his work, entitled a recent exhibit *Corpus Callosum*.

smile at some coming attractions and shudder at others. When I took a sabbatical in the 1990s, I gravitated through force of habit to California. However, it is no longer the edge of history. Because of multimedia and the internet, we have indeed moved into the global village, where, according to Marshall McLuhan, *the center is everywhere and the periphery is nowhere.* Sitting here in the Smart Room of my Electronic Cottage in the village of Hudson, with my computer potentially linked to millions of other computers around the globe, I am as central as anyone in New York or London or Cupertino, California.

Kristina Hooper-Woolsey was showing me around the Apple Multimedia Lab. One of her colleagues, on hearing I was from Montreal, embarked on an enthusiastic exposition on a project on Glenn Gould he had just seen there. It was by Henry See, who had started by working on my 128K Macintosh during the night when I was not using it. At a conference on Virtual Reality, Ted Nelson suggested I go to Glasgow to meet Liz Davenport, the European representative of his Xanadu Project. She introduced me to two colleagues at the University of Strathclyde who were publishing *Hypermedia* , the first academic journal in the area. They in turn suggested I go to Copenhagen to visit Jakob Nielsen who had just published his book in the area, *Hypertext and Hypermedia* [NIELSEN]. Despite the ironic fact that he, alas, was in California, it became clear that the global village had arrived.

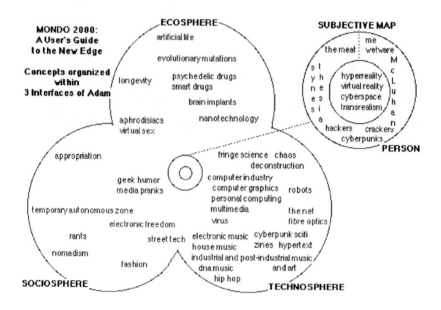

FIGURE 5-2
"NEW EDGE" CONCEPTS
ORGANIZED WITHIN TRIAD MODEL

The idea of media as extensions of the person reveals the falseness of the question *Is the body obsolete?* . It is not meaningful to talk about media without the body. This is like publishing an appendix without a book. Indeed, data can be stored in a computer and transmitted over telecommunications, but it does not become information until someone uses it to extend themselves. Thus a computer transmitting data over a modem to another computer is not a medium. It only becomes a medium when someone reads it and gives it meaning. -- *information is data which reduces entropy for a given individual.* Marshall McLuhan anticipated the impact of electronic technology as (quoting McLuhan) *the final phase of the extensions of man - (to) the technological simulation of consciousness, when the creative process of knowing will be collectively and corporately extended to the whole of human society* [HELSEL & ROTH, Page 15].

Far from the obsolescence of the body, McLuhan envisioned the extension of all our bodies into a social body. As we moved from the first generation of speech which is entirely within our individual bodies to a fourth generation of multimedia which is entirely outside our bodies, we have shifted emphasis from our individual memories as our private writing spaces to our collective memory as a public writing space [BOLTER].

McLuhan was criticized for being unscientific. There was no coherent theoretical framework but simply a series of probes. Now that his son, Eric, has published *Laws of Media*, which started out as a revision with his father of *Understanding Media*, he has presented a coherent theoretical structure. Now, it is dismissed as not a conventionally correct theory.

However, it is a theory designed not for the sociosphere or the ecosphere, the domains respectively of the social and natural sciences, but for the technosphere. This domain, which Herbert Simon calls the *sciences of the artificial* [SIMON], has been relatively neglected by philosophers and practitioners of science.

One principle that is clear, however, is that this is the domain of tools rather than of theories. This is what is implied by the statement that, in the MIT Media Lab, the motto is *Demo or Die* rather than *Publish or Perish* [BRAND]. You do not ask of tools if they are true but if they are useful. The **tetrad** (The major focus of *Laws of Media*) is a tool rather than a theory. This system of four questions requires us to think about the structural shift in the media system required by the assimilation of each medium. (By way of example, Figure 5-3 contains a tetrad for the medium of radio.) Is it useful? Emphatically yes. It permits us to consider systematically the complex structural shift produced by the introduction of a new medium on the system of media which precedes it. Each shift in our four generations of media is such a paradigmatic shift, yielding qualitatively different systems - from speech to speech-print to speech-print-video to speech-print-video-multimedia. This structural shift, rather than a sectorial shift, is the basic characteristic of organic systems.

To understand such a shift, we need a tool such as the tetrad. The ubiquitous is paradoxically elusive. The fish will be last to discover water. The tetrad introduces the fish to water, the person to the media in which we are immersed. Media may not be as broad as Eric McLuhan suggests (the over-generalization to all artifacts may be one reason why *Laws of Media* has been dismissed by critics), but it is broader than we tend to think. We tend to lose sight of media which is too close or too far. Thus, the first generation of speaking is so close that we see it as a part of ourselves rather than an extension of ourselves. Thus, the fourth generation of multimedia is so far, for those who are not yet familiar with it, that they see it as separate from themselves.

This brings us to a second distinguishing characteristic of the technosphere. Whereas the sociosphere has **observer effects**, the technosphere has **participant effects**. We are all anthropologists, participant observers in our own culture. Those who view multimedia as a tool to extend themselves see it as a means of liberation, those who view it as a constraining environment see it as a means of oppression. The debate continues because self-fulfilling prophecies provide both sides with evidence for their position. A medium only becomes an extension of those who use it. If you do not use it, it becomes an environment. Those who do not grasp it as a tool, and thereby extend themselves, are victims of it because its use by other people creates the environment in which they are living. If it is not part of your solution, then it is part of your problem. Or, as the cyberpunks more rudely phrase it, *if you are not part of the steam-roller, then you're part of the road.*

'diffusion' broadcasting:
the multilocational

**access to entire planet
everybody
everywhere**

tribal ecological environment:
trauma, paranoia

RADIO was an invasion of Western
culture, phasing out 2,500 years
of culture and literacy. It
brought to the surface an
'instictive' tribal sensitivity
to the dangers of alcohol...
a hypersensitivity to 'the
Demon RUM' Radio
was the hidden
ground to the
figure of
retrieved Prohibition

Orson Welles's
Invasion from Mars

world reverses
into talking picture:
audience as actors
participating in their own
audience participation
Global Village Theatre

**wires and connections
and physical bodies**

end of rational and lineal:

end of Euclidean space:

end of Western time
and space

ENH | REV
RET | OBS

ENH	What does it enhance or intensify?
OBS	What does it render obsolete or displace?
RET	What does it retrieve that was previously obsolesced?
REV	What does it produce or become when pressed to an extreme?

FIGURE 5-3   EXAMPLE OF TETRAD – RADIO

5.3   THREATS AND OPPORTUNITIES

So far, we have been telling the story of tele-communications. We started
with speech and memory. We use the distance senses of audition (for verbal
communication) and vision (for non-verbal communication).[4]   This is tele-
communications - that is, communications at a distance. It's communication at a

---

[4]   There is communication also using the close senses of touch, smell and taste. Helen
Keller, being blind and deaf had no access to the distance senses, yet lived a full life, graduating
from university, writing books, using only those close senses. However, this is a whole other
story. Though I've neglected it here, you may want to explore it on your own - in private.

short distance - we have to be within ear-shot and eye-sight of one another - but communication at a distance nevertheless.

The major opportunity provided by the assimilation of each generation of media is the further conquest of time and space. As argued in Chapter 3, the invention of tools for storing information outside our bodies - the second generation of print and film - increases our range. I can write a book in Montreal and you can read it in San Francisco (well outside the range of my voice). You can take a photograph in New Delhi and I can look at it a decade later in New York (well outside the range of my sight).   However, I can look at your photograph far away from where it is taken but not right away.   Books and films are physical objects which have to be transported from place to place.

The second generation of media is thus limited to the speed of transportation. The message could not travel any faster than the messenger, since the hardware (medium) and the software (message) were not yet separate [LEVINSON 1997, Page 192]. Thus, the Aztec system of having a relay team of trained runners posted every twenty miles was limited to the speed of running humans; the Pony Express was limited to the speed of galloping horses; the pigeon post was limited to the speed of flying pigeons.

The speed of transportation has only recently exceeded the speed of sound. Thus, unless you were sending a message from New York to Paris on the Concorde jet or had persuaded an astronaut to deliver a letter to the moon, your conquest of space and time was limited to the relatively slow pace of transportation - that is, below the speed of sound. Thus, the invention of tools for transmitting information outside our bodies - the third generation of telephone and television - further increases our range. We are now able to communicate at *essentially* the speed of light (the qualifier is added to allow for the friction as our message moves through air and along wires). For the first time in history, the message can travel faster than the messenger. Your voice on the telephone can be heard almost instantaneously at the other side of the planet; a television transmission can be received around the world at essentially the same time. I can speak into a telephone in Montreal and you can hear me in San Francisco right away. You can appear in a television studio in New Delhi and I can see you in New York right away.

As argued in Chapter 3, the institution that resisted the second generation of media was the Church. Resistance comes from the conservatives - that is, those who have something to conserve tend to see innovation as a threat. Priests wanted to preserve their power as interpreters of the Bible for their illiterate congregations. The institution which resists the third generation is the Academy. As we assimilated the second generation of media, power had passed from priests to professors, who wanted to preserve their power as the official producers and distributors of knowledge.

The university system, founded in the Middle Ages, welcomed print, the new media of the time. However, the Academy refused to cross the digital divide with the other institutions in our society. It still focuses on the first two generations of media - Talk and Chalk. The telephone has played no role at all and television only a minor role. When a teacher uses television in class, it is assumed that s/he is filling in time because s/he has not prepared a lecture and is not taken seriously by the students. Scholars tend to look down on television as a plebeian medium of popular culture for entertaining the masses. This third generation of media introduces a class distinction between those who get their information through print and those who get their information through television, between high and low culture, between lives devoted largely to enlightenment and lives devoted largely to entertainment.

There is, however, nothing about television as a medium which predisposes it towards entertainment rather than enlightenment. This emphasis is due to historical accident. There was much discussion in the early days of television about how it would be financed. In Great Britain, it was decided to finance it publicly by selling licenses to the owners of television sets; in the United States, it was decided to finance it privately by selling screen time to corporations for advertising. In the latter case, it therefore became a tool for delivering audiences to corporations. Since entertainment is more popular than enlightenment, then the emphasis was placed on entertainment.[5]   If the television corporations could lure large audiences for their corporate clients with talking-head discussions of post-modern theory, then we would be inundated with talking-head discussions of post-modern theory. It is the responsibility of the educational system to raise public enthusiasm for enlightenment (or rather not to dampen the intrinsic interest in enlightenment).

One of the few scholars who advocates the use of video in the classroom is Camille Paglia. An enterprising (and brave) editor at *Harper's Magazine* arranged a lunch meeting between Camille Paglia and Neil Postman who favors print over video. Their debate was a very articulate, and surprisingly polite, discussion of the usual issues [HARPERS].

I personally find a combination of both media ideal. Figure 5-4 lists a number of books which accompany various television series. My strategy is to read a chapter before viewing the corresponding episode. This reassures me as a compulsive academic that I have the names and the references and all the scholarly apparatus available. The video complements the text. There are many cases in which it is better to show than to tell. This permits me to fire on both my cylinders - the right and the left hemispheres.

---

[5]   I explore this at length in another book - *Turning Teaching Inside-Out* [GARDINER 2005]. However, you need only imagine a television program entitled "*Enlightenment Tonight* " surviving for 20 years on prime-time television or two billion people watching a televised version of the presentation of the Nobel Prizes, the enlightenment analog of the Oscars, to realize that entertainment is indeed more popular than enlightenment. The recent critical and commercial success of documentary films by Michael Moore – *Bowling for Columbine, Fahrenheit 9/11* – is an encouraging sign of change.

James Burke
Connections
New York: Little, Brown, 1995
(VIDEO: John Black, Director
10-hour documentary on the history of technology).

Joseph Campbell
Betty Sue Flowers, Editor
The Power of Myth
New York: Doubleday, 1988
(VIDEO: Bill Moyers, Interviewer
6-hour conversation with Joseph Campbell at George Lucas' Skywalker Ranch)

Robert X. Cringely
**Accidental Empires: How the Boys of Silicon Valley Make Their Millions,
Battle Foreign Competition, and Still Can't Get a Date**
New York: HarperCollins, 1996
(VIDEO: Robert X. Cringely, Narrator
Triumph of the Nerds 3-hour documentary on the recent history of the computer)

Daniel Goleman, Paul Kaufman, & Michael Ray
The Creative Spirit
New York: Dutton, 1992
(VIDEO: 4 one-hour videos on creativity:
• Inside Creativity • Creative Beginnings • Creativity at Work
• Creating Community)

Wim Kayzer & Oliver W. Sacks
A Glorious Accident:
Understanding Our Place in the Cosmic Puzzle
San Francisco: W. H. Freeman, 1997
(VIDEO: 1-hour interviews with • Daniel C. Dennett • Freeman Dyson •
Stephen Jay Gould • Oliver Sacks • Philip Sheldrake • Stephen Toulmin)

Tom Lewis
Empire of the Air: The Men Who Made Radio
New York: HarperCollins, 1991
(VIDEO: Ken Burns, Director, Jason Robarts, Narrator
2-hour documentary on history of radio)

FIGURE 5-4   BOOKS AND ACCOMPANYING TV SERIES

Because of its resistance to the third and fourth generations of media, the educational system has become a gigantic qwerty phenomenon. Just as the typewriter keyboard was designed for another time but persists into the present because so many people have been trained on it, so the educational system was designed for the agricultural society but persists into the present because teachers continue to teach the way they were taught[6]

When information was largely in the heads of teachers, it made sense to sit people in rows and tell them things. When only teachers had access to books, it made sense for teachers to read those books and for students to write theirs. Those talk-and-chalk methods no longer make sense. If we continue with those traditional methods, the university will become increasingly peripheralized and irrelevant. In her autobiography, Margaret Mead states that My grandmother wanted me to have an education, so she kept me out of school.   Marshall McLuhan expressed a similar sentiment: The information level outside of school is so much higher than inside the school, that one interrupts one's education by going to school. Those statements were made many decades ago. In the interval, the information level outside school (that is, in the Media) has increased dramatically, whereas the information level inside school (that is, in the Academy) has shown little change. Those statements were startling then. However, they are so obviously true now, that they have become clichés.

We are very familiar with descriptions of generations in terms of demographics - e.g. the boomer generation born after the Second World War - or in terms of decades - e.g. the 60s generation. However, a more meaningful

---

[6]   A small example may help illustrate this. The long Summer vacation was originally designed to enable students to help with the harvest. I asked one class how many of them needed the Summer vacation to help with the harvest. Only one of them raised his hand, explaining that he was from Saskatchewan, but later John told me he was putting me on. Our schools and universities are thus sitting essentially vacant for a third of the year. If we had a trimester system in which teachers and students chose two out of three terms, we could make better use of our facilities, and some of us could get out of here during the Canadian Winter. Alas, we've got to tote those bales!

distinction between generations is in terms of the media with which they grew up. I don't remember watching television or using a telephone before I left Scotland at 20. My friend and neighbor, Trisha Santa, who is forty years younger than me, wipes me out at the computer game, *You Don't Know Jack*, not just because it is based on movies and television she grew up with, but because she is so much more at home with keyboard and mouse and screen. (She bought her first computer at 20, I bought my first computer at 50.) On the other hand, I always (so far) beat her at Scrabble, since print was the medium I grew up with. Hard on *her* heels is the Net Generation, even more at home with the fourth generation of media they have grown up with.

In her book *Culture and Commitment: The New Relationships Between the Generations in the 1970s*, Margaret Mead makes the distinction between **postfigurative cultures**, when the future repeats the past, **cofigurative cultures**, in which the present is the guide to future expectations, and **prefigurative cultures,** for the kind of culture in which the elders have to learn from the children about experiences which they have never had. *"We are now entering a period, new in history, in which the young are taking on new authority in their prefigurate apprehension of the still unknown future."* [MEAD, Page 13].

This new type of culture she saw emerging with the 70s generation is now fully here with the 90s generation. Don Tapscott, in his book *Growing up Digital: The Rise of the Net Generation* describes the generation born in the 1980s (and thus about to arrive at our universities soon) as one which has grown up with computers and thus is totally at home with them [TAPSCOTT].[7]   A university designed for postfigurative cultures, in which the old pass on their

---

[7]   During an interview with Pamela Wallin, he describes the reaction of his 12-year-old son Alex to his statement that he is teaching people how to surf the net. *"Why not give them a course on using the telephone when you are at it? "*   His 13-year-old daughter Nikki chimes in *"Yeah, Dad, how about another course on using the refrigerator? "* [TAPSCOTT, Pages 39-40].

wisdom to the young because they have experience of the life which the young will live in the future, is no longer appropriate. When this **net generation** arrives at the university and finds me standing in front of a blackboard with a piece of chalk, the excrement is really going to impinge on the ventilation device!

In Chapter 15, I advocate a new university based on all four generations of media. However, I'm not advocating a university in which the young are the professors and the old are the students. Nor would I look forward to a day in which the arrogance of youth is no longer balanced by the arrogance of experience. The old still have much to offer the young - the really important lessons of life are the same in whatever culture - be it prefigurate, cofigurate, or postfigurate. Those who have been on our planet longer are more at home on it, if they have been paying attention, than those who have just arrived. However, we are all *"immigrants in time"* (to use the delightful phrase of Margaret Mead). We all suffer future shock, as Alvin Toffler tells us, - that is, culture shock in our own culture because it is changing so rapidly [TOFFLER 1971]. The Net Generation suffers less from future shock because they have grown up with computer-based media and can help the old feel at home in this alien (and potentially alienating) culture.

The university of the future I am proposing is a community of scholars, young and old, where we all teach one another, regardless of age. Ageism is as offensive as sexism and racism and is equally offensive when it is directed by the old against the young as when it is directed by the young against the old.[8] The young have a conspiracy against the old - they are planning to outlive us. It is essential then that we perform the basic function of parents and teachers - to plan our own obsolescence.

---

[8]   One interesting difference between ageism and the more familiar prejudices of sexism and racism is that you eventually become a member of the group you demean. Imagine Archie Bunker becoming a black woman.

Immigration in time is even more threatening than immigration in space. You can't just "stay home" in the present. There is no alternative to moving into the future. The old can help the young move confidently into the future (in which they have a greater investment and, therefore, presumably interest) and the young can help the old feel more at home in a present (in which they are often bewitched, bothered, and bewildered).

CHAPTER 6

THIRD GENERATION -
TELEPHONE AND TELEVISION

6.1 PRECURSORS - TELEGRAPH AND RADIO

6.2 THE INVENTION OF TELEVISION

6.3 THE INVENTION OF TELEPHONE

6.4 TELEPHONE VERSUS TELEVISION

When television has fulfilled its ultimate destiny, man's sense of physical limitation will be swept away -- With this may come a new horizon, a new philosophy, a new sense of freedom, and greatest of all, perhaps, a finer and broader understanding between all the peoples of the world.

David Sarnoff, April 1931

I think it will be admitted by all that to have exploited so good a scientific invention for the purpose and pursuit of entertainment alone would have been a prostitution of its powers and an insult to the character and intelligence of the people.

John Reith, First President of the BBC, 1932

6.1   PRECURSORS - TELEGRAPH AND RADIO

The third generation of media, in which information is transmitted outside the body, is exemplified here by telephone and television, its most salient current examples. In doing so, however, I neglect the historical role of two other media - telegraph, which could be considered as a precursor of telephone, and radio, which could be considered as a precursor of television.

The various exemplars of transmitting information outside the body - that is, the third generation of media - can be considered as more sophisticated versions of two kids communicating with two tin cans joined by a piece of string. Telegraph permits communication by transmitting tappings on one can to be received by the other can. Telephone aspires to improve the tin cans and the string, so that the more sophisticated signal of the human voice can be transmitted. Radio aspires to throw away the string and transmit the message through the air (hence, its original name - *wireless*). Television aspires to transmitting light waves as well as sound waves through the air.

Indeed, if I were to trace the genesis of this generation to its roots, I would have to tell the stories of Benjamin Franklin and his kite, of Luigi Galvani and his frog, of Thomas Alva Edison and his light bulb, of Nikola Telsa's challenge to Edison in their battle over the relative merits of direct current (DC) and alternating current (AC), of Volta, Ampére, Ohm, Joule, and Hertz, whose contributions earned them immortality as measures - that is, the story of the capture and control of the power of electricity. Figure 6-1 lists the many contributors to this story, which is a prequel to the story told here.[1]

---

[1]   It could be argued that Thomas Alva Edison should be included as a major figure in the history of media. His work on electricity laid a foundation for the third generation of media. An enthusiastic advocate of telegraphy, he spelled out his proposal to his future wife on her hand

1544	1603	**William Gilbert**
		Coined the term "electricity"
1706	1790	**Benjamin Franklin**
		Lightening is electricity
1736	1806	**Charles Augustine de Coulomb**
		Torsion balance for measuring electricity
1737	1798	**Luigi Galvani**
		Effect of electricity on nerves
1745	1827	**Count Allesandro Volta**
		Electric battery
1775	1836	**André-Marie Ampère**
		Electric current produces magnetic field
1777	1851	**Hans Christian Oersted**
		Magnetic field around wire
1789	1854	**Georg Simon Ohm**
		Measurement of electrical resistance
1791	1867	**Michael Faraday**
		Electromagnetic induction and rotation
1818	1889	**James Prescott Joule**
		Amount of heat related to resistance
1821	1894	**Hermann L. F. von Helmholtz**
		Nerve impulses in visual and auditory systems
1831	1879	**James Clark Maxwell**
		Light is electromagnetic wave
1847	1931	**Thomas Alva Edison**
		Light bulb, Direct current electricity
1856	1943	**Nikola Tesla**
		Alternating current electricity
1856	1940	**Sir Joseph John Thompson**
		1908 Nobel Prize for electricity in gases
1857	1894	**Heinrich Rudolf Hertz**
		Electromagnetic waves at speed of light
1868	1953	**Robert Andrews Millikan**
		1923 Nobel Prize for single electron charge

FIGURE 6-1   PREQUEL - THE STORY OF ELECTRICITY

---

using the Morse Code and he named the subsequent two children Dot and Dash. His light bulb provided better access to the second generation of media. Our planet was dark for, on the average, half the time, until his light bulb enabled us to read when the world was dark.

All those media which enabled us to transmit information outside our bodies rest on this foundation of a new form of energy beyond mechanical energy. Let us assume that we have discovered how to pass an electric current along a wire. All we need now is some method of using this device to transmit messages. We are then poised to cross the digital divide from the first and second generations of media, based on mechanical energy, to the third and fourth generations of media, based on electrical energy.

Although many telegraph systems existed before, Samuel Finley Breese Morse (1791-1872) gets most of the credit, because he developed the simple code which bears his name. The message was contained in the breaks in the electric current passing along the wire.[2]   In the **Morse code**, each letter of the alphabet was represented by a series of such short (dots) and long (dashes) breaks. This code, thus, piggy-backs on the second generation of writing which in turn piggy-backs on the first generation of speaking.

A number of such **codes**, designed to overcome some limitation, in the transmitter or receiver, use such a piggy-back strategy. Thus **semaphore** is used to communicate at a distance beyond the range of the human voice by having an arrangement of flags represent each letter of the alphabet. **Braille** is used to communicate with blind people by having a pattern of raised dots represent each letter of the alphabet. **American Sign Language (ASL)** is used to communicate with deaf people. It is a full language but an aspect of it - hand-signing - is a code in which a particular hand signal represent each letter of the alphabet.[3]   Those

---

[2]   That is, it is the *absence* of current rather than its presence which contains the message. The fact that this solution is counter-intuitive may explain why it took so long to emerge.

[3]   I'm indebted to Dr. Edgar Zurif for this distinction. He kindly read the manuscript and made a number of valuable suggestions for its improvement. Hand-signing is equivalent to spelling out words. My neighbor, Dana, used it the other day. She: *I'm going for a W A L K.*

various codes are presented in Figure 6-2.[4]

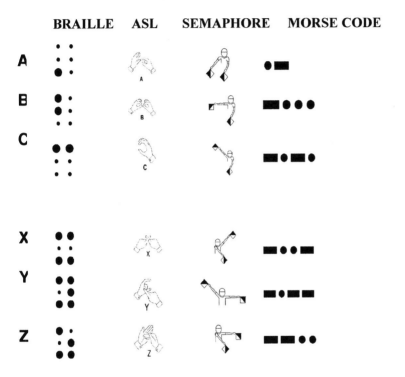

FIGURE 6-2

VARIOUS CODES PIGGY-BACKING ON THE ALPHABET

Me: *I know how to spell 'walk'.*   She: *But she doesn't* (pointing to her dog Soda who had picked up her leash and was barking at the door).

[4]   The problem with piggy-back bilingualism, as discussed in Section 2.2, is that the second language is more a code than a genuine language.

6.2   THE INVENTION OF TELEVISION

The invention of television is a complex story with a cast and plot which is more dramatic than most dramas which have appeared *on* television. This story is well-told in *Tube: The Invention of Television* [FISHER & FISHER]. Let us focus on three major characters, at the risk of slighting the large supporting cast of eccentric geniuses and enterprising businessmen.

Like many good stories, it's about a Scotsman, an American and a Russian. They shared a common dream - to send visual signals over air waves. John Logie Baird (1888-1946), Philo Taylor Farnsworth (1907-1971), and Vladimir Kosmo Zworykin (1889-1985) all made major contributions to the invention of television. All three are credited by their supporters as THE inventor of television. Although their invention has in the interval created many millionaires, only one of them was to die rich and honored. The other two died broke and broken men.

John Logie Baird was an eccentric Scottish inventor whose inventions, except for an undersock, had so far never worked. He had migrated to Hastings in the south of England because of his delicate health (even his body didn't work very well). There he began to build what would become the world's first working television set

> by purchasing an old hat box and a pair of scissors, some darning needles, a few bicycle lamp lenses, a used tea chest, and a great deal of sealing wax and glue. The contraption that he assembled from these variegated pieces of equipment soon "grew and filled my bedroom. Electric batteries were added to it, wireless valves and transformers and neon lamps appeared, and at last to my great joy I was able to show the shadow of a little cross transmitted over a few feet."
> [FISHER & FISHER, Page 31] [5]

---

[5]   The main event in Hastings, according to traditional history, is of course the Battle of Hastings in 1066. I would like to argue that this more obscure event of the first TV image projected by John Logie Baird in 1923 is, in the long run, more important. If the Big Story of

It turned out that Baird was on the wrong track. As we discovered when talking about film (see Section 4.2), the illusion of movement takes advantage of the physiological phenomenon of persistence of vision. That is, the fact that the sensation lingers after the stimulus has gone. However, the image lingers for a very short time and thus the images must follow one another very quickly. If the rate is below the critical flicker frequency (CFF), required to delude the eye into reading a series of still images as a moving image, the illusion is lost. This CFF can not be reached by means of mechanical energy - it is necessary to use the new electrical energy.

However, his demonstration that the transmission of images over space was possible encouraged his competitors to seek a solution, but by electrical means. A 14-year-old farm boy called Philo Taylor Farnsworth, inspired by some old copies of *Science and Invention* he found in the attic of the farmhouse and by the back-and-forth pattern of his ploughing, realized that the CFF could be reached by snaking an electronic beam over the object. Previous attempts by people who had never ploughed a field were hung up on writing and thus returned to the beginning of the next line without taking advantage of the return trip.[6]

Farnsworth had the necessary technical skills to come up with the idea but lacked the necessary social skills to take the idea to the market. That required the entrepreneurial genius of a Russian immigrant to the United States, Vladimir

---

historical time is the co-evolution of the person and media as extensions, as argued in this book, this was a major episode in that Big Story. Harold may have lost an eye in 1066 but we all gained an eye in 1923.

[6]   However, if they had done their homework on the history of writing, they could perhaps have been inspired by **boustrophedon script**. Egyptian hieroglyphs could be read from left to right or from right to left (you could tell which by observing the direction the animals were facing) or alternating between the two (boustrophedon means as the ox turns in ploughing). The latter option was usually chosen for large documents on long walls - the reader did not need to walk back to the beginning to continue reading [ROBINSON, Page 94].

Kosmo Zworykin. He had contributed to the technical development of television but he also had the social skill to interest another Russian immigrant, David Sarnoff, later President of RCA, in providing financial backing for his inventions, and the business skills to market television. That's why *he* was the one who died rich and honored.

Simultaneous discoveries and inventions suggest that the times are ripe for this discovery or invention. The pieces are available - it requires only someone to come along and put them together - if not Baird, then Farnsworth; if not Farnsworth, then Zworykin; if not Zworykin, then some one else.   This phenomenon - called the **Zeitgeist** (German for *the spirit of the times*) - suggests a sort of technological determinism.   However, it suggests only that the technology may be inevitable. It says nothing about the way in which this technology will be used. Nor does it say that this technology will determine that it will use people rather than that people will use it. Anticipating a further charge of technological optimism, I also plead guilty as charged. Media is intrinsically good, since it brings people together. This is not to say that people can't fiendishly find ways to use it to evil ends.

6.3   THE INVENTION OF TELEPHONE

The invention of the telephone is more clear-cut. It was invented by Alexander Graham Bell (1847-1922), who took out a patent on it in March 1876. For the sake of simplicity, it is tempting to believe that he had a dream of improving the telegraph so that one could transmit the more complex waves created by the human voice, just as the various inventors of television shared the dream of improving radio by enabling one to send images as well as sounds through the air. However, unlike Baird, Farnsworth and Zworykin, Bell did not set out to invent the telephone. He had no vision of sending speech over wires. Since both his mother and his wife were deaf, he was strongly motivated to seek tools for the deaf. It was while searching for such a tool that he stumbled on the telephone. Two principles are illustrated here.

Emotion plays as much a role in the history of science and technology as reason. The motivation for discovery and invention is often very subjective though the procedures aspire to be objective. Emotion and reason are not, as conventionally assumed, in conflict - emotion is the engine and reason is the steering-wheel. Both are needed to get wherever you want to go. You need both idealistic ends (emotion) and realistic means (reason).

Where you arrive, however, is not always where you set out to go. Many discoveries and inventions are a result of **serendipity** - the fine art of finding something while looking for something else.[7]   This phenomena of serendipity is also illustrated by the discovery being triggered by a chance environmental event. Newton sees an apple fall and discovers the universal theory of gravitation. It's important to note, however, that serendipity strikes only the prepared mind. Many people saw apples fall before Newton. However, he could transmute this trivial local event into the significant universal principle of gravitation, because he had thought deeply about the mutual attraction of objects. He had shed the 99% perspiration to earn the 1% inspiration. He had drunk deeply of the spirit of the times.

Archimedes sees water overflow from his bath and discovers the theory of specific gravity. He runs naked through the streets shouting *"Eureka"*, illustrated

---

[7]   Horace Walpole's *Three Princes of Serendip* were the original inspiration for this word. His three princes wandered around the world finding things they were not looking for.

once again that reason and emotion are not incompatible.[8]   This sudden illumination has thus been called the **Eureka Effect**. Arthur Koestler prefers to call it the "**aha phenomenon**". and argues in his book, *The Act of Creation*, that the effect is not confined to science - it is the same as the "ah phenomenon" in art and the "haha phenomenon" in humor [KOESTLER].

6.4   TELEPHONE VERSUS TELEVISION

Telephone had a half-century headstart on television. Bell took out his patent in 1876 whereas Baird, Farnsworth, and Zworykin were working on television in the 1920s. However, a number of factors delayed the penetration of the telephone into society.

There was much resistance from the telegraph industry which was well-established when Bell took out his patent. They had a vested interest in delaying an invention which threatened their turf. Some advocates of telegraphy (writing at a distance) may have genuinely believed that the public would not be interested in telephone (speaking at a distance) because there would be no record of the transaction. Even the inventor was apprehensive about a technology which could be viewed as invasive. [9] He believed that it would be accepted by business but

---

[8]   *Eureka!* is Greek for *good God, that water's hot!*   Archimedes thus discovered the law of specific gravity and invented streaking on the same day.

[9]   He was not entirely wrong. It is a very invasive technology. As one who did not grow up with the telephone, I'm horrified at how people are so compelled to answer it. I once took advantage of this when, standing in line for some information about university registration, I

only if it was limited to an hour or two a day; he believed that it would not be accepted at all in homes and thus installed his first telephones in corner stores so that people could leave their homes to use them in emergencies [POOLE].

The two systems - telephone and television - developed side by side during the 1940s, 1950s, 1960s, and 1970s. There were no very significant changes. The telephone receiver, originally a standard black device, blossomed into a variety of forms and colors. The television set, originally small and in black and white, evolved into larger screens in color. The fact that minor shifts from rotary to push-button dialing in telephone and from black-and-white to color images in television were hailed as major innovations demonstrates how stable the situation was. Both technologies penetrated into the home until, in industrialized countries, their penetration had reached an asymptote of over 90%.

Whatever thought was devoted to the differences between those two systems focused on the part we could see - the telephone handset and the television set. They were largely seen as pieces of furniture which communicate. Playwrights sometimes wrote them into their scripts. Thus, they were clearly seen as "special" pieces of furniture but little consideration was given to the differences between them.

If we can tear ourselves away from the superficial visible aspects of the systems, we could consider the deeper distinction between an auditory system (telephone) and a largely visual system (television). They capitalize, respectively, on the two distance senses of our species. We have already

---

noticed that the clerk serving my line would interrupt her conversation to answer the phone. I jumped the queue by phoning her. A reporter, sent to cover a story in which a man holed up in his apartment was having a shoot-out with police, phoned the man. The gunman answered the phone, and answered his questions, with apologies for his abrupt answers since he was "very busy". The horror story continues as I watch people carrying a cellular phone like an electronic leash. A couple having brunch interrupted their tete-a-tete repeatedly to use their respective phones for outgoing as well as incoming calls.

considered, in Section 3.2, the dramatic differences between an oral culture (based on the ear) and a print culture (based on the eye).

Sound and light are both waves. However, a deeper distinction is between waves transmitted over wires (telephone) and waves transmitted through air (television). This distinction broke down, however, with the development of satellite-based telephone, which enabled us to receive telephone signals through the air as well as over wires; and with the development of cable television, which enabled us to receive television signals over wires as well as through the air. Communication over wires and communication through air both have their unique problems.

The basic limitation of communication using waves through the air is that waves travel in straight lines whereas our globe is round. The range of radio stations is about 40 miles. This is roughly the distance from any point on our planet to the horizon, and is the limiting factor in any line-of-sight system of communication. Thus, the waves must be passed on like a baton in a relay race with relay stations every forty miles. Or some means must be devised for bouncing waves off some "relay station" outside our globe. It turns out that the ionosphere conveniently bounces long-range air waves back to earth at a point considerably further than 40 miles away. The launching of the first satellite by Russia in 1957 suggested another option. Since then, air waves have been bounced back to earth by **satellites**.

Another option is to send the waves along wires and bend the wires around the globe. The story of the laying of the first trans-Atlantic cable was told in Section 5.1. Since then, our planet has acquired a girdle of criss-crossing cables. The basic limitation of communication using waves along wires is that copper wire has a limited bandwidth. Replacement of copper with **fiber optics** does for the wire option what satellites did for the air option. As the air-wire war continues, we will most likely see some compromise emerge with information being transmitted by a combination of the two strategies.

Another distinction is between **synchronous** and **asynchronous communication**. Both telephone and television were originally synchronous. That is, you and I had to be at the respective ends of our phone line at the same time for us to talk. Bill Gates points out that, if you wanted to see the *Beatles* or Elvis Presley on the *Ed Sullivan Show,* you had to be in front of your television set at eight o'clock on the designated Sunday evening [GATES]. Both telephone and television have since become asynchronous. You can leave your message in my voice-mail box and I can pick it up later. Time-shifting is possible with both television and telephone. My dates with *Felicity* and *Ally McBeal* need not necessarily be at 7 p. m. on Sunday and 9 p. m. on Monday respectively[10] - I can record and meet them both on Tuesday. You can leave me a v-mail message about the logistics of meeting on Sunday, I can pick it up on Monday, and meet you face-to-face as planned on Tuesday.

A deeper distinction is that the telephone is a two-way communication system where the television is a one-way communication system. Lately, television has touted itself as interactive. The viewer with a set-top box mediating between his cable company and his television set can choose one of four camera angles as he watches a hockey game or choose four alternative endings as she watches a drama. However, this very limited interactivity is little more liberating than the "interactivity" involved in choosing between brands of breakfast cereals. They are essentially the same and are often produced by the same corporations.

Going even deeper, we encounter the distinction between the telephone infrastructure consisting of a network of interlinked nodes and the television infrastructure consisting of a few sources connected to many destinations. In the telephone system, everyone is a source as well as a destination. Once again, as in

---

[10]   To my embarrassment, I've become addicted to two prime time soap operas! To my regret, they are now long-gone!

the case of the second generation of media, we find democratic and autocratic versions of media. The underlying infrastructure of telephone is like that of the Post Office, whereas the underlying infrastructure of television is like that of the newspaper.

Paradoxically, this democratic infrastructure is created by building a hierarchy. If Rob creates a "telephone system" with a string and two tin cans so as to communicate with his neighbor Mary, he needs only 1 string. However, if Sam asks to join the network and insists on his own tin terminal, they now need 3 strings - one between Rob and Mary, one between Rob and Sam, and one between Mary and Sam. An invitation to a fourth kid, Milly, would require 6 strings - one between Rob and Mary, one between Rob and Sam, one between Rob and Milly, one between Mary and Sam, one between Mary and Milly, and one between Sam and Milly.

This is beginning to get out of hand - so let us reduce it to a formula. Since each kid must be linked to each other - the number of links is the number of kids times the number of others (that is the number of kids minus one). However, since the link from Rob to Mary is the same as the link from Mary to Rob, the result must be divided by two. Figure 6-3a shows the relationship between the number of kids and the number of links between them. As you can see, the number of links increases quickly as the number of kids increases slowly.

The number of telephone handsets in the world was estimated at 400 million in 1980, and it has grown considerably since then. The number of telephones has grown linearly, but the number of links between telephones has grown exponentially. The solution to this huge problem is to link them in groups rather than in pairs. Figure 6-3b shows the simple case in which 10 telephones are linked in 2 groups of 5. This reduces the number of links from 45 (10x9/2) to 11 (count them). The nodes in this network are called switching devices and the think wire between them is called a trunk line.

This hierarchical organization of the telephone system enables you to zero in very quickly on one of the 400 million handsets. Let us say you want to call from Canada to your mother in Scotland. You dial 011 which gets you Great Britain, then 44 which gets you Scotland, then 505 which gets you Renfrewshire, then 843 which gets you Lochwinnoch, and then 364 which gets you the handset in your mother's home. Hello, Mum! (Actually, it is not that tidy but the example does serve to demonstrate the principle of zeroing in on a specific item from a large number by moving into smaller and smaller categories to which it belongs).

Note that the same principle is applied in getting a letter to one of the millions of homes in the world. You write the categories in reverse order - Mrs. J. K. Brown, 9 Calder Drive, Lochwinnoch, Renfrewshire, Scotland, Great Britain - and the mail system works backwards through this set of categories to deliver it. Hello, Mum! The Zip Code is an attempt to allow machines to automate mail delivery just as they have automated telephone call delivery. You may be familiar with the same divide-and-conquer principle in the game of *Twenty Questions.*

In the early 1980s, there was a flurry of excitement around a technology called **videotext**, which was a sort of hybrid of telephone and television. Various nations were touting their version of videotext as a standard for the globe. Japan has its Captain, Great Britain its Prestel, France its Minitel, and Canada its Telidon. The Canadian videotext system, Telidon, was technically superior to the French videotext system, Minitel. However, Telidon failed and Minitel flourished [MARCHAND M].[11]   This could have been due simply to the poorer marketing of Telidon (just as VHS videocassettes triumphed over the better technology of BETA videocassettes because of the poorer marketing of BETA by Sony).

---

[11]   Incidentally, the victory turned out to be a mixed blessing. The penetration of the internet into France has been slowed down by the fact that many people are satisfied with the limited version of the internet embodied by the Minitel system.

NUMBER OF NODES	NUMBER OF LINKS
2	1
3	3
4	6
5	10
6	15
7	21
8	28
9	36
10	45
100	4,950
1,000	499,500
10,000	49,995,0000
100,000	4,999,950,000
1,000,000	499,999,500,000

(a) RELATIONSHIP BETWEEN NUMBER OF NODES AND
NUMBER OF NODE-TO-NODE LINKS IN A COMMUNICATION SYSTEM

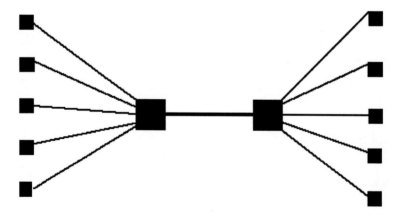

(b) USE OF SWITCHES AND TRUNK LINES TO REDUCE LINKS

FIGURE 6-3   NODES AND LINKS, SWITCHES AND TRUNKS

There may have been a deeper reason. Telidon was viewed and developed as an extension of television, whereas Minitel was viewed and developed as an extension of telephone. Touting *"two-way television "* was not a good move, especially just before 1984![12]   Perhaps the most important distinction is between the democratic infrastructure of the telephone system as opposed to the autocratic infrastructure of the television system. Those distinctions are summarized in Figure 6-4.

TELEPHONE	TELEVISION
Handset - furniture you talk into	TV set - furniture that talks
Ear - sound waves	Eye - light waves
Waves over wires	Waves through air
Synchronous communication	Asynchronous communication
Two-way communication	One-way communication
Democratic infrastructure	Autocratic infrastructure

FIGURE 6-4
ESSENTIAL DIFFERENCE BETWEEN
TELEPHONE AND TELEVISION

We saw in Section 3.2 how television did not wipe out *its* precursor, radio. Applying the evolutionary framework of this book, we may perhaps understand the difference in terms of the ecological niche of each media.   Radio

---

[12]   It is not surprising that the various dystopias - *1984, Brave New World* - are based on television rather than telephone. Big Brother could hardly control the population by calling each of us. We are unlikely to be lulled into a passive state by talking to one another on the telephone.

has certainly been reduced in importance by the assimilation of television. The family now gathers around the television set rather than around the radio. This era can be recaptured by those who did not live through it by renting Woody Allen's *Radio Days* from the local video store (which, incidentally is forcing television in turn to redefine *its* niche). Radio has carved itself out a new and narrower niche for situations in which it is more appropriate to use the ears rather than the eyes - while driving, while doing dishes, while dusting furniture, while dancing or romancing, etc. It was a godsend during the recent Ice Storm since it served to keep people informed and in touch with one another when more sophisticated communication systems were disabled.

Nor did the telephone wipe out its precursor - the telegram. Whether their resistance was due to a genuine belief or simply due to their investments, the apprehension of the telegraph industry was indeed justified. When was the last time you sent or received a telegram? Even the language of the telegram - the Morse Code - has recently been declared obsolete [IMMEN]. Telephone triumphed over telegraph because it was the fittest in the same niche. (Fitness has, in this context, nothing to do with the gymnasium - it means the best fit to the environment.) Telegraph persisted alongside telephone for some time because it provided a concrete record of transactions. However, fax moved into this niche and dealt the death-blow to telegraph. Sometimes it takes a one-two punch before a technology goes down.

CHAPTER 7
SHIFT 3 - ASSIMILATING
THE FOURTH GENERATION

7.1 IS THE CURRENT SHIFT CLEARER NOW?

7.2 TORONTO SCHOOL - NEW MCLUHANS

7.3 THREATS AND OPPORTUNITIES

The ease of entering and changing text on a screen, the nearly instant speed of the transmission - all in contrast to the difficulty and slowness of such applications when conducted on paper - conspire to make online communication a speech-like medium, a hybrid in which our fingers not only do the walking but do the talking, from its inception.

Paul Levinson, DIGITAL MCLUHAN, Page 33

What a bore it is, waking up in the morning, always the same person.

Logan Pearsall Smith

7.1   IS THE CURRENT SHIFT CLEARER NOW?

Away back in Chapter 1, I argued that we can't get a clear look at this third shift, as we assimilate the fourth generation of media (Multimedia and Internet), because it is happening now. We are still in the turbulent throes of this third transition. It's happening all around us. We are too immersed in it to see it clearly. The ubiquitous is paradoxically elusive. The fish will be last to discover water. I suggested back then that we may be able to see more clearly by going far back into our past and taking a long look at our present. Is it clearer now? I think so. It's clearer to me after writing this history, and I hope it's clearer to you after reading it. This fish, at least, is beginning to get to know the water.

Within the long perspective, we can see that the turbulent transition of the present is a logical continuation of a long process. It is the latest (and, I'll argue later, last) chapter in what I call the Big Story of historical time - the co-evolution of the person and media as extensions. That process is the adaptation of our social system and media system over historical time to the challenges of the environment. We shifted to an agricultural society and acquired media to store information outside our bodies; we shifted to an industrial society and acquired media to transmit information outside our bodies; we are now shifting to an information society and acquiring media to both store and transmit information outside our bodies.

Those shifts may perhaps best be understood within the challenge-and-response model of history proposed by Arnold Toynbee [TOYNBEE]. As we moved from a hunter-gatherer to an agricultural to an industrial to an information society, the response to the challenge of such dramatic shifts in society was the development of the second, third, and fourth generations of media, respectively. We are now in the throes of the third shift and may perhaps get some insight into the current turbulent transition by looking at the previous two shifts.

As we moved into an agricultural society, nature was not able to keep up with this social evolution and we had to invent our own media system in response to this challenge. We settled down but goods moved around and we needed tools to record goods we have stored and shipped to others. As Schmandt-Besserat has demonstrated (see Section 4.3), this need to keep records of excess food stored and traded in the emerging agricultural society evolved into writing [SCHMANDT-BESSERAT]. Tokens representing various goods were wrapped in clay envelopes with symbols etched on them to represent the contents. Those symbols evolved into writing.

The second shift to electronic media based on electricity was a response to the challenge posed by the globalization of trade (in goods and ideas) and thus the need for instantaneous communication around the globe. As we moved into an industrial society, it was necessary to have more instantaneous communication on a global scale as raw materials were collected from around the globe and finished products distributed around the globe. Telegraphy and its descendants in the third generation of media were developed as a response to this challenge.

As this globalization shrunk the planet into a Global Village, there was a need for an infrastructure for communication within this village. Needs generate markets. Entrepreneurs take over from innovators to develop the satisfiers of those needs to generate wealth for themselves and for others. As we now move into an information society, information must be integrated and distributed around the globe so that we can interact with it wherever we are. As we have come to realize that information is itself an important resource, we need means of packaging and distributing it around the globe. Just as we needed to store food to use later and to trade, as we moved into the agricultural society, so we need to store information to use later and to trade, as we move into the information society. The fourth generation of multimedia and internet is the response to those challenges.

Which is cause and which is effect? Those who say technology is the cause are dismissed as technological determinists and those who say society is the cause are dismissed as cultural determinists. This process, of which our current turbulent transition is a part, is a process of continuous discontinuity, like the process of phylogenetic development, as described by Charles Darwin, and the process of ontogenetic development, as described by Jean Piaget. As in those cases, the continuity is function, in this case communication, and the discontinuity is structure, in this case, different media emerged to deal with different challenges. To ask which is more important is like asking which of the three legs of a three-legged stool is most important. The three shifts are different stages in the process by which our species has extended our nervous systems through our co-evolution with media This is what I call the Big Story of historical time.

Now that the similarities in our three transitions are stated, the differences become clear. This third transition is, as argued in Section 5.1, no more important than the other two. Indeed, it could be best viewed simply as the dropping of the other shoe. Once a means of transmitting information electronically was available, it was only a matter of time and technology before the means of storing information electronically was devised. The third transition differs from the first and second, because it shifts us into an information society, in which media is central. The information society is defined in terms of media. It is no longer simply a means to an end but an end in itself. Power has shifted from violence (in an agricultural society) to money (in an industrial society) to knowledge (in an information society) [TOFFLER 1990].

This lends support to the argument that the Big Story of historical time is the co-evolution of the person and media as extensions. Life is led forward but understood backward. Now that we can see history as culminating in an information society, then it is imperative that we revision history in terms of communication rather than in terms of conflict. Much conflict is a footnote to communication - case studies of failures of communication.[1]

Another common theme in the three transitions is the piggy-backing of each generation on the previous ones. As argued in Chapter 3, the second generation of writing piggy-backs on the first generation of speech by using a foundation of graphemes which correspond (roughly) to phonemes. As argued in Chapter 5, telegraph, the prototype for the third generation, piggy-backs in turn on the second generation by using a code of dots and dashes corresponding to each grapheme. The fourth generation of multimedia and internet picky-backs in turn on the third generation by using a code of 0s and 1s to correspond not only to graphemes but to numbers and images and sounds. Each generation of tele-communications thus capitalizes on the power of the first generation, which is the invention of nature.

Once again, as the similarities are described, the differences become clear. Since this same code is used for the storage and transmission of information in the fourth generation, it integrates storage and information within the same system. Thus the plagiarism of nature continues in the fourth generation in a more dramatic way. This fourth generation brings us back, in a sense, to the first generation, in which storage (memory) and transmission (speech) are integrated within the human brain. The extrasomatic transmission of the third generation is integrated with extrasomatic storage in the fourth generation. Which leads to a whole other story.

Another story was continuing in parallel to our story of tele-communications - the story of artificial intelligence. Until very recently, they were separate stories. The third shift into the fourth generation of media is due largely to the convergence of computer and tele-communication technologies.

---

[1]   Cool Hand Luke hinted at some deeper causes of conflict when he said to the sadistic guard *"We have a failure of communication"*.

Those two stories now merge into one story. We should perhaps have predicted this merger. Tele-communications is the story of the technological extension of language; artificial intelligence is the story of the technological extension of thought. Their convergence was inevitable.[2] Few futurists predicted it. Perhaps if we had been thinking in terms of evolutionary psychology, we would have.

As the histories of computers and of tele-communications converged, the extrasomatic tool for storing information (the computer) and the extrasomatic tool for transmitting information (tele-communications) merged into the same system. Let us call this system **informatics**. The penetration of informatics into society has triggered the shift from an industrial society, based on energy, to a post-industrial society, based on information (Figure 7-1).

During the early 1980s, I kept a record of the processes which had been converted to this informatics system. See Figure 7-2 for a list collated from *The Globe and Mail* between 1980 and 1983. I had to abandon this project because of the exponential growth of this conversion process. The penetration of informatics into industrialized society has been so dramatic that it has produced a paradigmatic shift to a post-industrial society (Figure 7-3). Thus this third shift is not simply a continuation of the conquest of space and time as in the first and second shifts but a qualitative change in the whole society. We are in the midst of a paradigmatic shift from an industrial society, based on energy, to a post-industrial society, based on information. Thus we are in the midst of a turbulent transition into a society, which is not just influenced by media but is defined in terms of media. The basic function of an information society is the storage and

---

[2]   This story parallels the twice-upon-a-time structure of many Hollywood movies. We are introduced to him, we are introduced to her, then we see their lives converge . The convergence of computer and tele-communication technologies was, in hindsight, just as predictable. The question now is *"will they live happily ever after?"* This is just as predictable. They will indeed live happily together or die unhappily together. Every time there is a downturn in the New Tech industry, some people speculate that the informatics infrastructure and the new economy based on it was just a fad. However, it is here to stay. It is the culmination of a long historical process representing the unfolding of the human potential.

transmission of information.

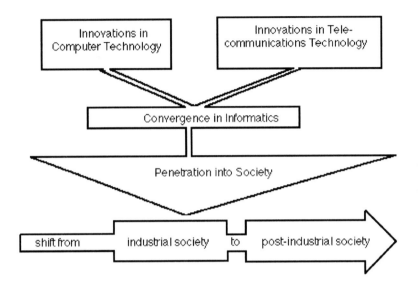

FIGURE 7-1   FIVE PROCESSES OF CHANGE

Informatics is the infrastructure of this information society. The anti-trust case brought against the Microsoft Corporation is based on the principle that no individual or institution should own the infrastructure. The infrastructure of the industrial society is the transportation system. Imagine the confusion and corruption if the highways were owned by a corporation (or perhaps, even worse, by many corporations, as they were essentially in the early days of transportation). You wouldn't be able to travel if you couldn't afford to pay the tolls. Even if you could pay, your trip would be constantly interrupted as you stopped to pay at the toll-booths set up by each corporation. If you had a feud with someone who owned a particular road, you could be banned from traveling on it, no matter how much you paid and how willing you were to wait. Informatics was once

18 February 80	10	Monitoring house to secure against fire and theft
23 October 80	15	Teaching blind and crippled to read and write
17 November 80	10	Facilitating face surgery
03 December 80	05	Replacing missing limbs (bionic hand)
17 February 81	B 3	Operating a sawmill
23 February 81	11	Presenting text/images on electronic blackboard
24 February 81	10	Creating electronic music
04 March 81	11	Comparing structure of songs to settle cases of plagiarism
04 March 81	12	Dispensing drinks and cooking roast beef
28 March 81	03	Automatic control during Sabbath for Orthodox Jews
30 March 81	10	Guiding blind
21 April 81	03	Increasing library security
09 May 81	B 1	Controlling inventory and maintenance in vending machines
01 June 81	13	Warning divers of danger
01 June 81	13	Creating three-dimensional images
17 June 81	B 9	Helping airline and travel agent sales
30 July 81	B 9	Storing maps
26 August 81	04	Playing chess
23 January 82	21	Writing musical scores
13 February 82	B 3	Providing up-to-the-minute annuity rates
22 February 82	B 9	Regulating fuel consumption on ships
27 February 82	06	Keeping time in "tickless, tockless" clocks
20 March 82	B16	Typesetting books
12 April 82	11	Researching in computerized library
24 April 82	06	Bartering, using, electronic bulletin board
25 May 82	B11	Keeping records of companies
28 July 82	B10	Managing a fleet of trucks
02 July 82	B 1	Scanning prices in supermarket
15 July 82	10	Communicating with victims of cerebral palsy
07 August 82	06	Voice paging people across country
26 August 82	09	Choosing a car or boat
03 September 82	06	Giving verbal instructions to users of photocopiers
24 September 82	R 4	Auditing and accounting
08 October 82	10	Changing sounds into images for deaf
01 November 82	T 1	Planning business and vacation trips
23 November 82	06	Dispensing Coca-Cola, with spoken instructions
26 November 82	09	Preserving the choreography of dance
26 November 82	11	Animating cartoons (Heidi)
08 December 82	B 1	Simulating flight
08 December 82	B 4	Shopping, electronically, at home
13 December 82	B 9	Controlling inventories for direct selling company
15 December 82	09	Consulting doctor
11 March 83	10	Monitoring prisoners with electronic ankle bracelets
16 April 83	02	Milking cows
06 May 83	06	Knitting
17 August 83	07	Checking text for neologisms to enter in dictionaries
16 September 83	06	Wearing as earrings, cuff-links
26 September 83	01	Calculating doses for diabetics
13 October 83	12	Apprehending criminals
10 November 83	13	Charting the zodiac

FIGURE 7-2 COMPUTER-AIDED EVERYTHING

described as the " *electronic superhighway*". This much-maligned term has gone out of favor.[3]   However, it is an important reminder that informatics is the infrastructure. Since we all share the infrastructure, we should all own it. The supremacy of a democratic system over an autocratic system is most evident in the case of the infrastructure.

7.2   TORONTO SCHOOL - NEW MCLUHANS

A number of current scholars, each heralded by their supporters as the "*new McLuhan*", are carrying on the Toronto School tradition of Innis and McLuhan. Whereas Innis focused on the first transition, McLuhan on the second transition, those young scholars are focusing on the third transition which is currently taking place.

The first of those (in order of seniority) is Robert Logan (1939-   ). His three major books within the Toronto tradition are *The Alphabet Effect* [LOGAN 1986], *The Fifth Language* [LOGAN 1995], and *The Sixth Language* [LOGAN 2000].

The second is Paul Levinson (1940-   ). His most recent books are *The Soft Edge: A Natural History and Future of the Information Revolution*

---

[3]   Some people protested that they were bored with the term - *electronic superhighway*. This is another symptom of our emphasis on entertainment over enlightenment. This is like dismissing the equation - $E = M.C\ squared$ - because it is boring. Both the term and the equation are designed to enlighten us - not to entertain us. Electronic superhighway served the purpose of reminding us that the infrastructure of the information society is tele-communications by emphasizing the parallel with the infrastructure of the industrial society - transportation.

[LEVINSON 1997] and *Digital McLuhan: A Guide to the Information Millennium* [LEVINSON 1999].

The third is a McLuhan literally as well as metaphorically. Eric McLuhan (1941-   ), a son of Marshall McLuhan, worked with his father on *Laws of Media* [MCLUHAN M & MCLUHAN E]. Although this book started out as a revision of *Understanding Media: Extensions of Man,* it finished up when finally published 8 years after his father's death to contain as much of the point of view of Eric as of Marshall. Eric has since published a book on his own entitled *Electric Language* which continues to explore his perspective [MCLUHAN E].

The fourth is Arthur Kroker (1945-   ) who, as the only Montrealer in the Toronto School, is appropriately more flamboyant. After a traditional book, *Technology and the Canadian Mind* in which he presented an excellent survey of the work of Innis, McLuhan and George Grant [KROKER 1984], he has produced a spate of un-traditional books on the fourth generation of media - for example, *Spasm: Virtual Reality, Android Music, Electric Flesh* [KROKER 1993] and *Data Trash: The Theory of the Virtual Class* [KROKER & WEINSTEIN].

The fifth is Derrick de Kerckhove (1946-   ), who was a student and colleague of Marshall McLuhan before taking over his position as Director of the *McLuhan Program in Culture and Technology.* His two major contributions to the Toronto tradition are his recent books - *The Skin of Culture: Investigating the New Electronic Reality* [DE KERCKHOVE 1995] and *Connected Intelligence: The Arrival of the Web Society* [DE KERCKHOVE 1997].

The "baby" of the group is Bruce W. Powe (1955-   ). He wrote a book describing Marshall McLuhan (along with two other Canadians, Pierre Trudeau and Glenn Gould, an almost-Canadian born on a yacht off Amherst, Nova Scotia, Wyndham Lewis, and an Italian, Elias Canetti) as *The Solitary Outlaw* [POWE 1987]. No doubt impressed by a country in which the Prime Minister for 16 years can creditably be described as a *"solitary outlaw"*, he went on to do a very unCanadian thing - he presented a glowing picture of our country as *A Tremendous Canada of Light* [POWE 1993]. His exploration of the impact of the fourth generation of media continues with *Outage: A Journey into Electric City* [POWE 1995].

Although his major focus is the role of the intellectual in a world of declining literacy, Powe could be better described as a poet rather than a scholar. Of the other five *"new McLuhans"*, only Levinson is trained within the discipline of communication studies. The others are scholars in various different disciplines - Logan is a physicist, Eric McLuhan followed his father into English Literature focusing on the work of one of his father's heroes, James Joyce, Kroker is a Political Scientist, and de Kerckhove was a Professor in the Department of French. In this sense, they also follow in the Toronto tradition - Innis studied political science and McLuhan studied English Literature. All members of the Toronto School transcended their disciplines to become generalists. The diversity of points of view they therefore bring to Media Studies accounts for much of the richness of the tradition. The continuation of the Big Story of historical time - the co-evolution of the person and media as extensions - is in good hands.

7.3   THREATS AND OPPORTUNITIES

When we analyze Toynbee's Challenge into Threats and Opportunities, we find that our long look at the first and second transitions help us better understand our current third transition. It is essentially a continuation of the first two, but with its own uniqueness.

The major opportunity in our story of tele-communications so far is the increase in human freedom by the progressive conquest of time and space. In

Chapter 3, we learned that the invention of tools for storing information outside our bodies - the second generation of print and film - increases the range of our distance senses - vision and audition. In Chapter 5, we learned that the invention of tools for transmitting information outside our bodies - the third generation of telephone and television - further increases our range. We are now able to communicate at *essentially* the speed of light (the qualifier is added to allow for the friction as our message moves through air and along wires) rather than under the speed of sound.

The invention of tools for both storing and transmitting information outside our bodies - the fourth generation of multimedia and internet - can not continue this conquest of space and time. There is no place on our planet which is not potentially accessible to print and film, telephone and television. Nothing moves faster than the speed of light.[4]   Some have argued that it permits us to escape the constraints - not of time and space - but of our identity [STONE, TURKLE 1995]. Surfing around on the internet without our bodies on, we can try on other personalities. No one knows what sex we are, what color we are, how old we are - that is, there is no basis for prejudice (sexism, racism, ageism, respectively). We can not be pre-judged.

Logan Pearsall Smith pinpoints one aspect of the human predicament when he says: *What a bore it is, waking up in the morning, always the same person.* We are condemned to be one person in one place at one time. Media permits us to be, at least vicariously, other people in other places at other times. This is part of the explanation why there is such a huge appetite for stories. The

---

[4]   Nothing, that is, but in a sense the human mind. Albert Einstein imagined himself traveling faster than the speed of light and created the theory of relativity. The speed of light can not only be exceeded by human imagination, it can be squared! The C in $E = M.C$ squared is, of course, the speed of light. In our enthusiasm for our inventions of extrasomatic tools, we must be careful to recognize that the ultimate invention was nature's invention of the human mind. Our various extrasomatic tools are pale copies plagiarized from nature.

life we lead is only one of millions of possible lives we could have led.

Each decision we make cuts out many possible lives.[5]   Of course, if you feel that the one life you happen to have led was a misspent life, then you are even more attracted to living your missed lives vicariously.   That is perhaps why dedicated devotees of Star Wars and Star Trek movies are often advised to get a life.   The movie classic *It's a Wonderful Life* explores the alternative poorer lives people would have led if the hero had not lived.   A number of recent movies - for example, *Run, Lola, Run, Sliding Doors, The Family Man* - depict how trivial events can result in vastly different lives.

As always, there is resistance to this new generation of media from those who perceive it as a threat.   However, this time the resistance is not from the immediately previous generation of media, as in the first and second transitions. As we saw above, the telephone and television industries are welcoming this new generation with open antennae. Far from resisting, both industries are vying to incorporate fourth generation digital features. The reason is clear. Once you have a means of transmitting information electronically, it would be useful also to have a means of storing it electronically.

Resistance comes from the second generation of media - lovers of books and film argue against the storage and transmission of information by digital means. This next step was inevitable. We should perhaps have been waiting apprehensively for the other shoe to drop, but we certainly should not have been startled when it did. Resistance is from the second generation because this fourth

---

[5]   On the morning of my twentieth birthday, I woke up discontented that I had not yet traveled much. I leapt out of bed, picked up the Sunday Post which opened at an ad for the Hudson Bay Company: *Find fame and fortune in the Canadian North* . Six weeks later, I was standing on the docks in Montreal. I had cut out all my lives I would have led had I stayed in Scotland. The Hudson Bay Company had enough recruits by the time they came to Lochwinnoch (they started at the North of Scotland because people were more used to cold climates). Thus I was cut off from all the lives I would have led had I spent the contracted two years in the Arctic. Is it any wonder that I read many stories set in Scotland and in the Arctic?

generation offers an alternative means of storing information. What makes it even more threatening is that it is more compatible with the third generation. The fourth generation is an opportunity for the third generation of Telephone and Television but a threat for the second generation of Print and Film.

Otherwise very intelligent people - Robertson Davies, E. Annie Proulx, Gore Vidal, etc. - boast about their resistance to the word-processor. At the mere mention of an electronic book, one of my students invariably argues that you can't take it to bed with you, that they like the feel and smell of books.[6]   Publishers have been very slow to recognize that they are in the information business and that the book is just one of the ways to package it.[7]   For some purposes, you may want to package it physically in a book, for other purposes, you may want to package it electronically on a CD-ROM or on a web site, and for yet other purposes, you may want to consider a combination of physical and electronic storage - a book with a companion CD-ROM inserted in the back cover or a CD-ROM in a box with a book enclosed.[8]

---

[6]   I have very depraved students, who lie in bed fondling and sniffing books.

[7]   A very useful book called *The Originals* identifies the real people on whom over 3,000 fictional characters are based [AMOS].   Since I am interested in the psychology of creativity, I used it to explore the process by which authors transmute real people into fictional characters. To facilitate my research, I made an electronic version, which enabled one to search by author and title. I sent my electronic version to the publisher asking if they would be interested in using it as a supplement to the book. Since there was no reply after six months, I went to their office in London to discuss it in person. Being British, they would not talk to me because I didn't have an appointment. I finally persuaded a secretary to accept the floppy disk containing the electronic version. When I got back to Canada, there was a lawyer's letter threatening to sue me. I replied that I would not have flown to London to present them with the evidence if I was planning to rip them off. I may be a scholar but I'm not stupid. Since then, silence. Just noticed at amazon.com that the book is out of print. Perhaps, over a decade later, I should try again!

[8]   This would perhaps help defuse the disappointment one invariably feels when the big box is opened and found to contain a small CD-ROM. It's pointless to point out that a CD-ROM can contain the equivalent of 500 500-page books. It's a small object in a large package and one feels cheated. Even a t-shirt would alleviate this impression. Better would be a book which contains the essence of the contents of the CD-ROM for those occasions in which one happens not to have a cumbersome computer.

The film-is-dead issue is not as familiar as the book-is-dead issue. However, many film-lovers are appropriately apprehensive about the fourth generation of media which has invaded the production of films. Computers play a huge role in all stages of film making - pre-production, production, and post-production. It is now moving beyond production into distribution. The **digital versatile disk (DVD)** holds 14 times as much information as the CD-ROM.[9] The difference is however not merely quantitative. Since it is now possible to store a full-length movie electronically, the videocassettes in your local video store will gradually be replaced by DVDs. Since the video and audio quality of a DVD approaches that of film, movies can be distributed and projected electronically. My local bar has a DVD theater which could be distinguished from a traditional movie theater only by the most discriminating connoisseurs of film.

As argued above, the fourth generation of media continues the piggy-back strategy of the second and the third. It uses a code in which each letter of the alphabet is translated into a series of 0s and 1s. Thus, A is 0110001 and Z is 0011001. We saw in Chapter 2, how the number system emerged out of logic - the rules for combining sentences to create meaningful discourses. The fourth generation also piggy-backs on the number system, by using a code in which each number is a sequence of 0s and 1s. Thus, 1 is 0001 and 9 is 1001. Images can be represented as a pattern of 0s and 1s (Figure 7-3). Video and audio can be represented as sequences of 0s and 1s. By reducing everything to a lowest common denominator of 0s and 1s, the fourth generation can represent each of the previous three generations.

Another threat is the threat to democracy. We have found that, whereas the first generation of media is essentially democratic, the second and third

---

[9]   The cynics who dubbed DVD *"doubtful very doubtful"* have been silenced.

generations have democratic and autocratic options. That is, the second generation has the post office (democratic) and the newspaper (autocratic); the third generation has the telephone (democratic) and the television (autocratic). What about the fourth generation? Since it piggy-backs on the telephone system, it is initially democratic. Anyone who can afford a computer and an Internet Service Provider (hence not fully democratic) can be source as well as destination of e-mail (the most popular function of internet). In Section 4.3, the unsung heroes who created the democratic Post Office were listed. The fourth generation of media has also been built by such unsung heroes (see Figure 7-4).

However, there is some pressure towards making the internet more like television. Many corporations are trying the create WebTV in which the internet simply supplies additional channels to an essentially passive audience. Without naming names, those organizations aspire to set up Gates on the internet and Bill us for going through them. In his book *The Virtual Community: Homesteading on the Electronic Frontier*, Howard Rheingold describes the early days of the internet as parallel to the early days of the settlement of the American West [RHEINGOLD 1993]. They were days of anarchy but also of neighborliness. However, he sensed even then the electronic analogs of the Railway and Cattle Barons on the horizon. They are now very much with us, as cable television companies mock people with only telephone access and offer the higher channel capacity of their fiber-optic cables. Alas, traffic on those cables is largely one-way as they download movies-on-demand to us. Such systems are interactive in the limited sense that we can choose the movie or the camera angle we prefer on watching a hockey game. Just as a consumer society is democratic in the limited sense that we can choose between different brands of soap flakes and breakfast cereals.

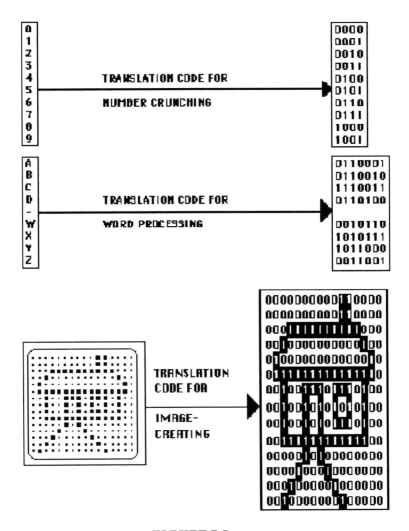

FIGURE 7-3

LOWEST COMMON DENOMINATOR OF 0s AND 1s

Marc Andreessen	Netscape browser
Bill Atkinson	First popular authoring system (HyperCard)
Charles Babbage	Conception of computer
John Bardeen & William B. Shockley	Electronic transistor (Nobel Prize 1956)
Bob Berner	ASCII, Backslash, Escape button
Tim Berners-Lee	World Wide Web
Jeff Bezos	amazon.com
Dave Bradley	CONTROL-ALT-DELETE (to restart frozen computers)
Dan Bricklin	First spreadsheet (VisiCalc)
Sergey Brin Larry Page	Google search engine
Vannevar Bush	Memex
Ada Augusta Byron	First Programmer
Jim Clark	First browser (Mosaic)
Martin Cooper	Cell phone
Donald W. Davis	Packet Switching
J. Presper Echart Jr. & John W. Mauchley	First electronic digital computer in North America (ENIAC)
Douglas Engelbart	WIMP interface
Shawn Fanning	First site to exchange MP3 sound files (Napster)
Justin Frankel	Code for compressing sound files (MP3)
James Gosling	Platform-independent language (Java)
Ted Hoff	Microprocessor
Grace Hooper	COBOL computer language
Steve Jobs Steve Wozniak	Apple Personal Computer
Mitch Kapor	First database management system (Lotus 1-2-3)
Alan Kay	Graphic User Interface (GUI)
Gary Kildair	First microcomputer operating system (CP/M)
Jaren Lanier	Virtual reality headset
Gordon Moore	Moore's Law
Ted Nelson	Hypertext
Robert Noyce	Integrated circuit
Pierre Omidyar	eBay.com
Adam Osborne	First portable personal computer
Jean Armour Polly	Vacuum tube
Dennis Ritchie	C computer language
Ed Roberts	First PC (Altair)
Larry Roberts & Bob Taylor	Internet
George Stabitz	First digital computer
Ivan Sutherland	Three-dimensional computer graphics
Ray Tomlinson	First e-mail message (sent to himself, of course)
Linus Torvalds	Linux Operating System
Dave Winer	Idea-processor (Think Tank, More)
Alan Turing	Turing machine, Turing Test
Phil Zimmerman	Pretty Good Privacy (PGP)

FIGURE 7- 4   UNSUNG HEROES IN COMPUTER HISTORY

The corporate culture, which embodies this pseudo-democracy of person as consumer rather than person as citizen, has recently dramatically increased its presence on the internet.[10] The great hack attack closed down many of their commercial sites. The hackers were vilified in the press as "terrorists" or "vandals" or at least "pranksters". When it was revealed that the great hack attacks were perpetuated by young hackers to impress their friends with their competence, no one in the media pointed out that this was better than trying to impress them with the brand names of their clothes. Better they demonstrate what they have *in* their heads than the brand name of the cap *on* their heads.

Steven Levy subtitles his classical book *Hackers: Heroes of the Computer Revolution* [LEVY]. Why have they suddenly become the villains? Rheingold's subtitle *Virtual Community: Homesteading on the Electronic Frontier* provides a clue. Hackers were the homesteaders who first colonized the new frontier of cyberspace. However, as Rheingold warned, the railroad and cattle barons have moved in. Suddenly the original pioneers who built the internet are the villains. In his *Matrix Trilogy*, William Gibson gives us a preview of coming distractions [GIBSON W 1984, 1987, 1988]. He depicts a world in which power is in the hands of various multinational corporations. His heroes are console cowboys who are outside the system battling the hired guns for those corporations.

Hackers are not unethical. They just have a different system of ethics. The basic principle of the hacker ethic is that "*information wants to be free*". They share their information with others and expect others to share with them. We are moving into a psychology of abundance from a psychology of scarcity. You can give information away and still keep it. This hacker ethic is going to have to deal with the fact that people who create information need to have some

---

[10]   It was inevitable that the meeting-place becomes also the market-place. It's interesting to compare the Internet with the Agora. This was the market-place, which became the meeting-place for Socrates and his philosopher friends.

mechanism of being recompensed for it so that they can look after the mundane maintenance matters. Otherwise they can't continue to create information. But it is better than the corporate ethic that information is merely a commodity to be bought and sold on the market.[11]

---

[11]   Not being a hacker, I'm not as upset by the invasion of the internet by the corporate culture.   However, I am upset at its invasion of the University, where I've spent most of my life. McGill University next door had to fight hard to prevent Coca-Cola from dictating what drinks were available on the campus.   My own university has advertisements in the university washrooms.   At this most intimate moment in front of the urinal, one is confronted by ads.   It's especially upsetting to be staring at an ad which proclaims "*your future is in your hands*", reminding me rudely that, in my case, its my PAST that is in my hands.

CHAPTER 8
FOURTH GENERATION -
MULTIMEDIA AND INTERNET

8.1   A SHORT HISTORY OF THE COMPUTER

8.2   THE ULTIMATE EXTENSION

8.3   THE THREE INTERFACES OF NEGROPONTE

In the post-literate society, literacy could function as a DEW line: the distant early warning of overload, saturation, and dissolution of individual integrity. Literacy kept you critically conscious; it could restore the balance to the inbalance of instantaneous information. The printed word could be a weapon against unconscious drift. The eighteenth-century focus on language, education, and debate could work like a still point in the electronic wave.

B. W. Powe, THE SOLITARY OUTLAW, Page 183

No medium is inherently better than any other. --- It's all in what you do with it.

Michael Chabot,
THE AMAZING ADVENTURES OF KAVALIER AND CLAY,
Page 363

8.1   A SHORT HISTORY OF THE COMPUTER

The third generation of media involved the invention of extrasomatic tools for transmitting information - telegraph and telephone for transmitting information over wires and radio and television for transmitting information through the air. The fourth generation of media is largely the story of the invention of one extrasomatic tool for storing information - the computer. This automation of thought (computers) then converges with the previous automation of language (tele-communications). This convergence requires the digitization of our various extrasomatic tools for transmission of information so that they can "talk" to the computer for the storage of information.

We must imagine something before we create it. Every invention appears first in the subjective map of someone before it appears in our common objective world. The machine, like the person, must be conceived before it is born. The automation of thought by means of computers emerged from imagining a simulation of ourselves. This section of our story began then with two teen-age girls.

Mary Wollstonecraft Goodwin (1797-1851), while still a teenager, had run off to Europe with two poets - Percy Bysshe Shelley and George Gordon, the notorious Lord Byron. They were holed up in a chateau in Switzerland during a very rainy Summer. To entertain themselves, they decided to write horror stories. The two poets, being experienced writers, started writing right away, and taunted Mary who could not even get started. One night, however, she had a dream and started writing a story the next morning, which quickly evolved into the familiar famous story of *Frankenstein* [SHELLEY].

Back in England, Ada Augusta Byron (1815-1851), the daughter of Lord Byron, upset that her father had deserted her when she was only one month old, turned from art to science. She attended a demonstration by an eccentric inventor called Charles Babbage (1791-1871) of his Difference Engine. Although only 17, she recognized its importance right away. Babbage had invented the computer. Ada Byron (later, Lady Lovelace) worked with Charles Babbage for the rest of her life [RHEINGOLD 1985].

He worked on the hardware and she worked on the software. Alas, Babbage never could get his machine to work. However, if he had, the software written by Ada *would* have worked. She had discovered all the major basic principles of programming. "Ada" is now the name of a computer language named in her honor as the world's first programmer. Two major cyberpunk authors - William Gibson and Bruce Sterling - surprised their fans by getting together to write a Victorian novel. *The Difference Engine* was an alternative history which explores the repercussions on society if Babbage had been able to get his machine to work over 100 years before someone else finally managed to build one that did work [GIBSON W & STERLING B].

Another eccentric Englishman contributed to our conceptualization of the computer. Alan Turing (1912-1954) presented us with the **Turing Machine** and the **Turing Test**. He imagined a device through which one could thread an infinite loop of squares [TURING]. Each square contains either a 1 or a 0. The machine can either change one symbol to the other or leave it the same. He argued that any problem which can be expressed clearly in terms of logical statements could be solved by this machine. The Turing Test involved communication between a person with a terminal linked to two other terminals which are out of sight, operated respectively by a person and by a machine. If the person could not tell which was which, the machine had passed the Turing

Test.[1]

Alan Turing put his theory into practice during World War 2. He was invited to join a group which was attempting to break the code of a machine used by the Nazis to transmit coded messages. Turing reverse-engineered the Enigma machine which created the code, from a description of the machine given him by a disgruntled former employee of the Nazis who had been dismissed because of he was Jewish. As a result, the Allied Forces were able to read captured Nazi messages throughout most of the war. Many have argued that Alan Turing did more to win that war than anyone else including Winston Churchill who considered the breaking of the code so valuable that he did not warn people about a bombing raid for fear of alerting the Nazis that their code had been broken.

One of Turing's eccentricities was that he was an outed homosexual at a time and place where this was dangerous. (This homophobic society had jailed one of our greatest playwrights, Oscar Wilde, essentially for homosexuality at the height of his fame only a few decades earlier.) Dismissed from his job and abandoned by those who could have saved him because his contribution was still classified information, he committed suicide by biting into an apple laced with cyanide.[2]

As Turing realized, the best code for a computer consists of two letters - 0

---

[1]   This means, of course, that the computer would sometimes have to act stupid in order to appear human. If given two 6-digit numbers to multiply, it would have to "pretend" to take some time. An instant answer, which it could provide, would be suspect.

[2]   This apple deserves a place alongside Newton's in the annals of famous apples in science. Turing's work was just de-classified in the 1970s. Since then, his story has been told in a number of media - for example, a cyberpunk novel, *Cryptonomicon*, by the current star within this genre [STEPHENSON 1999], a documentary, *Breaking the Code*, starring Derek Jacobi as Alan Turing, and a film, *U-571*, about the capture of Enigma from a German submarine (with Americans replacing the British who "starred" in the real story, since it's an American movie). Mick Jagger of the Rolling Stones has taken out an option to make the movie, *Enigma*, based on a book about the work of Turing and his colleagues.

and 1.[3]   Thus computer technology - no matter how esoteric it may seem - is simpler than 1, 2, 3. It's 0, 1. A computer can thus be created using any device which can toggle between two stable states, representing 0 and 1. In the first generation, the device was a vacuum tube; in the second, it was a transistor; in the third, it was an integrated circuit; in the fourth, it was a microprocessor (many integrated circuits on a single chip). Each of those devices supplanted the previous device, in contrast to the generations of tele-communications, in which each generation simply supplemented the previous generations.

We are currently awaiting the fifth generation. Perhaps it will be a chip made of gallium arsenide rather than silicon, which gets too hot at the current speed of operation. Perhaps it will be a biochip, made of organic rather than mechanical material. Whatever it will be, the saga of the incredible shrinking chip will continue. Computers are getting smaller and smaller, faster and faster, cheaper and cheaper, smarter and smarter, and friendlier and friendlier. **Moore's Law**, that the speed of a chip will double and the cost of a chip will half every 18 months, has continued to apply over the last few decades of the 20th century and promises to continue in the 21st century.

The computer had a long gestation period. Though conceived by Charles Babbage in the early 19th century, it was not born till over a century later. However, once born, it grew (or shrunk?) rapidly. Indeed, so rapidly that its history can be described within a single life-time - for example, mine.

1955   My first steady job after getting off the boat from Scotland was as a clerk in the Canadian Pacific Railway's offices at Windsor Station. CPR had

---

[3]   It may initially appear surprising that such a powerful language can be created using only two letters. Speech - the language of the first generation - consists of 44 units (the phonemes), and print - the language of the second generation - consists of 26 units (the graphemes - i.e. the letters of the alphabet). However, the "language" in which you and I are written - the genetic code - consists of only 4 letters - A (Adenine), G (Guanine), C (Cytosine), and T (Thymine). The complexity of a system is thus not directly correlated with the number of elements it contains.

just got its first computer [CANADIAN TRANSPORTATION, SPANNER]. It filled a huge, air-conditioned room, cost millions of dollars, had a score of priest-engineers attending to it, and all we clerks were terrified that it was going to take over our jobs. This was, of course, only seven years after the first working computer was built at the University of Pennsylvania in 1948.[4]

1969   A group of West Indian students, protesting what they perceived as racism, took over my classroom H-110 in the Hall Building of Sir George Williams University and then moved, along with many of my students, to occupy the Computer Center upstairs. This site was chosen because the computer was viewed as the tool of the oppressive "System" (the military-industrial-academic complex) which was violating human rights. The computer was still a massive device which had to be fed a stack of cards to be processed by the engineers who returned results days later. *"Do not bend, staple, or mutilate"* was one of the slogans of the protesters, who threw the cards out of the windows when the police stormed the Computer Center.

1984   Fifteen years later, I buy my first computer - the 128K Macintosh. Though its power and price ($3000) is laughable now, it had more power than that first computer at CPR and sat on my desktop. The big step however was not the next installment in the saga of the incredible shrinking chip but the improvement in the interface. It was like improving your ax by getting a new handle rather than a new head. There was no essential difference in the inside of the computer (I opened it up to check and found that it was mostly empty) but in the relationship between the computer and myself. This **WIMP** (Window-Icon-Mouse-Pulldown menu) **interface** replaced the previous **MACHO interface** (Figure 8-1) and

---

[4]   Actually the release of the classified information about the work of Alan Turing and his colleagues in deciphering Nazi codes during World War 2 reveals that this group had built a computer earlier.

    Thanks to my neighbor, Ron Ritchie, of the Canadian Pacific Railway, for finding those sources for me.

reduced our dependence on the high priests attending to the computer.

1997   My computer is now powerful enough to enable me to make a silicon clone (siliclone) of myself and download it on to a CD-ROM. The big breakthrough during the intervening decade is a shift from an emphasis on **artificial intelligence (AI)** to an emphasis on **intelligence amplification (IA).** There is no need to simulate natural intelligence (that we already have) but to supplement it with artificial intelligence. The siliclone is an extension of Scot. Thus it fits within the framework of the Toronto School of Media Studies in which media is viewed as an extension of the person.

FIGURE 8-1   WIMP VS MACHO INTERFACES

8.2   THE ULTIMATE EXTENSION

The principle contribution of the Toronto School presented in this book is the consideration of media as extensions of the person. Its founder, Harold Innis, considered the case in which we extend ourselves by storing information outside our bodies; Marshall McLuhan, the most famous member of the school, considered the case in which we extend ourselves by transmitting information outside our bodies; various current scholars, touted by their supporters as the new McLuhan, are considering the case in which we extend ourselves by both storing and transmitting information outside our bodies.

We have noted a number of times in telling the story of media that our inventions are often found, in retrospect, to be plagiarisms of nature. Making paper out of trees was inspired by watching a wasp eating wood and secreting paper to build its nest [AUF DER MAUR, Page 123].[5]   Radar simulates the echolocation systems of bats and whales. The history of film is the story of the gradual movement towards the mind movie the nervous system is making throughout our life-time. I look forward to the day when some inventor designs a vehicle which can travel on land, in water, and through the air, only to realize that s/he has re-invented the lowly duck. Much of this plagiarism is unconscious. However, recently, many scholars are consciously exploring the copying of nature in a process called **biomimicry** [BENYUS].

In graduate school, I remember the eye being compared unfavorably with the camera - the film is in backwards, there is a hole in it, the camera wobbles up and down, and so on. Subsequently we find that all those features are functional.

---

[5]   Aware that Nick's stories - like you and I , cheese and wine - tend to improve with age, I hesitated to include this reference in a "scholarly" book. However, I glanced up from reading this story in a local restaurant and saw Don May, who had just received a Wallenberg Prize (industry's equivalent to the Nobel Prize also bestowed by the King of Sweden) for his contribution to the physics of paper production. Don confirmed the story and filled out the details for me.

Physiological nystagmus, the wobbling up and down, is necessary to refresh the neurons firing for the stimulus. When it is eliminated, the image fades [PRITCHARD ET AL]. The eye is thus able to take millions of sharp snapshots throughout a lifetime without changing the film and with only a little help late in life in adjusting the focal length. Rather than arrogantly dismissing nature's inventions as inadequate versions of our own, we should look to nature for inspiration. The Leica is a lousy eye.

The plagiarism of nature continues in the fourth generation of media. The first generation of memory and speech (nature's invention) integrates storage and transmission of information within the same system. The fourth generation of multimedia and internet imitates this first generation by integrating storage (multimedia) and transmission (internet) within the same system. The fourth generation is more like the first generation than either is like the second and third generations. Whereas the second generation separates text (print) from image (film) and the third generation separates the ear (telephone) from the eye (television), the fourth generation re-integrates them. The computer could be considered as the corpus callosum, the structure joining the left hemisphere (text) and the right hemisphere (image), since it can deal equally well with both. Since it can also simulate audio and video, as patterns of 0s and 1s over space and time, it re-integrates the ear with the eye. Like the nervous system, it is a analog-to-digital converter as it converts the various analog signals from the visual and auditory receptors into a common digital language.

Phylogenetic development (that is, from animal to human) and ontogenetic development (that is, from child to adult) could be best described (if one must describe it in a sentence) as the progressive emancipation of the organism from the tyranny of the environment. The first generation of media (memory and speech) begins this story and the subsequent generations of media, in which we extend the nervous system using extrasomatic tools, merely continue it.

In escaping the constraints of time and space and personality, the informatics infrastructure is once again emulating the nervous system. We have always been able to collapse time and space into the present as we contain the past in memory and the future in imagination. We are the time-binding and space-binding animal. Our imagination has always allowed us to be other people in other places at other times. The past, present, and future of the objective world is all potentially present in the subjective map. *The past is history, the future is mystery, but the present is a gift. That's why it's called the present.* When we unwrap our conception-day present, we find that it contains the past in the form of memories and the future in the form of hopes and fears.

Now that each of us has potentially at our fingertips the computing power that was available only to multi-corporations for millions of dollars only a few decades ago, we have to ask how we may best use it. Most of us use it as a typewriter. It is a very good typewriter. However, we may want to consider going beyond this limited use. Idea-processing allows us to go beyond word-processing, by focusing on the hierarchical structure of thought underlying the sequential presentation of language. Examples of idea-processors are *Think Tank* (later called *More* when more was added to it) for the Macintosh and *Framework* for the IBM and its clones. Those programs enable you to write stream-of-consciously every topic you can think off within the domain of a paper or speech you are writing. You can move topics up and down the list as the best order emerges and left and right in the list as topics are recognized as subtopics of other topics. Gradually an outline emerges. Content can be placed appropriately within the outline by opening a window within each topic.

The limitation of idea-processing is that moving from node to node within the hierarchy requires that you climb the tree and descend the appropriate branch. Authoring programs permit you to link any node in a network directly with any other node. The first generally available such authoring program was HyperCard.

One of the days the universe changed was 11 August 1987 when the Apple Corporation launched HyperCard. Bill Atkinson, who wrote the program, insisted that it be given away with every Macintosh computer sold. For a while then people were using a computer as a computer. However, Bill Atkinson left the company and Apple returned to bundling a word-processing program instead and people tended to revert to use the computer as a typewriter (MacWrite) and an easel (MacPaint). More sophisticated programs have since emerged, but still largely devoted to doing things we could do before but more efficiently - making slide shows (PowerPoint), making movies (Premiere), and so on.

HyperCard enables you to build a stack of cards. Each card can contain text or images or a combination of text and images, and buttons linking to any other card. It sounds simple. However, it has enormous reverberations. Whereas word-processing is one-dimensional, idea-processing is two-dimensional, authoring is three-dimensional (Figure 8-2). That is, any node in the network (card) can be linked to any other node. At any node, one can go deeper and deeper into a third dimension by linking it to cards containing footnotes and footnotes to footnotes. We now have a three-dimensional media mediating between our three-dimensional brain and our three-dimensional world. It enables us to map that world in our mind. The nodes and links are isomorphic with the structure of the internet with its computer nodes and its telecommunication links and with the structure of the mind with its concept nodes and its relationship links (Figure 8-3). We finally have a positive prosthetic which is a perfect fit. Many more sophisticated authoring programs have emerged since HyperCard. However, they are all based on the same principles. You will note that the Internet is a huge set of interlinked stacks.

Now that we finally have a positive prosthetic that fits, the **user interface** is thus very important. The excitement generated by the introduction of the Apple Macintosh in 1984 had nothing to do with the computer per se but with the interface between the computer and the person. The WIMP interface was much easier to use than the previous MACHO interface (see Figure 8-1). This allowed us to get rid of the middle (muddle?) men who mediated between us and our media extensions. It is hard to imagine an easier interface after using it over the intervening years. Jef Raskin, who headed the creative team which developed this WIMP interface for the Macintosh, has just published a book, *The Humane Interface*, in which he argues that we need an even simpler interface [RASKIN]. The metaphor is indeed very mixed (Figure 8-4) and a coherent metaphor would make the computer even more user-friendly.

The concept of media as extensions of the person, as articulated by the Toronto School, has a valuable down-to-earthing effect. The appendix is not meaningful without the book. Media have meaning only as they extend the person. Mind is meaningless without body. It can not be uploaded into a computer and downloaded into another body, as if it was a mere container. After wandering around without their bodies on, some people, however, get carried away. They begin to claim that the body is obsolete. A usually intelligent magazine ran a cover story under the title *Is the body obsolete?* [WHOLE EARTH REVIEW]. If you are shocked that the question is asked, you will be even more shocked that half of the respondents answered *yes* . This is the most recent among the many ingenious devices we have created to deny death. Many of them are cataloged by Ernest Becker in his brilliant Pulitzer-Prize-winning book, *The Denial of Death* [BECKER].

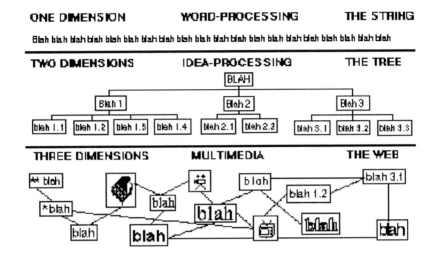

FIGURE 8-2
ONE-, TWO-, THREE-DIMENSIONAL USE OF COMPUTER

The emerging fourth generation of media - multimedia and internet - is a solution in search of a problem. Various problems, to which informatics is the solution, are proposed as **killer applications.** Some recent candidates are e-mail [CROSARIOL], video telephony [BROCKMAN], video-on-demand [PILLER], group scheduling software [KANE] and even Wired Magazine [WHITE].[6] Each of those are useful functions. However, they simply enable us to better do things which we could do before, and they certainly won't sustain a billion-dollar industry. I appreciate my word-processor, my spreadsheet, my database manager, my graphics program, my e-mail, my browser. They certainly have been "killer" enough to keep me and others buying computers and opening ISP accounts. Bill

---

[6]   Some have even nominated on-line gambling as the next killer app [MOORE].   Anyone who knows a compulsive gambler well will be horrified at the prospect of a "service" which enables gamblers to indulge their vice without getting out of the house or even out of their pajamas.

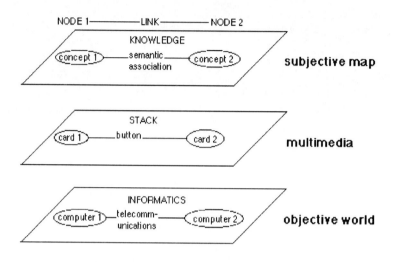

FIGURE 8-3   ISOMORPHISM OF NODES AND LINKS

Gates characteristically defines killer applications as applications which sell a lot of computers [GATES, Pages 74-76]. The Apple Corporation has been saved from bankruptcy by simulating the second generation electronically - **desktop production (DTP)** - and now by simulating the third generation - **desktop video production (DTVP)** or **digital video (DV)**.

FIGURE 8-4   WHERE AM I?

However, what I am looking forward to is the moment when the computer finds its niche in doing things which could not be done before. *My* candidate for killer application is thus the **siliclone** - that is, a silicon clone of oneself [JUSTER].   This is the inevitable culmination of the co-evolution of the person and media as extensions. That is, it is the happy ending to the story being told in this book. The siliclone is the ultimate extension. It aspires to a completely integrated and interactive representation of the information contained in your nervous system.

This is, of course, impossible. The story will always be a to-be-continued story. However, the journey is more important than the destination. The most important aspect of your information is the conception-day gift which can not be cloned. However, it need not be cloned, since you already have it. What <u>can</u> be cloned is the footnote you have added during your life-time. This is your contribution to the wisdom. By building the siliclone, you can leave your contribution behind for your survivors. Our function as teachers and parents is to plan our obsolescence.

We are essentially re-inventing ourselves. That is why it is not unreasonable to consider cloning oneself using the fourth generation of media. This clone is not an example of artificial intelligence (AI) but of intelligence amplification (IA). There is no point in simulating yourself when you already have yourself. However, there is a point in creating an artificial extension of yourself which is able to do well things which you do poorly. For example, memorizing details. My siliclone has all those details at his (sorry, my) fingertips. The aim is to develop the optimal synergy between natural intelligence (Scot) and artificial intelligence (Siliclone). Scot and Siliclone are partners. As in any partnership, we each focus on what we do well. Siliclone is good at memorizing content, whereas Scot is good at putting this content into context. Thus, we can put raw data in context to get information, information in context to get knowledge, knowledge in context to get understanding, and understanding in context to get wisdom. This is how value is added to raw data in the information society. The evolution and function of the Siliclone will be discussed in more detail in Section 15.2.

One fascinating development in the fourth generation is the extension of ourselves into the internet in the form of **avatars** in virtual worlds [DAMER]. In the early stages, we characteristically dress ourselves as avahunks and flirt with avatarts in virtual bars. However, I can do that in the local bar with potentially more concrete results. In the virtual world, I would like to do things which I can't do in the real world. Now that I have cloned myself, I can go out as myself and hang out with dead people.

My killer application will involve not only people cloning themselves but people cloning others who were born too soon to clone themselves. My siliclone is of no great interest. I propose it only as a model for preserving the wisdom of more illustrious members of our species.

Like, for example, Bertrand Russell. In one of his many essays, Russell described a nightmare in which a librarian holds the last copy of his last remaining book in his hands as he decided whether to toss it into a trolley containing a pile of books to be destroyed or to return it to the shelf. He wakes up, shivering and sweating as the book is poised between those two fates. In a sense, his nightmare has come true. Since his death in the 1970s, I've heard very little of him. No doubt his work is still alive in the minds of some scholars of philosophy. However, Russell worked very hard in a long, productive life to make his work available to a larger audience. It would be sad to lose his wisdom.

Perhaps his footnote to human wisdom could be preserved by a project which we could whimsically call *Resurrecting Russell* or, for the lay public, *Bringing Bertie Back*. At first, perhaps, it could consist only of his books now in the public domain. Prolific as he was, they could fit easily on a CD-ROM or in a web site. Philosophers who are expert in his work could subsequently perhaps help integrate his work around answers to questions which can be posed to him. If those mega-corporations seeking killer applications were willing to hire such philosophers to help resurrect Russell, I'd be delighted to pay a fee to hang out with him. On the other hand, I'd not be willing to pay to order a pizza and a movie over the internet. That I can do in the real world already. What I can't do is forget about the movie and hang out with Bert instead.

8.3   THE THREE INTERFACES OF NEGROPONTE

Nicholas Negroponte used the diagram, depicted in Figure 8-5, to help persuade corporations to invest millions of dollars in his Media Lab at MIT [BRAND, Page 10]. He argued that the broadcast and motion picture industry, the print and publishing industry, and the computer industry would merge into a single mega-industry and that their corporation could become a big player in that industry if they invested in research on it by his Media Lab. He got it roughly right but there have been a number of surprises along the way. Let us, with thanks and apologies to Negroponte, use a revised version of his model, which could be called **The Three Interfaces of Negroponte**, to organize our thoughts on the current situation.

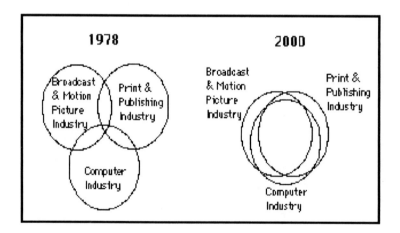

FIGURE 8-5
THREE INTERFACES OF NEGROPONTE

Figure 8-6 depicts the Three Interfaces of Negroponte as an inset in the fourth generation of The Four Generations of Media (see Figure 1-2) which could be considered as an inset in the Technosphere in the Triad Model (see Figure 3-2).

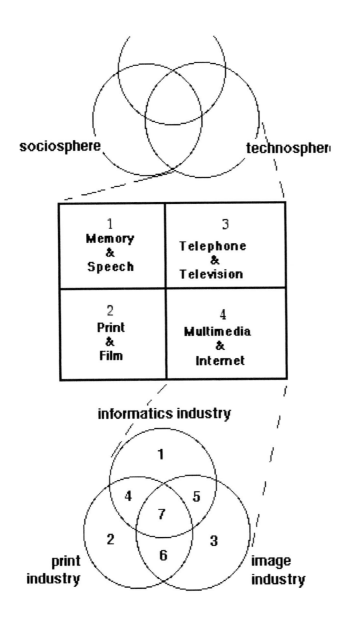

FIGURE 8-6   INSETS WITHIN INSETS

Note that in all cases, the model contains the optimal seven categories.   Let us look, in turn, at each of the seven categories in the revised Three Interfaces of Negroponte model.

1   *Informatics Industry.*

The convergence of computer and tele-communications industries into informatics was discussed above as the merger of the automation of thought and the automation of language (see Figure 7-1).   It is the resultant informatics industry, rather than simply the computer industry, which is depicted by this circle.

2   *Print Industry.*

Let us call Print and Publishing Industry simply the Print industry. This category represents the print industry still outside the influence of the informatics industry. Desktop production has been possible for some time. I produced a book - *The Ubiquitous Chip* - on my desk in 1987. Now, with the emergence of on-line, on-demand publishers, there is desktop production and distribution. I produced and distributed a book - *A History of Media* - from my desk in 2002. However, such books are not yet recognized by the academy as "real" books and they do not have access to the traditional peer-reviewing and distributing process. Negroponte may have underestimated the inertia of tradition.

3   *Image Industry.*

Let us call the Broadcast and Motion Picture Industry simply the Image Industry. This category represents the image industry still outside the influence of the informatics industry.   Much production of images has shifted from analog to digital but much still remains analog. Much of the production of films, including pre-production and post-production, is now digital. However, distribution is still mostly analog.   George Lucas, whose *Star Wars: Attack of the Clones* was entirely a digital production, made a pitch at the Cannes Film Festival for digital distribution. The vision of beaming a film, simultaneously and instantaneously, to all the theaters in which it is scheduled to appear rather than shipping huge film reels to each of them is tempting, but it will be some time before enough theaters are equipped to receive them. Here the inertia is caused not so much by tradition as by economics.

Those three categories could be considered as the analogues of the left hemisphere of the brain (print industry), the right hemisphere of the brain (image industry), and the corpus callosum which links them (informatics industry). The merging of those three industries could be considered as the emergence of a global brain. Let us look at the four remaining categories in our model, which represent the mergers.

4   *Merger of print industry and informatics industry.*
Desktop Production (DTP) has taken over much of the traditional print production industry, triggering the book-is-dead controversy, mentioned in Section 7.3. The process is digital but the product tends to remain defiantly analog. Despite a variety of attempts, electronic books have failed to challenge traditional books.

5   *Merger of image industry and informatics industry.*
Digital video (DV) has taken over much of traditional image production, triggering the film-is-dead controversy, also discussed in Section 7.3. Once again, the process is digital but the product tends to remain defiantly analog.

6   *Merger of print industry and image industry.*
We have had products combining print and image for some time. Within the print industry, there are books with illustrations and photo essays. Within the image industry, there are paintings with captions and films with subtitles. However, one has always been primary and the other secondary. The only medium where print and image have had more or less equal status is the comic book

There has been an incredible surge in the production of comics recently. Comics have become almost respectable. There are series of books, in comic form, introducing various scholars. Icon Books publishes a series on

Evolutionary Psychology, Chaos Theory, Postmodernism, and other such lofty topics. Scholarly books have been written, in comic form, about -- comics [MCCLOUD 1993, 2000]. Popular films have explored the lives of previously obscure comic book authors - *Comic Book Confidential* explores comic book culture from the 1920s to the 1950s with an emphasis on the work of Robert Crumb and *American Splendor* focuses on one of Crumb's proteges, Harvey Pekar. The comic book has now become a graphic novel, with star authors like Neil Gaiman with his *Neverwhere* and *Sandman* and Art Spiegelman, whose graphic novel *Maus* (on the decidedly unfunny topic of genocide) won a Pulitzer Prize. This shift of the comic book into the main-stream may be largely due to the fact that the computer can so easily integrate print and image.

In Section 4.4, the difficulty of transforming books into films was illustrated by the case of the novels of John Irving. Transforming *comic* books into films is not so difficult. This may be partly due to the fact that the stories are simple - after all, they were written for 12-year-old boys. It may be partly due also to the fact that they are already visual - the comic book itself is practically a story-board. The most popular comic books - Superman, Spiderman, etc. - are already into film sequels, and the less popular comic books - X-men, The Incredible Hulk, etc. - are being transformed into films.

7   *Merger of Informatics Industry, Print Industry, and Image industry.*

If we think of the technosphere as the most active domain in the triad model, of the fourth generation of media as the most active within the technosphere, and of the convergence of those three industries as the most active in the three interfaces of Negroponte, then this is the bull's-eye. This is where the action is.

However, if the Big Story of historical time is the co-evolution of the person and media as extensions, as argued in this book, then the conclusion of that story is an anti-climax. Our story ends up in this domain. The ending is disappointingly inconclusive. It is as if someone had invented the can-opener before someone else had invented the can. As argued above, this powerful tool is a solution in search of a problem.

The recent rash of mergers are a result of corporations combining into mega-corporations jostling to position themselves within the mega-industry represented by the triple overlap of those three industries. Some of those mergers would have been unimaginable only a few years ago. Corporations within industries which, until recently, were not in the same industry are merging so that the resultant mega-corporation has the facilities to compete within this emerging multimedia mega-industry. However, their efforts have been in vain - so far. Time-Warner (which had already merged print with image) merged with America On-Line (AOL). Time-Warner had the content and AOL had the carriage - millions of subscribers to its portal into the internet. Sounds like a license to print money, yet they lost a record 100 billion dollars in one quarter. John Motavalli describes how the big media corporations have lost billions searching for the problem [MOTAVALLI] and Gordon Pitts describes how the various kings of convergence in Canada were deposed by following a certain view of the solution [PITTS].

One such *"king of convergence"* was Jean Monty, who lost millions of dollars and his job as Chief Executive Officer of the parent company to Bell Canada. I've had a telephone account with Bell Canada for many decades. More recently, I acquired an account in their television company, Bell ExpressVu, and their computer company, Bell Sympatico. I assumed that they were converging on this vast new industry predicted by Negroponte. I assumed that they were forming an information utility. Hydro Quebec is my energy utility; Bell Canada would be my information utility. Alas, they have not yet been able to even "converge" my bills. Hydro Quebec does not send me separate bills for electricity to the kitchen, to the living-room, and to the bathroom. However, Bell Canada still sends me bills for information delivered to my telephone, to my television set, and to my computer. The particular device for storing and transmitting information is becoming increasingly irrelevant. It will take some time however before we have information utilities which make no distinction between those various devices.

The failure of international corporations to create an industry on the internet is encouraging news for those who are apprehensive about their increasing power. Despite their huge resources, they cannot penetrate because they do not understand the culture of the internet. The people who "live" on the internet dismiss them as boors crashing a hippie party flashing their big wallets at the women and their big egos at the men. The nerds are kicking silicon in the faces of the big bullies.

There are nevertheless success stories. However, they are about individual insiders with limited resources but good ideas. Jeff Bezos started by selling books (that obsolete technology!) and ended up with www.amazon.com [BAYERS]. Pierre Omidyar started with an internet ad to sell some trinkets collected by his girl-friend and ended up with www.eBay.com [COHEN]. The unprecedented cases of their companies yet to make a profit gaining billion dollar value on the market makes sense because they have positioned themselves strategically within that domain predicted by Negroponte. Although their companies have not yet been profitable, the value of their shares has multiplied hundreds of times in the few years they have been available on the market. In staking out its territory, those companies have made billionaires not only of their founders but of their parents and friends who lent them the few thousands dollars to get started.

However, the success stories are simply electronic analogs of familiar things - amazon.com is becoming the Wal-Mart of the internet and eBay.com is a gigantic global garage sale. When I ask my students to show me there favorite sites, they take me to absolut.com or bmw.com or similar sites which are flashy new ways to sell me booze and fast cars. The function of this domain was assumed to be the processing of information, but it has turned out that it's initial function has been to sell stuff. It is used simply to do things we did before by other means.

This is the typical pattern in technological innovation. Each new technology is defined in terms of some familiar old technology. Thus, the car was first called the *horseless carriage*, the telephone the *talking telegraph*, and the radio the *wireless*. The fourth generation of media is currently at this stage of being defined in terms of the previous three generations of media. Marshall McLuhan uses the metaphor of driving looking through the rear-view mirror to describe this phenomenon.

Our story is obviously a to-be-continued story. After a pause in the present (Section 2: The Present Chapter 9) to look , we will leap into the future (Section 3 The Future Chapters 10 -18). Each of those chapters will consider various alternative futures - various different endings to our to-be-continued story,. Or - to continue McLuhan's metaphor - we will turn on the headlights and see if, by looking ahead, we can anticipate how this fourth generation of media will enable us to do something essentially new.

CHAPTER 9
THE PRESENT - THE PERSON

9.1 CONTINUOUS DISCONTINUITY

9.2 BEHAVIORISM AND TRANSPORTATION THEORY

9.3 HUMANISM AND TRANSFORMATION THEORY

9.4 INTERACTIONISM AND TRANSACTION THEORY

9.5 FRAMEWORK FOR THE FUTURE

One importance reason for this worldwide convergence on liberal democracy had to do with the tenacity of human nature. For while human behavior is plastic and variable, it is not infinitely so; at a certain point deeply rooted natural instincts and patterns of behavior reassert themselves to undermine the social engineer's best-laid plans. Many socialist regimes abolished private property, weakened the family, and demanded that people be altruistic to mankind in general rather than to a narrower circle of friends and family. But evolution did not shape human behavior in this fashion. Individuals in socialist societies resisted the new institutions at every turn, and when socialism collapsed after the fall of the Berlin Wall in 1989, older, more familiar patterns of behavior reasserted themselves everywhere.

Francis Fukuyama, THE POSTHUMAN FUTURE, Page 14

No decision however determines his thought -- or any historian's thought -- more fully than his assessment of human nature.

John Barker, THE SUPER-HISTORIANS, Page 333

9.1 CONTINUOUS DISCONTINUITY

"The past is gone, the future may never come, but the present is a gift. That's why it's called the present." Familiar aphorisms such as this point to the importance of the present. The Turing Machine was described in Section 7.1 as a continuous loop of frames on each of which is either 0 or 1. The loop passes through a mechanism which can either leave the frame as is or change it. You could consider the present as the frame within the mechanism. Nothing is happening with all the cells which have already passed through (the past) nor all the cells which have yet to pass through (the future). It is at that single cell of the present that the future is transformed into the past. The present is where the action is. It is important but it is elusive. If I write about the present just now, it will not be the same present when this book is published nor the present when you read it. In this chapter, therefore, I will write about the *ever*-present, about the constant throughout time - past, present, and future. I will write about human nature.

Development appears to be both continuous and discontinuous. Charles Darwin resolved this paradox by describing development as a process of continuous discontinuity - continuous with respect to function and discontinuous with respect to structure. Phylogenetic development, says Darwin, is continuous with respect to function (organisms evolve through adaptation to their environments) and discontinuous with respect to structure (different organisms evolve to fit different environments).

Jean Piaget (1896-1980) has done for ontogenetic development (from child to adult) what Darwin has done for phylogenetic development (from animal to human). Like Darwin, he views the function of the nervous system as the adaptation of the organism to the environment. However, he goes further by arguing that adaptation involves the alternating processes of assimilation (in which the organism takes in information from the environment) and accommodation (in which the organism adjusts its cognitive structure, if necessary, to assimilate this information). Thus, ontogenetic development is continuous with respect to function (the person adapts to the environment through alternating assimilations and accommodations) but discontinuous with respect to structure (different structures emerge over time to accommodate what is assimilated).

Presenting Darwin's theory of evolution as the basic theory of psychology (see Section 1.2), places the person firmly where s/he belongs within the field of biology rather than physics, as an organism rather than a mechanism. The theory of Jean Piaget, places the person even more firmly within biology as an organism.

However, I would like to go further by arguing that the co-evolution of the person and media as extensions is also a process of continuous discontinuity. It is continuous with respect to function (communication) and discontinuous with respect to structure (different generations of media have emerged along with different social systems). The constant in the past, present, and future is human nature, with its fundamental need for communication. The invention of different generations of media and their corresponding social systems constitute the unfolding of the human potential. It is essential then that we have a full and accurate concept of the person.

Chapters 3, 5, and 7 are entitled respectively *Assimilating the Second, Third, and Fourth Generations*. This is obviously inspired by Piaget's theory. However, it implies that society changes to accommodate those three generations of media, and thus raises the issue of **technological determinism**. In Section 5.1, I switched to Arnold Toynbee's challenge-and-response model of history, implying that the second, third, and fourth generations of media were responses to the challenges of moving into an agricultural, industrial, and information society, respectively.   However, this got me from the frying-pan of technological determinism into the fire of **cultural determinism**.

The three major scenarios within the triad model (see Figure 3-2) were ecosphere-as-cause, sociosphere-as-cause, and technosphere-as-cause. It is clear now that the really important scenario is person-as-cause. There is a correlation between changes in the sociosphere and changes in the technosphere. However, correlation does not necessarily imply cause.[1]   It could mean that sociosphere causes technosphere (cultural determinism) or technosphere causes sociosphere (technological determinism) or that there is a third variable underlying both the changes in the sociosphere and the changes in the technosphere. That variable is the person in the center. The person is simultaneously creating new societies and new media. Necessity is the *father* of invention. The creative mind of our species is the mother of invention. The necessity of supporting a larger group when our species settled down was the seed which, nourished in the creative mind, produced the invention of both the agricultural society and its corresponding medium, print.

In media studies - as in education, economics, political science, and all the other social sciences - there is an underlying concept of the person. Apart from some vague, infrequent (and politically incorrect) reference to *economic man, political man*, etc., the concept of the person is usually implicit. I would like to make it explicit. The next three sections will explore three alternative concepts of the person - the behavioristic concept, the humanistic concept and the interactionist concept. They will be presented as thesis, antithesis, and synthesis [GARDINER 1980]. I will argue that the behavioristic concept of the person underlies traditional media theory and practice, that the humanistic concept of the

---

[1]   For example, there is a correlation between the salaries of professors and the consumption of alcohol. This correlation does not necessarily (hic! hic!) imply cause. Both variables are effects of an underlying cause - the general increase in wealth.

person underlies alternative media theory and practice, and that the interactionist concept of the person promises more integrated theory and more meaningful practice.

9.2 BEHAVIORISM AND TRANSPORTATION THEORY

The behavioristic concept of the person is presented as the system of five propositions listed below. Since each proposition implies the next, those five propositions constitute a system rather than simply a set.

- The person has only extrinsic needs
- The person is conditioned from the outside in
- The person is not responsible for behavior
- The person has only extrinsic worth
- The person has contractual relationships

The typical exposition of behaviorism consists of the first two propositions - *"The person has only extrinsic needs"* in courses on Motivation, and *"The person is conditioned from the outside in"* in courses on Learning. However, I go beyond this traditional exposition to demonstrate the implications of those first two propositions and to provide a contrast with the humanistic concept of the person in the next section.

- ### THE PERSON HAS ONLY EXTRINSIC NEEDS

The broad question in psychology is *What is the function of the nervous system?* and the broad answer provided by the theory of evolution is *To enable the organism to survive.*   The **theory of evolution** could thus be considered as the basic theory of psychology.[2]

The next question is *How does the nervous system enable the organism to survive?* and the classic answer is *It ensures that the organism will approach things which are good for it (for example, things that it eats) and that it will avoid things which are bad for it (for example, things that eat it).* The **need-reduction theory** explains the former mechanism and the **activation theory** explains the latter mechanism. Thus, the need-reduction theory and the activation theory could be considered as the means of fitting psychology within the basic framework of the theory of evolution.

You are alive. You are in a precarious state. Life is a narrow tightrope with death on either side. To stay alive, you must maintain yourself within a narrow range of temperature, blood-sugar concentration, metabolic rate, and so on. Let us focus on temperature.

You have been set by the great temperature-setter-in-the-sky at 98.6 Fahrenheit (or at 37 Centigrade if God has gone metric). You are allowed to vary a little bit around this optimal temperature. But, a bit too low, you die; a bit too high, you die. Certain physiological mechanisms enable you to maintain your optimal temperature despite variations in the temperature of your environment. If it gets too cold, you shiver; if it gets too hot, you sweat.

Consider, however, the alligator. It shivers not, neither does it sweat. Yet all alligators are not frozen alligators or boiled alligators. A group of alligatorologists organized an expedition to Africa to find out why. A few thousand miles and several thousand dollars later, they discovered the answer. When an alligator gets too warm, it slides into the cool water; when an alligator

---

[2]   The question and the answer are both open to debate. However, since behavior and experience are manifestations of the function of the nervous system, I prefer to consider our other subsystems as internal environment. As for the answer, I think it is time to place psychology within biology where it belongs.

gets too cold, it climbs on to a hot rock. Thus, the alligator maintains its optimal temperature by adjusting the environment to itself rather than by adjusting itself to the environment. It behaves.

The process by which an organism maintains itself in its optimal state is called **homeostasis**. When it deviates from this optimal state, it can return to it either by adjusting itself to the environment or by adjusting the environment to itself. Our species, of course, uses both mechanisms. We shiver and sweat *and* we buy furnaces and air-conditioners. Adjusting ourselves to the environment is the province of physiology; adjusting the environment to ourselves is the province of psychology.

Let us take a closer look at the psychological mechanism. Imagine a hypothetical contented organism which has just been wined and dined. It is in its optimal state. However, it can not remain thus for long. The mere passage of time conspires against its bliss. It gets thirsty. It gets hungry. This physiological state of deprivation is called a **need**. The need can be satisfied by appropriate behavior with respect to some appropriate object in the environment - by drinking water in the case of thirst and by eating bread in the case of hunger. Since the nervous system is the only system within the organism which knows the environment, the physiological state of deprivation in the digestive system must be transformed into some psychological counterpart in the nervous system. A need must be transformed into a **drive**. The drive orients the organism to some appropriate thing in the environment - the **goal**. By making the appropriate response to the goal, the drive is removed, the need is satisfied, and the optimal state is regained.

Let us turn now from the positive to the negative drives, from the tendency to approach things that are good for us to the tendency to avoid things that are bad for us, from the need-reduction theory to the activation theory.

There are two ways we can avoid things that are bad for us. We can remove the thing or we can remove ourselves. The first involves fight and the second involves flight. The emotion underlying the former is **rage** and the emotion underlying the latter is **fear**. Such primitive emotions must have played a dominant role in the early history of our species. Consider one of our remote ancestors confronted by a saber-toothed tiger. She has a tiger in her subjective map. She can remove it or remove herself. She can kill it or she can run away. The only good tiger is a dead tiger or a distant tiger.

An emotion-arousing stimulus has three broad effects - experiential (we feel angry or afraid), physiological (there are certain changes in our bodies), and behavioral (we fight or flee). Discovery of the function of a structure in the brain called the **amygdala** has clarified the interaction among those three effects.

The emotion-arousing stimulus, like all stimuli, acts directly on the cortex. The stimulus is transformed at the appropriate receptor (a set of cells specialized for this purpose) into nerve impulses, which are transformed at the appropriate projection area of the cortex (a set of cells specialized for this purpose) into a perception. This **cue function** of the stimulus has long been known. However, what is less known is that the emotion-arousing stimulus also acts indirectly on the cortex to perform an **arousal function**. It switches on the amygdala, which projects diffusely on to the cortex, to alert you that *something* is happening in your environment.

Thus, the arousal function alerts you that something is happening (the amygdala responds in the same way to sights, sounds, tastes, smells, and touches) whereas the cue function informs you precisely *what* is happening. The arousal function prepares you for an emergency. It acts upward on the cortex to produce the experiential effects (fear or rage) and downward on the autonomic nervous system and the endocrine system (responsible respectively for the physical and chemical aspects of your internal environment) to produce the physiological effects (increased heart rate, injection of adrenalin, and so on), to provide the motivation and the energy for the behavioral effects (fight or flight). The cue function informs you whether there is indeed an emergency. Must stimuli are not worth getting emotional about. In such cases, the cortex acts downward on the amygdala to inhibit the arousal function. Animals without a cortex get mad at every little thing. The cue function also informs you of the nature of the emergency so that you can respond appropriately. Otherwise, you might attack tigers and run away from rabbits.

The need-reduction theory and the activation theory are diagramed together to clarify the similarities and differences between them (see Figure 9-1). Both theories involve a negative feedback loop to maintain the organism in its optimal state. Both theories describe the nervous system as a mediator between the internal environment (that is, the other subsystems within the organism) and the external environment. According to the need-reduction theory, the function of the nervous system is to mediate between a state of deprivation in the internal environment (need) and a thing in the external environment which will satisfy that need (positive goal), so that the organism will approach that thing; according to the activation theory, the function of the nervous system is to mediate between a thing in the external environment (negative goal) and a state of the internal environment (an emotion), so that the organism will avoid that thing.

Since the nervous system is merely a mediator between internal and external environments, the person is extrinsically motivated. The person is pushed and pulled by external forces - pushed by needs and pulled by satisfiers of those needs, pushed by threatening things and pulled by emotions generated by those things. Behaviorists conclude that all human behavior is determined by those extrinsic needs. Secondary drives can however be established through association with those primary drives. Thus, monkeys will work for tokens if those tokens can be exchanged for food. Capitalism is established by making money the means to the end of satisfying the basic biological needs. The behaviorist would thus explain your behavior in reading this book by saying that

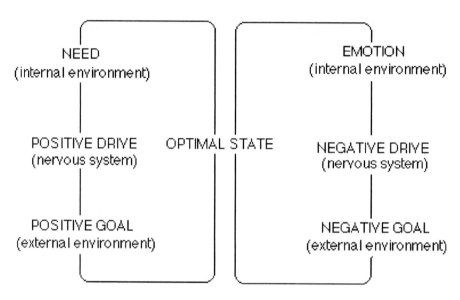

FIGURE 9-1
NEED-REDUCTION AND ACTIVATION THEORIES

you are reading this book to pass a course to get a degree to get a job to get money to buy food to remove your hunger drive to satisfy your hunger need to return to your optimal state to survive.

- ### THE PERSON IS CONDITIONED FROM THE OUTSIDE IN

It all started when Ivan Petrovitch Pavlov walked into his laboratory and a dog salivated, Most us would have been merely flattered. However, Ivan Petrovitch Pavlov was not like most of us. He devoted the next forty years of his life to understanding why. He had already won a Nobel Prize for his work in physiology. Most of us would have been satisfied. But Ivan Petrovitch Pavlov was not like most of us.[3]

Environment affects behavior. This statement is true but trivial. Pavlov suggested how it may be made more precise and thus more meaningful. Representing a dog or a person or whatever organism as a rather unflattering empty box, we could consider environment as a set of stimuli acting on it and behavior as a set of responses produced by it. Now we can substitute the precise statement "*Stimulus X elicits response Y* " for the vague statement "*Environment affects behavior*". We all know that an organism can come to behave differently in the same environment. That is, it can learn. How does it learn? Or, more precisely, how can stimulus X, which was previously neutral, come to elicit response Y?

Pavlov begins his answer by pointing out that, at birth, some stimuli are already capable of eliciting certain responses [PAVLOV]. If I tap you sharply below your knee, then you will raise your lower leg. The tap (stimulus) is prewired to the raising of the lower leg (response). No experience necessary. Such a prewired link between a stimulus and a response is called an **unconditioned reflex (UCR)**. If I blow a whistle, you will not raise your lower leg. However, if I were to blow the whistle, tap below your knee, blow the

---

[3]   Have you ever heard of Edward B. Twitmeyer? He was an American graduate student who stumbled on the same phenomenon before Pavlov, considered it footnoteworthy in his doctoral thesis, and went no further. Twitmeyer was like most of us!

whistle, tap below your knee, blow the whistle, tap below your knee, and so on and on, then eventually you would raise your lower leg to the whistle alone. Such an acquired link between a stimulus and response is called a **conditioned reflex (CR)**. It is acquired by the operation of presenting a stimulus that was originally neutral - the **conditioned stimulus (CS)** - together with a stimulus that is already wired to the response - **unconditioned stimulus (UCS)**. This operation is called **classical conditioning**.

Edward Thorndike provided another answer. He rounded up stray cats from the back alleys of New York City. He built a box with a door that could be opened by pressing a lever. Inside the box he placed a cat; outside the box he placed things that the cat liked (typically one or more of his famous three Fs - fish, friends, and freedom). The problem was to get out, and the solution was to press the lever. When first put in this **puzzle box**, the cat went through its repertoire of responses: clawing at bars, hissing at Thorndike, arching its back, spitting and snarling, smiling at Thorndike, purring and meowing, and so and so on, more or less at random. Finally, by chance, it hit on the Thorndike-ordained correct response. Each time it was put back into the box, it took less and less time to get out until eventually it went immediately to the lever and pressed it.

Thorndike described this process as **trial-and-error learning** [THORNDIKE]. His theory of learning was somewhat analogous to the survival-of-the-fittest principle which is central to Darwin's theory of evolution. In a population of organisms, some are fitter to survive in a given environment; in a repertoire of responses, some are fitter to survive in a given situation. The fittest response is the one leading to reward. Thus, we have a second answer to the question "*How does a particular stimulus, previously neutral, come to elicit a particular response?*" The response is a means of gaining access to a stimulus that already elicits some response that is intrinsically rewarding. This is **instrumental conditioning**. The two types of conditioning are diagramed side-by-side for comparison in Figure 9-2.

John B. Watson, the founder of behaviorism, elaborated on Pavlov's work in an attempt to explain all behavior in terms of classical conditioning [WATSON JO]. He extended the theory from simple local responses like salivation to complex general responses like fear; from single responses to strings of responses like habits. Talking is just a sequence or movements of muscles in the mouth and throat just as walking is a sequence of movements of muscles in the legs. Thinking is simply talking to yourself in a voice so low that no one else can hear. Thus, all behavior is explained in terms of classical conditioning.

B. F. Skinner, the most famous behaviorist, elaborated on Thorndike's work in an attempt to explain all behavior in terms of instrumental conditioning [SKINNER]. He renovated and automated the puzzle box into what has come to be called, in his honor and to his dismay, the **Skinner box**. The task was not to press a lever to escape from the box but to press a lever to acquire a food pellet. He was too poor to supply pellets every time the rat (or whatever organism) pressed the lever (**total reinforcement**) and thus supplied pellets only some of the time (**partial reinforcement**). He found that supplying pellets as a function of responses - say, every tenth response (**ratio schedule**) - produced a higher rate of responses than supplying pellets as a function of time - say, every ten seconds (**interval schedule**). He found that supplying pellets, on the average, every ten responses or every ten seconds (**variable schedule**) produced a higher rate of responding than exactly every ten responses or every ten seconds (**fixed schedule**). It's that variable ratio schedule that keeps us pulling that lever of those slot machines. As we saw in Section 2.2, verbal behavior is simply a means of acquiring those "pellets" through the mediation of other people. Thus, all behavior is explained in terms of instrumental conditioning.

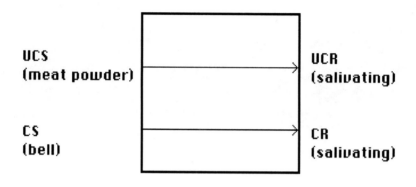

Pavlov and his dog

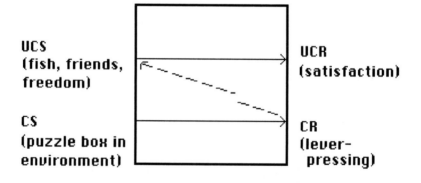

Thorndike and his cat

FIGURE 9-2
CLASSICAL AND INSTRUMENTAL CONDITIONING

- TRANSPORTATION THEORY OF COMMUNICATION

The communication theory associated with the behavioristic concept of the person is the Shannon-Weaver model of communication [SHANNON & WEAVER]. Information is transmitted by a source over a channel to a destination. It is called the **transportation theory of communication** since information is simply *"transported"* from the source to the destination. For example, right now I am the source, you are the destination, and we are communicating over the visual channel. The information transmitted by the source is not necessarily the information received by the destination. You may receive information which I did not transmit (**noise**) and I may transmit information which you do not receive (**equivocation**). The criterion of success is the percentage of **transmitted information** - that is, the overlap of information transmitted by source and information received by destination. (see Figure 9-3).

Let us say that you know my last name is GARDINER but you do not know my first and middle names. If I now tell you that my last name is GARDINER, I provide you with no information. You already knew this. Information from the source (in this case, me) to the destination (in this case, you) is thus a function of **uncertainty** at the destination. Let us now say that I tell you my first name is WILLIAM. I provide you with information, since you did not already know this. Let us now say that I tell you my middle name is LAMBERT. Once again, I provide you with information because you did not already know this. However, I provided you with more information when I told you that my middle name was LAMBERT than when I told you my first name was WILLIAM, because there was more uncertainty at the destination. That is, you were more likely to guess that my first name was WILLIAM (every Tom, Dick, and Harry is called WILLIAM) than to guess that my middle name was LAMBERT.

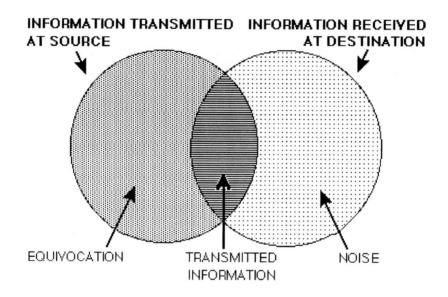

FIGURE 9-3

TRANSPORTATION THEORY OF COMMUNICATION

The amount of information transmitted from the source can thus be measured as a function of the amount of uncertainty at the destination. Information theorists define the **bit** as the amount of information which cuts uncertainty in half. Thus, if I toss a coin and tell you that it came down HEADS, I transmit 1 bit of information because there were 2 equally likely alternatives - HEADS and TAILS. With 4 equally likely alternatives, then, I transmit 2 bits of information; with 8, 3 bits; with 16, 4 bits; and so on. The amount of information when told the results of tossing a die is between 2 and 3 bits, of choosing a card from a pack is between 5 and 6 bits, of choosing a letter from the alphabet is between 4 and 5 bits (see Figure 9-4).

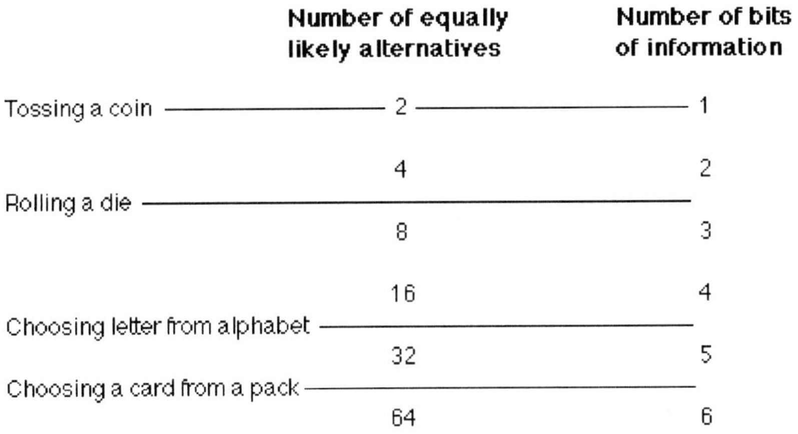

	Number of equally likely alternatives	Number of bits of information
Tossing a coin	2	1
Rolling a die	4	2
	8	3
Choosing letter from alphabet	16	4
	32	5
Choosing a card from a pack		
	64	6

FIGURE 9-4
INFORMATION AS FUNCTION OF UNCERTAINTY

In real life, however, the various letters in the alphabet are seldom random. They are usually encountered in context which reduces the amount of information provided by each letter. I am thinking of a four-letter word. It would no doubt take you a number of guesses before you got the first letter. It is Q. You can now get the second letter right away - Q is always followed by U in English. The third letter is easier than the first, since it must be a vowel. It happens to be "I". The fourth letter is also easier since there are only a few letters which fit. It happens to be "Z". This feature of language is called **redundancy** and explains why we can get the message even when it is not fully transmitted by filling in the gaps.

9.3 HUMANISM AND TRANSFORMATION THEORY

The behaviorists have grasped some truth but not the whole truth. Classical conditioning, determines some behavior; Instrumental conditioning determines some behavior; but those processes do not explain all behavior. It is necessary for us to continue to explore more and more sophisticated concepts of the person.

The humanistic concept of the person is presented as the system of five propositions listed below. Once again, since each proposition implies the next, those five propositions constitute a system rather than simply a set. Note that each of the five propositions negates the corresponding proposition in the behavioristic concept of the person.

- The person has intrinsic needs
- The person is growing from the inside out
- The person is responsible for behavior
- The person has intrinsic worth
- The person has intimate relationships

- THE PERSON HAS INTRINSIC NEEDS

Your nervous system is an element of you as a person and you as a person are, in turn, an element of your society. The nervous system has a very special role within this hierarchy of systems within systems, since it is the only system which can *know* your environment. It must know your environment in order to perform three broad functions - to mediate between your internal environment and your external environment (biological function), to interact appropriately with other people (sociological function), and to understand your environment and yourself (psychological function). Underlying each of those functions are certain organic needs - biological, sociological, and psychological, respectively - designed to ensure that your nervous system performs each of those functions.

The satisfier of the need to eat is food; the satisfier of the need for stimulation is novel stimuli. Just as you seek food when you are hungry, you seek novel stimuli when you have a need for stimulation. A number of studies have demonstrated that organisms explore and manipulate their environment in search of novel stimuli. Rats will often choose the long, scenic route over the short, dull route from the start to finish boxes within a maze. They spend more time around unfamiliar than familiar objects when they are placed in their cage. Monkeys will work hard to unfasten latches to open windows to see what's happening outside. Indeed, they will work hard to see nothing. They enjoy learning to open latches as an end in itself. The activity is its own reward.[4]

This need for stimulation may perhaps be explained in evolutionary terms. As long as things remain the same, you are in no danger. It is only novel stimuli which are potentially dangerous.   Exploration and manipulation of the environment makes the unfamiliar familiar. If it is indeed dangerous, then you can remove it or remove yourself; if is is not dangerous, then you have removed the threat of danger. Besides removing danger or threat of danger, exploration and manipulation incidentally enables you to get to know your environment. One peculiar property of novel stimuli may help explain why we have come to know more than we really need to know in order to merely survive. As we explore and manipulate a novel stimulus, it becomes less and less novel, and therefore less and less able to satisfy the need for stimulation. We must continually search for new stimuli in order to satisfy this need. Perhaps as our environment got less and less

---

[4]   One psychologist tried to study monkeys through a keyhole in their room. All he saw was one large, brown, baleful eye. A monkey was studying him!

threatening, then the incidental function of getting to know the environment got more and more important.

Psychologists once arranged to have observers infiltrate an organization whose members believed that the world would end at a particular time on a particular date. They were curious to discover what happened when that time came and went and the world remained. They found that those members of the group who were only peripherally involved ceased to believe, whereas those members who were strongly committed to the group (that is, those who had stated their beliefs in interviews with the press, who had sold their possessions, who had canceled their life-insurance policies, and so on) continued to believe. Those true believers argued that the destruction of the world had been postponed, that there had been a mistake in the date, that the apocalypse had been canceled because of their vigilance, and so on.

Leon Festinger, the leader of the group of psychologists, explained those findings as **cognitive dissonance** [FESTINGER ET AL]. When two items of information do not fit, there is a tendency for one of them to be changed. For example, the two items of information - *I smoke* and *smoking causes cancer* - are dissonant. Festinger found indeed that significantly fewer smokers than non-smokers believed that smoking causes cancer. People, with those two dissonant items in their subjective maps, either stop smoking or stop believing.

Whereas the need for stimulation provides the organic basis for knowing our environment, the need for consistency provides the organic basis for understanding our environment. Not only do we need to know, but we need to know what we need to know. What we know must be organized into a consistent body of knowledge. That is, we need not only to know but to understand. The need for stimulation and the need for consistency thus provide an organic basis for psychological growth.

Jean Piaget describes the process of mental growth as a series of alternating assimilations and accommodations. You assimilate information from your objective world and adjust your subjective map to accommodate that information if it does not fit. The need for stimulation is the organic basis for assimilation, and the need for consistency is the organic basis for accommodation. The need for stimulation ensures a fresh supply of new information from the objective world, and the need for consistency ensures that this information will be integrated into a consistent subjective map of that objective world.

- THE PERSON IS GROWING FROM THE INSIDE OUT

If the person has intrinsic needs, then the person grows from inside out. Every normal child has the potential to be fully a person, just as every normal acorn has the potentially to be fully an oak tree and every normal kitten has the potential to be fully a cat. Powered by the intrinsic system of needs, built into the nervous system, as described above, the child seeks satisfaction for them. In an appropriate environment, children are able to satisfy those needs and thus fully realize the human potential. The basic project of the child is to become an adult - not any old adult but a great and good adult. We therefore need not so much to explain the genius of Albert Einstein or Margaret Mead (or whoever you think has most fully realized the human potential) but rather why we are not *all* Einsteins or Meads.

We are all familiar with Freud's explanation for the stunting of the growth of so many of us. The ego, superego, and id (which can be identified respectively with psychological, sociological, and biological needs) are in perpetual conflict. Abraham Maslow proposes an alternative explanation. There is a **hierarchy of needs** and thus biological needs must be satisfied before moving up to sociological needs which must, in turn, be satisfied before moving up to psychological needs. Even at this level, the need to know can be frustrated by the fear of knowing [MASLOW].

- ## THE PERSON IS RESPONSIBLE FOR BEHAVIOR

If the person grows from the inside out, then the person is responsible for behavior. Whereas extrinsic motivation requires extrinsic control, intrinsic motivation permits intrinsic control. The constraints of society on a person with extrinsic motivation can be replaced by the restraints of a person with intrinsic control. One symptom of a shift from the behavioristic concept of the person based on extrinsic motivation to the humanistic concept of the person based on intrinsic motivation is a shift from an emphasis on extrinsic control to an emphasis on intrinsic control.

- ## THE PERSON HAS INTRINSIC WORTH

If the person is responsible for behavior, then the person has intrinsic worth. The person must accept blame for bad behavior but, on the other hand, can accept credit for good behavior. That is, a person can have intrinsic worth. People who consider themselves to have intrinsic worth are said to have **self-esteem** (that is, worth in their own eyes); people who consider themselves to have no intrinsic worth tend to seek **prestige** (that is, worth in the eyes of other people).

- ## THE PERSON HAS INTIMATE RELATIONSHIPS

If the person has intrinsic worth, then the person has **intimate relationships**. Since each person is unique because of their intrinsic worth, no person can be interchanged with any other within any social system, including that small society of two involved in an interpersonal relationship. All relationships are potentially intimate, since we recognize all other people as members of the same species on the same planet in essentially the same predicament. A stranger is just a friend you haven't met yet.

On the other hand, if a person has only extrinsic worth, then people are interchangeable elements within a social system. There can only be **contractual relationships** between people. Your relationship with your grocer is contractual. It does not really matter to you that this particular person sells you food and to him that this particular customer buys it. You take this food home and cook it for your mate. Your relationship to your mate would appear to be qualitatively different from your relationship to your grocer. Neither of you are interchangeable. It is important to you that you cook the food for this particular person and to him/her that it is you who is doing so.

However, the behavioristic concept of the person implies that this relationship is also contractual. You simply present a longer and more complex shopping list and your mate retaliates with an equivalent list. I'll scratch your back if you'll scratch mine. This cynical view of human relationships is not some 1984ish vision of a dehumanized world but a necessary deduction from the behavioristic concept of the person. B. F. Skinner explicitly states this view in his book *Verbal Behavior* [SKINNER]. There are two ways you can get things done - you can do it yourself (non-verbal behavior) or you can ask someone else to do it for you (verbal behavior). Verbal behavior is defined as behavior which gets things done through the mediation of other people. Other people are means to your ends.

The humanistic concept of the person implies that relationships are intrinsically intimate rather than basically contractual [MADDI & COSTI]. Instead of viewing your relationship to your mate as an extended contractual relationship, it views your relationship to your grocer as an unrealized intimate relationship. The latter is based not so much on an implicit contract to exchange food and money but on a tacit understanding not to realize the full potential intimacy. You each respect that fact that the other can handle only so much intimacy - even if only because the other has only so much time.

- TRANSFORMATION THEORY OF COMMUNICATION

Whereas the behavioristic concept of the person underlies the traditional transportation theory of communication, in which information is simply transported from the source to the destination, the humanistic concept of the person underlies an alternative **transformation theory of communication**, in which the information is transformed at the destination. A number of communication theorists - Roland Barthes [BARTHES], Walker Percy [PERCY], Tony Schwartz [SCHWARTZ T], Marshall McLuhan and Barrington Nevitt [MCLUHAN & NEVITT] - have recommended such a shift.

The transportation theory of communication, based on the behavioristic concept of the person, assumes that the audience is passive. A person is a couch potato - all eyes but no action. The big three television networks tend to view their task cynically as delivering a passive audience to their advertisers, with the programs between the ads merely a device to keep them amused until another ad can be administered to them. Critics of television tend to agree with this vision of the audience, and see themselves as condescending to save the slobs from themselves.

There has been, till recently, some justification for this point of view. If no action is possible, except switching to another almost identical channel or, in extreme cases, switching the television off, then the audience is necessarily passive.[5] However, recently we have had the revolt of the couch potato - remote control, VCR, interactive videodisk, desktop video production. Such new

---

[5]   The first colloquium I attended in graduate school was presented by Howard Liddell. He described research in which he was testing the intelligence of sheep using a covered maze. He admitted sheepishly that he had crawled in to clean it one day and had taken as long to get out as his stupidest sheep. He brightened up when he reported that the second time he got lost, he did much better. When the decision to turn right or left in a maze is purely arbitrary, our much-vaunted intelligence is of no help. There is no reason why Dr. Liddell should do better than his sheep. All our intelligence provides is the capacity to benefit from experience. Thus the experimenter did better than the subject the *second* time he got lost in the maze.

technologies promise to transform the passive couch potato into an active producer-director programming his/her own evening of enlightenment and entertainment.

9.4 INTERACTIONISM AND TRANSACTION THEORY

Interactionism could be viewed as a synthesis of this behavioristic thesis and the humanistic antithesis. The behavioristic concept of the person was presented as a system of five propositions, and the humanistic concept of the person was presented as a system of five propositions, which contradicted the corresponding propositions of behaviorism. Let us look at each pair of opposing propositions to suggest how the interactionist concept of the person can resolve those dichotomies (see Figure 9.5).

•   THE PERSON HAS INTRINSIC **AND** EXTRINSIC NEEDS

The basic proposition of behaviorism is *The person has only extrinsic needs*, whereas the basic proposition of humanism is *The person has intrinsic needs*. This distinction between extrinsic and intrinsic needs is thus the basic difference between the behavioristic thesis and the humanistic antithesis. The humanistic concept of the person subsumes the behavioristic concept. The behaviorists are right - the person does indeed have extrinsic needs - the nervous system mediates between the internal and the external environment. However, the nervous system has needs of its own. Those intrinsic needs include the need for stimulation and the need for consistency which are the organic bases, respectively, for the need to know and to understand.

BEHAVIORISM	HUMANISM
The person has only extrinsic needs	The person has intrinsic needs
The person is conditioned from the outside in	The person is growing from the inside out
The person is not responsible for behavior	The person is responsible for for behavior
The person has only extrinsic worth	The person has intrinsic worth
The person has contractual relationships	The person has intimate relationships

FIGURE 9-5 BEHAVIORISM AND HUMANISM COMPARED

Thus, the humanistic paradigm subsumes the behavioristic paradigm as Einstein subsumed Newton rather than replacing it, as Copernicus replaced Ptolemy. Einstein did not argue that Newton was wrong but that it was correct only within a limited domain. Interactionists would argue however that knowing and understanding involve not only input information, as the behaviorists argue, and stored information, as the humanists argue, but also fedback information, which determines the relationship between stored and input information.

•   THE PERSON IS GROWING FROM THE INSIDE-OUT **AND** BEING CONDITIONED FROM THE OUTSIDE-IN

Interactionists agree with the humanists that *The person is growing from the inside out* AND with the behaviorists that *The person is conditioned from the outside in.* However, just as they emphasize intrinsic motivation, so they also emphasize inside-out growing. This is the primary process. However, the person can not grow in a vacuum. This interactionist model was illustrated in the case of the acquisition of language (see Section 2.2). Noam Chomsky argues that the acquisition of a language is the unfolding of the language-acquisition device (LAD), and Jerome Bruner points out that this unfolding requires a language-acquisition support system (LASS). Interactionism is the description of this dance of various lads and lasses.

- THE PERSON IS RESPONSIBLE FOR **SOME** BEHAVIOR

The third propositions of behaviorism (*The person is not responsible for behavior*) and humanism (*The person is responsible for behavior*) directly contradict one another.   We see here the philosophical debate between determinism and free-will. Interactionists resolve this conflict by pointing out that they are both right. Behaviorists and humanists are self-fulfilling prophets. If you are determined to believe that your behavior is determined, then it is indeed determined. If you believe you have free-will (the first act of free-will is to believe in it), then you do indeed have free will.

Time after pompous time, in introductory textbooks in psychology, including my own, one reads "*this behavior is determined by some complex interaction between genetic and environmental factors*". Consider, however, the case of Chang and Eng. They were Siamese twins. Chang was a womanizer and an alcoholic, whereas Eng was practically celibate and a teetotaler. Their very different personalities could not be the result of genetic factors on environmental factors (they were genetically identical and their environments were as close as any two people ever had) or any "*complex interaction between genetic and environmental factors*".

We must consider a third factor - choice. Chang chose the short, happy life whereas Eng chose the long, miserable life. Poor old Eng had to die when Chang died as a result of his excesses. However, most of us are not attached to someone else and can make choices that help determine our lives. Most of us can organize a psychic coup d'etat to overthrow the tyranny of our genetics and our environments. We can write our own scripts.

•   THE PERSON HAS INTRINSIC **AND** EXTRINSIC WORTH

If people are responsible for their behavior, then they can take credit for good behavior but must also accept blame for bad behavior. The words *good* and *bad* tend to scare scientists into scurrying off in search of philosophers. There seems to be no place for values in a world of facts. Some scientists are however evolving a set of values based on natural laws rather than cultural rules - that is, the propositions we have derived to describe our planet and our selves rather than the propositions we have derived to prescribe our conduct on this planet. Here is a summary of those values, as expounded by such diverse thinkers are Teilhard de Chardin, Buckminster Fuller and Kenneth Boulder.

Whereas the industrial society had to deal with an energy crisis, the information society has to deal with an entropy crisis. Entropy - the spontaneous tendency of systems towards disorder - is increasing. Biological systems, within their limited space and for a limited time, defy the law of entropy. During their growth, they become more rather than less structured. Our species, the most complex biological system, is the greatest anti-entropic force in the universe. Each of us is a defiant little package of anti-entropy fighting our brave battle against the forces of chaos.

Consciousness emerges as a function of complexity and provides the ultimate weapon against entropy. It enables us to assimilate and accommodate to information to create a microcosm of the universe within ourselves. The fuller and more accurate this subjective map of the objective world, the better we fight the good fight. It is ultimately futile, of course, we can win battles but must lose the war. Eventually, we die and get recycled as the air our survivors breathe and the water they drink. However, it is not futile for the species. Each of us spawns other defiant little packages of anti-entropy in our books and movies and children and students, which continue the war.

We have intrinsic worth, then, because we are important elements in the complex system of the universe. We are a part of nature rather than apart from it. Our criterion of success is not wealth but health. We are healthy insofar as we realize our function in the universe - to move up the hierarchy of needs, to satisfy our biological, sociological, and psychological needs, to know and understand our selves and our planet, to build a full and accurate subjective map of the objective world.

- ### THE PERSON HAS INTIMATE **AND** CONTRACTUAL RELATIONSHIPS

Whereas the contractual relationship is based on the rules of human beings, the intimate relationship is based on the laws of nature. We recognize other people as members of the same species on the same planet in essentially the same predicament as ourselves. If God is dead, then there is no one here but us. Other people are the only personal element in an impersonal universe. They hold out the only hope of empathy, of understanding, of caring.[6] We all have intimate and contractual relationships. The important distinction however is whether you believe relationships are basically intimate or basically contractual. Those who see relationships as basically intimate live in a world of saints and sinners. They

---

[6]   Those two basic attitudes towards other people are nicely represented by two gestures I encountered while traveling in Nepal. The traditional gesture is to hold your hands as in prayer, bow, and say *"namaste"* which means *"I honor the divinity in you"* . The other gesture - alas, in urban areas where Western values have pervaded - is to hold out one hand palm up and say *"rupee"*.   The shift from *"namaste"* to *"rupee"* is symptomatic of a shift from intimate to contractual relationships.

tend to see me as a saint. Those who see relationships as basically contractual live in a world of smart guys and suckers. They tend to view me as a sucker. I hang out with the former group and avoid the latter group.

• TRANSACTION THEORY OF COMMUNICATION

The interactionists view the person as dealing not only with input information, as in the transportation theory of communication, or not only with input and stored information, as in the transformation theory of communication, but with input and stored and fedback information. S/he is actively exploring and manipulating the environment in order to know and understand it. The exploration is guided by fedback information from the environment as a result of his/her actions. Their position could be viewed as a balance between the extreme outside-in position, with its over-emphasis on input information, and the extreme inside-out position with its over-emphasis on stored information. The relationship between input information and stored information is orchestrated by fedback information.

George Miller, Eugene Galanter, and Karl Pribram present the interactionist model in their famous book *Plans and the Structure of Behavior* [MILLER ET AL]. They argued that the behaviorists are the optimists in psychology - they aspire to explain human behavior in terms only of input information; the humanists are the pessimists since they argue that we need to add stored information to explain behavior. In other words, we need to put a box representing stored information within the box the behaviorists use to represent the person. They argue further that the humanists are not pessimistic enough - we need to add a third category of fedback information. In other words, we need to put a second box within that behaviorist box.

Here they turn to the analogy of the computer. The computer has a box for stored information (they called it the image) and it also has a box for instructions to process input and stored information (they called it the plan). The basic plan is to remove the discrepancy between input information and a desired state in stored information. Hence in the simple case of the plan to hammer in a nail, the person tests to see if the head of the nail is flush with the surface (test), if not s/he hammers the nail (operate), tests again (test), and so on around this feedback loop until the nail is flush, and then the plan is discontinued (exit). Their **TOTE unit** (Test-Operate-Test-Exit) is diagramed in Figure 9-6.

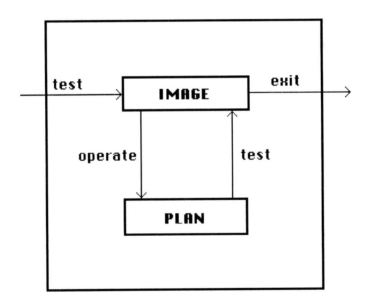

FIGURE 9-6   THE TOTE UNIT

The **transaction theory of communication** could be viewed as communication between TOTE units, each of which is processing input, stored, and fedback information according to their various plans. In a conversation then, your output is my input and my output is your input information. Your output can also be my fedback information if it is a response to my output, and vice versa.

Our plans may be complementary, if for example we are seeking understanding of a topic of mutual interest, or they may be in conflict, if for example, I am trying to persuade you to do something you don't want to do or you are trying to sell me something I don't want to have.

9.5 FRAMEWORK FOR THE FUTURE

The behavioristic, humanistic, and interactionist concepts of the person, as presented in the last three sections, provide progressively more and more adequate bases for media theory and practice. The person is seen as dealing with input information (behaviorism), input-stored information (humanism), and input-stored-fedback information (interactionism). However, the concept of the person is, in all three cases, still as an information-processing system, by analogy with the computer.

It is necessary to go beyond the concept of the person as a mechanism to the concept of the person as an organism. We need an emergent model of the mind rather than an information-processing one [TURKLE 1995, Page 178]. This is provided by Jean Piaget.

As we saw above, there is much empirical evidence which points to a need for stimulation, providing the organic basis for assimilation, and further empirical evidence which points to a need for consistency, providing the organic basis for accommodation. That is the need to know and the need to understand (that is, to have a consistent body of knowledge) is built into our nervous systems, as the humanists argue. The unfolding of this genetic potential from the inside-out , powered by those built-in needs for stimulation and consistency, is the primary process. However, this process has to be "fueled" by input from the outside, as the behaviorists argue.

The theory of Jean Piaget clearly places the inside-out process of growing as primary and the outside-in process of conditioning as secondary. The child is unfolding naturally from the inside-out but will not do so unless that process is "fueled" by appropriate information from the outside-in.[7]   Piaget clearly favors the smorgasbord to the set menu, as will be advocated in Section 15.4. Turning media theory and practice inside-out could be rephrased as replacing the traditional set menu with a smorgasbord.

As we move into the future in the next nine chapters, we will take this concept of the person with us. This is the constant throughout past, present, and future. It will help explain why utopias have not worked in the past (Chapter 13) and why that ultimate utopia in which we live for ever will not work in the future (Chapter 12); why a corporate culture is inadequate (Chapter 14) and how universities can become more adequate (Chapter 15), why some people aspire to a lo-tech future and some to a hi-teach future (Chapter 10).

---

[7]   When he presented that unfolding process at Cornell University during my time as a graduate student, the first question he was asked was *"how do you speed it up?"*   He took his pipe out of his mouth and said *"Ah, the American question!"*   Apparently this is the first question he was always asked when talking to a North American audience. His answer was, essentially, that one should let the process unfold and not rush it.

CHAPTER 10
HI-TECH AND LO-TECH FUTURES

10.1 WHAT IS THE FIFTH GENERATION?

10.2 HI-TECH FUTURES

10.3 LO-TECH FUTURES

10.4 PREVIEW OF COMING ATTRACTIONS

From the origin of human language 100,000 years ago until the invention of writing 5,000 years ago, the oral tradition had been the principle creator, conserver, and communicator of human knowledge. Our brains are biologically adapted to the tempo of oral interaction in real time.

Steven Harnard, 2003

(Death has dropped by to recruit War to ride to the Apocalypse. War invites him to stay for lunch. Mrs War is not amused.)
We're having rabbit, she said, and added in the voice of one who has been put upon and will extract payment later,
I'm sure I can make it stretch to three.
War's big face wrinkled. *Do I like rabbit?*
Yes, dear.
I thought I liked beef

No, dear, beef gives you wind.

Oh. War sighed. *Any chance of onions?*
You don't like onions, dear.
I don't?
Because of your stomach, dear.
Oh.
War smiled awkwardly at death. *It's rabbit,* he said. *Erm .... dear, do I ride out for Apocalypses?*
Mrs War took the lid off a saucepan and prodded viciously at something inside.
No, dear, she said firmly. *You always come down with a cold.*
I thought I rather, er, liked that kind of thing ...?
No, dear. You don't.
Despite himself, Death was fascinated. He had never come across the idea of keeping your memory inside someone else's head.

Terry Pratchett, THIEF OF TIME, Page 275

10.1 WHAT IS THE FIFTH GENERATION?

In my course on the history of media, I present my model of four generations of media with three shifts as the second, third, and fourth generations are assimilated. This model is presented in this book as Chapters 1 to 8 and summarized in the 2x2 matrix of Figure 1-2. The most-frequently-asked question by my students is *What is the fifth generation?* My most-frequent-answer is that there is no fifth generation of media but there may be a fourth shift. That is, a shift back to the first generation. There is growing dissatisfaction with the indirect, mediated communication of the second, third, and fourth generations and yearning to go back to an emphasis on the direct, face-to-face communication of the first generation. Many people want their communication (like their food) fresh rather than canned. They argue that, despite Alan Watts advice: *"The word is to the world as the menu is to the meal. Don't eat the menu"*, we have become menu-eaters.

This answer triggers a debate between those who advocate becoming more deeply immersed in the fourth generation (Section 10.2 Hi-tech futures) and those who advocate a return to the first generation (Section 10.3 Lo-tech futures). Some students whose vision of a fifth generation was direct telepathic communion between people concede that this future may best be viewed as a return to the first generation. Other students, whose vision of a fifth generation involves implanting information directly into the nervous system, argue that my resistance to a fifth generation is simply squeamishness. I concede that I plan to die with the same number of holes in my body as when I was born, and that they - many of whom are tattooed and pierced - are more comfortable with this vision of the future. However, I do not concede that this is the next step in evolution or even involves a fifth generation of media. This vision of the future is presented in Chapter 11 Cyborg Futures. Other students argue that I am not able to think outside my little 2x2 box. Chapter 12 Eternal Futures is an attempt to think outside this box and explore the possibility that there is indeed a fifth generation of media, involving our creations which escape from the box and surpass us.

10.2   HI-TECH FUTURES

Students who advocate a hi-tech future look forward to becoming more and more immersed in the fourth generation of media, which they tend to see as a projection into the future of trends which are already apparent. The saga of the incredible shrinking chip will continue. Thus, the computer which has moved from the floor-top to the desk-top to the lap-top to the palm-top will continue to the next obvious location, the wrist-top. We will soon be chuckling at the olden days when we lugged around a large piece of equipment containing one piece of information - the time. Already, most young people check the time on their cell phones. Watch-makers, who face a future in which watches are worn largely as status-enhancing jewelry, are hustling to include more information on their watches. Every major watch-maker has an electronic version which is essentially a computer on the wrist. Microsoft recently got into the act with their version.

The computer is thus worn rather than carried. When things are worn, care is devoted to fit. The interface becomes more important. Keyboards are obviously poor interfaces for wrist-top computers and will be replaced by toothpicks and voice-activated software. Now that we are used to people talking into their cell-phones, we'll have to adjust to people talking, like Dick Tracy, to their wrists. The traditional pick-up line *What's the time?* will be replaced by a variety of queries - *How's the weather?*, *Who won the hockey game?*, *What's playing at the Paramount?, May my wrist take your wrist to the movies?*

Advocates of hi-tech futures also anticipate, with delight, some shifts in emphasis as a result of innovations in the fourth generation of media. Let us look, in turn, at three such shifts - from person to environment, from observer to participant, and from entertainment to enlightenment.

•   FROM PERSON TO ENVIRONMENT

The two basic parameters of the objective world are time and space. Computers have always known what time it is. Recently, they have learned where they are. A **Geographical Positioning System (GPS)** built into the computer can tell it where it is in latitude and longitude by triangulating using satellites. Scholars focusing on **locative computing** are exploring the theoretical and practical implications of this development.

One implication is that information can be embedded in the environment as well as worn or carried by the person. As our hi-tech world gets more complex, we will need not only to extend the person but to enhance the environment. Thus, a person with a location-aware computer can leave a message (whimsically called "cyber-graffiti") at a location which can only be read at that location by another person with a location-aware computer. As usual, of course, we first use the technology as a toy rather than as a tool. Internet treasure hunts are organized at websites. If a participant correctly follows the clues provided at the website, s/he will reach a location where they can acquire a further clue or find a treasure. On finding a treasure, the participant, in the collaborative spirit of the Web, typically adds a trinket to the treasure as a calling-card and perhaps a clue to finding another treasure which s/he hides.

The technology can also be used as a tool to "*annotate*" places of interest. I've published a book which serves as a walking tour of Main Road, Hudson, the street on which I live. As the reader walks along the Main Road, s/he can see an old picture, a new picture, and some history of each house of historical interest. As location-aware computers become more common, I'll augment or replace this book with a more extensive history readable only when standing in front of that particular house. No doubt such devices will become available at heritage sites, museums, and art galleries.

Another use of this technology is collaboration among groups of people who do not necessarily know one another. Howard Rheingold has described such groups as *"Smart Mobs"* [RHEINGOLD 2003]. Once again, at first, they get together to play. One teenager finds Prince William in a bar and suddenly he's surrounded by a "swarm" of teenagers. Groups of people (*"flash mobs"*) suddenly converge on a particular location, do something bizarre, and then disband. There are more serious applications. Protest groups have been successful in disrupting various conferences organized by the World Bank, World Trade Organization, and other advocates of globalization, because they can communicate instantly and move quickly. A corrupt President in the Phillipines was ousted by such a Smart Mob.

- FROM OBSERVER TO PARTICIPANT

In Section 4.3, the history of film was described in terms of a closer and closer approximation to the "mind movie". Work continues towards making the movie a more and more accurate simulation of the real world. Douglas Turnbull has created a number of reality rides in various hotels in Las Vegas which immerse the audience more fully in a simulated environment. The entire visual field is stimulated, as in Omnimax, as is the entire auditory field with 360-degree sound. However, the local senses are invited into the simulation - the chair moves to correspond to the experience played to the distance senses of vision and audition. (One theater in the local Paramount complex is equipped with such seats.) Various reality rides at the various Disneylands are designed to invite the audience to become totally immersed in the worlds of Disney movies.

There has been a parallel development in art. Just as some film-makers aspire to move from a detached viewer looking at a film in a distant frame, so some artists aspire to move from a detached viewer looking at a painting in a frame. They too want to invite the viewer in so that s/he can be totally immersed in the world of the artist.

Experiments in Art and Technology (EAT) was an organization based in New York in the late 1960s which invited artists and scientists to work together. Their efforts culminated in their creation of the Pepsi Pavilion at the World Fair in Osaka in 1970. Artists were invited to program the environment for an audience passing through the pavilion on a sort of horizontal escalator. With the relatively primitive technology of the time, they were able to totally immerse the audience in some interesting experiences. By the 1980s when Myron Krueger came to Montreal for a conference on convergence, he was able to use computers to create very interesting responsive environments [KRUEGER]. Each square in the floor responded with a sound and the shadows of the viewer on a screen responded visually. Laurie Anderson, another participant at the conference, was delighted to find that she could play her environment as she danced around the room.

I met Myron Krueger at a conference on Virtual Reality in San Francisco in 1990. *What do you wear in cyberspace?* was the title of his talk and *Nothing* was its conclusion. Most of the other participants were wearing goggles and gloves. Those "garments" enabled them to become totally immersed in a simulated environment. Just as enterprising researchers had made a pocket version of the Ganzfeld, so they had made a pocket version of Myron's responsive room.[1] Videogame creators are pushing the frontiers in creating more and more

---

[1]   I raised my status at this conference by mentioning that I had studied with J. J. Gibson, whose perceptual theory was the basis of their programs to simulate the changes in the environment as a

realistic simulations of our environments. This industry, bigger than the film industry, is now merging with it.   Each major Hollywood movie is now supplemented with a CD-ROM containing the sound-track, a DVD containing the movie and extras about the making of the movie, and a videogame to enable people to totally immerse themselves in the world of the film.   There are movies based on games (e.g. *Final Fantasy*) and games based on movies (e.g. *Matrix*). Now I can watch Sony movies on my Sony TV and participate in those movies on my Sony PlayStation 2.   I'm not longer simply a passive viewer but a participant observer in a simulated world created by Sony and paid for by me.   I can buy those experiences at Future Shop or rent them from Jim's local video store.

•   FROM ENTERTAINMENT TO ENLIGHTENMENT

The focus of this development in media is, of course, entertainment.   We can amuse ourselves - if not to death - at least into debt.   This is what sells.   A program called "*Enlightenment Tonight*" would not have survived for 30 years on prime time TV and would not have inspired a rival network to create a competing program "*Inside Harvard*".   Reasons why entertainment is so much more popular than enlightenment will be explored in detail in another book - *Turning Teaching Inside-out* [GARDINER 2005].   Here, however, let us just consider briefly how this powerful new generation of media could be used for enlightenment.

I once (mis)spent a weekend totally immersed in a simulated world, as I explored the fictional island of *Myst*.   When I emerged, I wondered what it would be like to become as totally immersed in a simulation of some real place.   Shortly after, I was invited to produce the edutainment section of the CD-ROM to accompany the movie *Rob Roy*.   My initial plan was to create a time-space matrix so that people could explore a simulated Scotland and thus learn about its history

---

goggled participant moved around in their simulated environments. They didn't need to know that I never understood what he was talking about!

and geography. It turned out there was not enough time or space for such an over-ambitious project, and we had to settle for flying a helicopter around the Trossachs area where Rob Roy lived and having icons emerge from the mist which obscured the landscape from time to time. I'm now shifting focus down to the village of Hudson where I live. All the information I can accumulate about the village will be organized into a Virtual Village. Visitors can explore it at their leisure and thus become at home in it. Students of all ages will, in the future, become at home in such virtual villages rather than memorizing facts about it.

I once collected the ten top reasons why the virtual world is better than the real world (see Figure 10-1). This was a whimsical exercise. However, the virtual world is indeed better than the real world under certain circumstances. Pilots of large planes are trained in flight simulators. It is much too expensive to have them learn on a real plane (even if they don't crash it). They can crash the flight simulator as often as is necessary for them to learn how to fly the plane at no cost. Potential pilots graduate from the simulator to the real plane as co-pilots the first time they are in the plane. Medical students can learn on virtual cadavers. A slip of the knife which would destroy a real cadaver merely requires a "reset" or "undo" to try again. No need any more to rob graves for a steady supply of bodies for medical training. There is no reason why much more of our education could involve simulations of the various aspects of the real world we will later have to become at home in.

Those simulations capitalize on the powerful properties of the fourth generation of media. It is integrative and it is interactive. Both of those properties contribute to making it immersive. Integration of light, sound, text, etc. contributes to the creation of a total environment and interactivity makes it responsive to the user. Total immersion is the recommended method for language learning. However, every discipline is essentially the learning of its language. While learning Hebrew totally immersed in Hebrew, the medium and the message are consistent. The medium is the message.

The downside is the danger of media blur. That is, as we get better and better at simulating reality, people will find it more and more difficult to separate virtual from real worlds. Bill Kuhns used my apartment while I was off on a trip to write a book away from the distractions of his home. The manuscript he left on my desk for me - *Twice as Natural* - focused on media blur. During my trip, someone had shot John Lennon, because the assassin was Lennon and the real John Lennon had to go. Shortly after, someone shot at President Reagan in order to impress Jodie Foster who admired a character in a movie who had shot a president. This is the tip of an iceberg of media blur. Actors who portray doctors and lawyers on television are constantly asked for medical and legal advice. Actors who save the world in movies are elected governor!

1   There is no musical score or laugh track.

2   You have to do all your own stunts.

3   It's always in Technicolor. You can only have black-and-white
movies at night.

4   There is no UNDO function, RESET button, or
ESCAPE KEY.

5   You can't REWIND, FAST FORWARD, PAUSE, or have
SLOW-MOTION INSTANT REPLAYS. Your eyes can PAN
but they can't ZOOM.

6   Your marriage lasts till *"death do you part"* rather than until
the film is in the can or the TV series is canceled.

7   You can't channel-surf through your various other
possible lives.

8   You can't shop for a new body, head as you can for your avatar.

9   Your mobile movie studio doubles as a movie
theater but there is only one seat.

10   You can only die once and you have to leave it till the end.
There are no happy endings.

FIGURE 10-1
THE TEN TOP REASONS WHY REALWORLD IS INFERIOR
TO VIRTUAL WORLD

10.3   LO-TECH FUTURES

Live concerts are more popular than ever, despite the fact that fans can hear (and see) their bands better in the comfort of their homes. At the concert, the band members are distant dots on a postage-stamp stage pumping out sound which is almost drowned in the ambient noise. Ironically, the best view is on a giant screen but still with poorer resolution than their television screen. They are there, however, to belong to a tribe. Some fans of groups like *The Grateful Dead* and, more recently, *Phish* do not simply attend a concert when the band is in the neighborhood, but follow their bands from concert to concert around the globe. A Rock and Roll concert is a return to tribalism. Participants in raves are returning to the roots of our species which lived for most of our history as tribes of hunter-gatherers. Bruce Chatwin advocates a return to nomadism - the life-style before we settled down, claimed certain land as our own and started squabbling over it [CHATWIN].

In his book *Faster*, James Gleick bemoans the fact that our lives have speeded up so that we can match the speed of our various extensions [GLEICK]. Carl Honore, in his book *In Praise of Slow*, surveys the movements devoted to slowing us down again [HONORE 2004]. Such movements need not go back to a hunter-gatherer existence corresponding to that first generation of media. We can now be "hunters and gatherers" of information. The hi-tech hi-touch life-style uses the new extensions to facilitate a simpler, slower life. Being an information junkie, I had to live in cities because that was where the information was. The internet now enables me to live a simpler, slower life in the country. Information is as accessible to me here in the village of Hudson as it is in New York or London or Cupertino, California. This is electronic cottage country. Many of my neighbors have gone back to the cave. Unlike our hunter-gatherer ancestors, we don't need to leave our cave to hunt and gather.

As we assimilate each generation of media, we gain something and we lose something. Some people are arguing that what is gained is not worth the sacrifice of what is lost. The various extensions of the second, third, and fourth generations have "numbed" our natural senses and cluttered up our lives so that we neglect the face-to-face communication of the first generation. All of us have horror stories of families out of touch with one another as each member is immersed in their various media. Father is in one room watching the sports channel, mother in another room watching a soap opera, daughter in a third room glued to the phone talking to her friends, son in a fourth room playing games on his computer.

•   TELLING AND LISTENING TO STORIES

There is a universal need to tell and hear stories. The biological function of stories is clear. They allow us to benefit from the experience of others. It is teaching rather than learning which best distinguishes us from the other animals. A story from Uncle Lefty about waking a slumbering bear in a cave (hence Lefty) increases the odds for survival. However, stories may have a further psychological function. The life we lead is only one of millions of possible lives. Stories enable us to live our missing lives vicariously. *The unexamined life is not worth living* says the scholar, but *the unlived life is not worth examining*.

For every teller of stories there must be a listener. It is equally important to learn to listen as it is to learn to talk. We tend not be good at it. We forget that we have two ears and one mouth so that we can listen twice as much as we talk. A conversation is too often an alternation between speaking and waiting to speak, two parallel monologues rather than a dialogue. Listening is seldom on the official curriculum. However, it is what one does most of the time in school and university. Any illusion of intelligence in an "educated" person is due to the fact not that they talk well but that they listen well.[2] Scholars, who stray away from the academy, are frustrated when they find that they are not allowed to speak for more than 30 seconds without being interrupted. Sound bites is not simply a media phenomenon. Note that successful communication with animals as well as humans is due to good listening rather than good talking – Monty Roberts entitles his book *The Man Who LISTENS to horses* [ROBERTS].

•   LISTENING TO THE VERY LOCAL NEWS

An operating manual for species homo sapiens that I wrote in the 1960s was essentially an operating manual for the nervous system (the only subsystem which can be "operated" directly). It contained sections on biofeedback to enhance the signal from the autonomic nervous system and on meditation to reduce the noise from the central nervous system so that I could listen to the very local news from my body. I have realized, after 20 years in media studies, that I was guilty of *tabula isola*. Most of the operating manual should be about learning the skills and operating the tools of media as extensions of the nervous system. However, I've got so distracted by those flashy media which bring news from the outer world that I've been neglected, in practice and in theory, the news from the inner world.

Those media use the distance senses of vision and audition, which tend to overshadow the close senses of taste, smell, and touch. Even those powerful

---

[2]   Dr. Harry Harlow came to Cornell University when I was a graduate student to talk about his famous research on love in infant monkeys. He came around to the offices of the graduate students to ask if we had any questions. Later, one of my professors told me that Harlow was impressed by my intelligence. During his visit to an office I shared with three other graduate students, I hadn't said anything! However, I was very interested in his work and very impressed that this distinguished scholar would come to talk to us, and had listened very intently. Any impression of intelligence in university-educated people is due more to the fact that they have learned to listen than that they have learned to talk. If I had said anything, I would have blown my reputation!

distance senses are very limited. They pick up only a sliver of the electromagnetic range of stimuli. We got a glimpse of this during Operation Iraqi Liberation (OIL) when special glasses enabled the American troops to see in the dark. Even when we see clearly within the limited range of human vision, we observe very little. I once set myself to observe on the short trip from my home to my office that I had walked many times. On that trip, I noticed that three of the four corners at a busy intersection were occupied by banks, that a maternity wear store was called *Great Expectations*, and that there were many pigeons on the ledges of one church but none on the ledges of the church next door, even though the former church had spikes on the ledges to discourage them. (I discovered later that this had nothing to do with their religious preference but simply due to the fact that the pigeons traditionally rested at one church, that the spikes had been added later, but this was not enough to overcome the inertia of tradition.)

Another *"experiment"* alerts me what a limited sliver of the information available in our environment we take in. One of my neighbors, Dr. David Sorenson, is one of the world's foremost authorities on Thomas Carlyle. When I discovered this, I knew little about Carlyle - that he was Scottish, that he lived in the nineteenth century, and that he wrote something or other - and I knew nothing about his wife, Jane Welsh. Since then, I've noticed that this couple keeps popping up here and there in my reading. Some examples from my Carlyle File are presented in Figure 10.2.

The Carlyle File is a useful concrete example of the phenomenon of **selective perception** (Sometimes called the red-headed-woman effect - you fall in love with a red-headed woman, and suddenly the world is full of red-headed women.) The significance of selective perception is that it suggests we are conscious of only that small sample of the vast amount of information potentially available to us to which we are paying attention. Thomas Carlyle and Jane

MARRIED
17 October
1826

THOMAS CARLYLE
1795 - 1881

JANE WELSH
1801 - 1866

Richard D. Altick
The Scholar Adventurers
New York: The Free Press, 1950
Page 226   Story of housemaid (code-named Betsy Baker by scholars) who
burned the Manuscript of Carlyle's *The French Revolution.*
Page 250   Carlyle's famous bad temper attributed to illness.
Page 268   If (Quoting Carlyle) genius is an infinite capacity for
         taking pains, it is also an infinite capacity for enduring them.

William S. Baring-Gould
The Annotated Sherlock Holmes (Volume 1)
New York: Clarkson N. Potter, 1967
Page 155   Dr. Watson quotes Thomas Carlyle in *A Study of Scarlett* and
         Sherlock Holmes asks who he is. Watson points to an
         obituary. Annotation suggests Holmes was feigning
         innocence, citing evidence that he quotes Carlyle himself later   in the story..

Saul Bellow
It All Adds Up: A Non-fiction Collection
New York: Viking, 1994
Page 141   Carlyle's famous essay on Robert Burns in which he
         writes *"Let me write the songs of a people, and you may write   its laws."*

David Denby
Great Books: My Adventures with Homes, Rousseau, Wolfe, and Other Indestructible
Writers
New York: Simon & Schuster, 1996

Page 421   Impact of the publication of *The French Revolution.*

Merlin Donald
A Mind So Rare
New York: W. W. Norton, 2001
Page 61   Carlyle's famous aphorism quoted: *Under all speech that is*
          good for anything there lies a silence that is better. Silence is deep as Eternity; speech is
shallow as Time.

Lives Lived
Globe & Mail, 24 December 1996, Page A20
          Carlyle quoted in pseudo-obituary of Tiny Tim Cratchet.

Chris Hables Gray (Editor)
The Cyborg Handbook
New York: Routledge, 1995
Page 4   It was Carlyle who labeled his own time, the Machine Age.

Stephen Leacock
Too Much College
New York: Dodd Mead, 1939
Page 32   Cites Carlyle's argument that a university is just books.

Alberto Manguel
A History of Reading
Toronto: Alfred A. Knopf Canada, 1996
Page 256   Anecdote about Jane Welsh, wife of Thomas Carlyle,
          suffering through repeated readings of his long poem *Maud* by Alfred, Lord Tennyson.
Page 301   Quote by Carlyle in defense of the scholar-reader,
          Johann Geiler von Kayserburg.
Page 318   Anecdote about Jane Welsh taking risqué novels out of the
          library and signing *Erasmus Darwin.*

Phyllis Rose
Parallel Lives: Five Victorian Marriages
New York: Random House, 1984
Pages 21-44   The Carlyles' Courtship. Prelude to one of those
          Victorian marriages.
Pages 239-259   Back to the Welsh-Carlyle marriage.

Carolyn Zilboorg
Richard Aldington & H.D.: The Early Years in Letters
Bloomington: Indiana University Press, 1992
Page 88   Neitzsche is a kind of epigrammatic Carlyle.

FIGURE 10-2   THE CARLYLE FILE

Welsh were present in my reading before I got interested in them but I had not noticed them. Evolutionary psychologists point out that we pay attention only to that sliver of information available in our environment which is relevant to our survival. As survival becomes less crucial, we have the luxury of paying attention to the Carlyles but the same principle applies.

Much empirical evidence has been gathered indicating that the information of which we are *not* aware has an effect on our behavior. Sigmund Freud has been criticized for his focus on the unconscious. However, if anything, he under-estimated the profound effect of the unconscious - the effect of information of which we are not aware.

Selective perception permits us to focus on topics of interest. The focus can, however, be too sharp. We tend to find what we are looking for. When writing about biotechnology, I suddenly found the topic everywhere - in the business section of The Globe and Mail, in the Montreal Business Magazine, in Harper's Magazine on the newsstand and Salon Magazine on the Internet, in a novel I was reading - Zadie Smith's *White Teeth*. This was obviously an important topic but its importance was not *obvious* until I started to pay attention to it. This book is thus biased since the information potentially available is sieved through my selective perception.

I've also come across references to Thomas Carlyle in popular culture from *Seinfeld* (*Oh, ya, old Tommy Carlyle* – says George trying to impress a new intellectual girl-friend, who has mentioned him) and in the movies *Wonder Boys* and *Memoirs of a Dangerous Mind.* We are all familiar with the *Arrangement in Grey and Black, Number 1* - James Whistler's portrait of his Mother. We are not so familiar with *Arrangement in Grey and Black, Number 2*, his portrait of -- Thomas Carlyle.

I hesitated about including the reference to the book by Phyllis Rose, since

I didn't chance upon it. Kathryn Lamb, a friend, directed my attention to it. However, I included it since this is simply an extension of the selective perception phenomenon. Your friends know your interests and direct you to sources. We all (like Mr. War in the Terry Pratchett quote at the front of this chapter) store some of our information in the minds of our family and friends.

We neglect the very local news from our bodies at our peril. Our various organs work quite well on their own. From time to time, however, they have to alert us that something needs attention. Pain is the friendly reminder. Can you imagine how difficult life would be if your digestive system had no way of telling you that your tanks are full. You would have to be constantly alert that you do not overflow. A friend once went to a garage because he was worried about a warning light. The mechanic took out the bulb and said playfully *"Now it won't worry you any more!"* Modern medicine too often takes out the bulb - that is, it treats the symptoms rather than the disease.

• COMMUNION UNDERLYING COMMUNICATION

A number of scholars have argued that the mind is larger than the brain. I argue in Section 1 The Past (Chapters 1-8) that the Big Story of historical time is the co-evolution of the person and media as extensions [GARDINER 2002]. My mind is thus not contained in my brain but also in those various extensions in the media I use. Andy Clark also argues that we should consider our mind as including our various extensions [CLARK]. His loss of a laptop felt like an amputation. However, other scholars have gone beyond us in the extension of the mind, or rather see each of our minds as extensions of some larger entity. They are thinking even further outside the box of the brain. They believe the mind is extended by biology as well as by technology.

That entity has been described as a global brain [BLOOM H], world brain [RUSSELL], the collective unconscious [JUNG], cosmic consciousness

[BUCKE], noosphere [DE CHARDIN], nervous system of our planetary organism [LOVELOCK], and so on. We have tended to dismiss such concepts as mere expressions of hope that there is some basis for communion within our species underlying communication. They are mere metaphors, in the subjective maps of their creators, with no empirical evidence for their existence in the objective world. However, the evolutionary perspective opens the door to the possibility of mental entities beyond individual brains, because it emphasizes the fact that we have hundreds of thousands of years of shared experience. Philip Sheldrake, who has impeccable scientific credentials, is finally gathering empirical evidence for such an entity [SHELDRAKE].

We all have had experiences which give us the impression that there is someone in here that knows more than you do. Here are some of mine. You no doubt have similar anecdotes from your life. Dreams release the dramatist in us. In one of my dreams, the word "*postprandial*" was used. I didn't know what it meant. Being a scholar, I got out of bed to check its meaning. Suddenly, I realized that I didn't know what it means but someone in here must know. Since I was already at the Ps, I persisted and found that it meant "*after a meal*" and had been used appropriately in the dream.

I once had a series of dreams with different contents but the same message - *Cool it!* In one of them, I'm in a rural school-yard when a bell rings. I amble into a classroom and the teacher says: *You're late but that's okay!* Back in the school-yard, I'm climbing over a fence while a young boy looks at me quizzically as he walks out a gate.in the fence. I find myself in a hut where I'm climbing out the window as the same boy walks out the door. Suddenly, I realize that the hut is one I lived in before leaving Scotland and that the boy is my former self. When those dreams occurred, I had just completed a five-year plan to get my B. A., a five-year plan to get my Ph. D., and a five-year plan to write my first book. The dreams inspired me to abandon my next five-year plan and take a decade off!

The *Paris Review* publishes a series of interviews with famous authors. Many of those authors describe themselves as portals for their productions, as mere conduits for something larger than themselves. This does not mean that they simply wait for this to happen. They must shed the preliminary 99% perspiration to receive the 1% inspiration. However, the perspiration comes from them but the inspiration comes from somewhere else. Such phenomena require no spooky explanation. Our collective experience is coded into our DNA which we all share as members of our species. It has been so deeply encoded into our experience that we are not conscious of it. However, we may have access to it, if we go deeply enough into this well of human experience. The fact that there are only a few stories which are told, in some form, in all cultures is further evidence of such a common source.

10.4   PREVIEW OF COMING ATTRACTIONS

Science fiction has been a useful complement to science fact in considering the future. Unlike scholars, scifi writers are not reluctant to speculate about the future. They provide a *"preview of coming attractions"*. Isaac Asimov is the most famous scifi writer and his most familiar scifi novels are in the Foundation Series. Many subsequent novels and films (most recently *I, Robot*) follow up on his discussion of robots. Donald Kingsbury, who resigned from the Mathematics Department at McGill University to write science fiction, expands on Asimov's more obscure concept of psychohistory in his scifi novel, *The Psychohistorical Crisis* [KINGSBURY].   This novel illuminates some of those issues in the above debate between advocates of hi-tech and lo-tech futures.

The novel has an unhappy beginning. The hero - Eron Osa - is executed. It turns out however that being "*executed*" in this far-in-the-future universe means having one's "*fam*" (an electronic extension of one's self) detached and destroyed. Life in this future has become so complex that "*famlessness*" is death. There is no way that one can survive as one travels between planets, without this device which enables one to quickly acquire the diverse languages and cultures of each planet. We have evolved to be quick studies of novel environments. However, our environments in this future have become *so* novel and so numerous that biological evolution must be supplemented by technological innovation.

The rest of the novel is about how our famless hero manages nevertheless to survive and even thrive. He survives because he re-discovers the long-lost qualities of the "*naked brain*" and he thrives because he thus has a firmer foundation for his new fam than his opponents who have lost touch with their un-augmented brain. Helping also in his survival is his mentor, Murek Kapor, whose fam is so complex that it contains a whole other personality, Hiranimus Scogil, an "*imposed persona*" (158) not subject to Murek's control.

The fam is a tool which is worn rather than carried or implanted. It continues the progression mentioned above (see Section 10.2), due to miniaturization, from floor-top to desk-top to lap-top to palm-top to wrist-top to brain-top. Fams vary in quality from the standard government-issue (18) to those custom-designed by fam-making experts like Nemia of l'Amontag (157).

Fams combine the functions of various current tools - VCR-PVR-camcorder - which can be set at *accelerated assimilation* (36), fax machine, copier, sleeping pill (137), alarm clock (361), telescope - eye-fam set at high magnification (174) - and various people - therapist (244), tutor (227), research assistant - *Eron's educated fam absorbed details of erosion and weathering and concluded that the cataclysm couldn't have happened more than a million years ago* (136), Girl Friday (247) and secretary (362).

One very important function which has no clear-cut analog in current technology is to annotate and edit the environment - *"weasel"* (54), *"sim overlay"* (166) and *"robocomment"* (304). To survive and thrive in the complex world of the future, not only must you be augmented but your environment must be annotated. We get an early glimpse of such devices built into the dashboards of cars. Such systems know where they are using global positioning systems, where you may want to go - the nearest Holiday Inn, MacDonald's restaurant, etc., and can show you how best to get from here to there. Steve Mann, who will be introduced in Section 11.4, wears such a device to annotate and edit his environment.

The fam is potentially in touch with many external information-processing devices in an information-rich environment. It can of course communicate directly with the fams of other people - *"fam-to-fam link"* (331). There are also *"tri-vid maps"* (222), *"archival consoles"* (446), *"map-readers"* (375), *"weasels"*(54) - like the owls in Harry Potter, *"fonepad"* (44), *"sim overlay"* (166), *"personal capsule"* (45, 147, 235), *"wall emitters"* (26), *"wall screen"* (60), *"holo illustrators"* (113), *"mnemonifier"* (313), *"terminals"* (139), *"house telesphere"* (162, 333), all of which can feed the fam.

The fam is attached at age 3 in a coming-of-age ritual (78) - better than some coming-of-age rituals in which something is sliced off - and is fully functional by 12 so that the child is ready to ride the turbulent teens. The organic brain and the fam have a symbiotic relationship (372, 457), with the fam being subservient to the organic brain. One wonderful metaphor for this relationship is of a legless person in the knapsack on the back of an armless person (469). Brain and fam can be de-coupled and re-coupled without losing personality (155) but the brain is helpless in dealing with the complex environment on its own.

The unaugmented organic brain is described as the *"naked brain"* (18), as primitive (98), capable only of *"monkey business"* (374). Amazement is expressed at the culture created by the famless Helmerians (146). The naked brain is however good for one thing - wild, primitive sex (359). *"She did something preposterous - she took off her fam to do it the wild way"* (171). There is some value too in disconnecting the fam from time to time to *exercise your naked brain to keep it animal-sharp* (19). Sensory and perceptual experience is richer.

In contrast with the fam, traditional media are hopelessly inadequate. A book is described as archaic because it has no fam-jack (71) and thus its user must be eye-fed rather than fam-fed (18, 21, 81). Murek expresses horror at paying air-freight for a hard-copy book when it could be stored on the head of a pin (79). This is not so far off. Already the advantages of storing and searching information on a CD-ROM or DVD is so far beyond storing and searching on books that it is laughable that the publication of so many reference books persists so long.

The necessity which is the mother of the invention of the fam is the management of complexity. Government is by psychohistorians who can predict the future because they (aided by their fams) can manage the complexity generated by the many variables which determine the future. Much apparent complexity is actually just clutter which the fam can filter out to avoid chaos (277). The fam is also capable of *"complexity compression"* (265). Since the naked brain is stupefied by complexity (316), it must subcontract out various functions to the fam.

This vision of a far-off future may help us better design our immediate future. Lo-tech and hi-tech futures are not necessarily either-or alternatives at the ends of a lo-hi-tech dimension. They may be creatively combined in a hi-tech hi-touch future. Since leaving my village in Scotland, I've gravitated to cities, because I'm an information junkie and cities are where the information is. Or, rather, cities WERE where the information WAS. With the fourth generation of media, I'm as central in the Smart Room of my electronic cottage in the village of Hudson as anyone in New York or London or Cupertino, California. The Global Village of Marshall McLuhan, where the center is everywhere and the periphery is nowhere, is finally here. So I'm back in a village where I know my neighbors rather than in an APARTment in a city. I can now greet every person I pass in the street. (My teeth were freezing during my first Winter in Montreal when I was trying to smile at everyone I passed.)

CHAPTER 11
CYBORG FUTURES

All I can do is assure you that the cyborg is not to be found in the realm of hypothetical eventualities and hyperbolic horrors -- it is real; it is now. Each scenario in this book encounters wearable technology; each scenario postulates a new interface, a new relationship, between the human being and technology; each scenario demonstrates how present day extensions of human ability through technology affect the shape of society; and each scenario speaks to the way we live our lives now, as opposed to the way we can expect to live our lives in some potentially disastrous future.
Steve Mann with Hal Niedzviecki, CYBORG, Page xi

I was born human.
This was merely due to the hand of fate, acting at a particular place and time. But while fate made me human, it also gave me the power to do something about it. The ability to change myself, to upgrade my human form with the aid of technology. To link my body directly with silicon. To become a cyborg -- part human, part machine. This is the extraordinary story of my adventure as the first human entering into a Cyber World; a world which will, most likely, become the next evolutionary step for humankind.
Kevin Warwick, I, CYBORG, Page 1

11.1 WHAT KIND OF CYBORG DO YOU PLAN TO BE?

In the middle of the 16th century, Nicolaus Copernicus plucked us from the center of the universe and placed us on a broken-off fragment of a suburban star. Late in the 19th century, Charles Darwin removed us from our exclusive niche as the creation of God and put us where we belonged on the same scale as the other animals. Early in this 20th century, Sigmund Freud informed us that we are not even rational animals but moved largely by irrational forces of which we are not even aware. Each of those theories could be considered as challenging a reassuring discontinuity - between our planet and the rest of the universe, between ourselves and the other animals, and between rational and irrational creatures. Bruce Mazlich argues that we are now being confronted by a challenge to a fourth discontinuity - that between the person and the machine [MAZLICH].

It is not surprising then that so much focus has been placed recently on the **cyborg**. This entity - part-person and part-machine - lies somewhere along this dubious dimension between person and machine, and thus challenges the dichotomy of person and machine.   It has been a staple of science fiction for some time, especially in the sub-genre of cyberpunk. However, it is beginning to appear more and more in popular culture. A spate of recent feature films have 'starred' various cyborgs - for example, *Terminator*, *Robocop*, *Cyborg*, *Lawnmower Man*, *Johnny Mnemonic*, *Solo*.

Even scholars have shown some recent interest in cyborgs under various aliases - e.g. post-human [HAYLES] or micromen [PASK & CURRAN] or metamen [STOCK].   Kevin Kelly proposes a *"new biology of machines"* [KELLY]. We even have a Cyborg Handbook [GRAY] and a Cyborg Manifesto [HARAWAY]. Of course, the fact that the academy has 'discovered' the issue could mean - as some cynics say - that it is passé! However, this academic for one thinks the cyborg issue will be with us for some time, and that the cyborg will become a major metaphor during the 21st Century.

At a conference in Baden Baden, Germany, I argued that we are all cyborgs [GARDINER 1997]. We can 'look forward' to becoming more and more cyborgian as we age and require glasses, false teeth, a hearing aid, insulin shots to control our diabetes, a pacemaker to charge up our heart, perhaps even an artificial limb or two.   The machine parts we may require as we age are, of course, prosthetics to replace malfunctioning organic systems.   While perhaps inevitable, this may not be the type of cyborg we aspire to be. I suggested that we replace the perennial question *What do you want to be when you grow up?* with the question *What kind of cyborg do you plan to be?*

The argument that we are all cyborgs sensitizes us to the bewildering smorgasbord of cyborgs we encounter in day-by-day life: a courier on a bicycle, a kid on a skateboard, a middle-aged man reading a book, a teenager carrying a boom-box, a cybernaut with goggles and gloves exploring cyberspace, and so on. Those are all temporary cyborgs who pick up and put down their appendices or, in the case when they wear their appendices, put them on and take them off. From time to time, someone advocates they be permanently implanted.   Younger people, who have no qualms about tattoos and body piercing, may find this option of implanted intelligence interesting. Indeed, there seems to be no shortage of candidates with a *'desire to be wired'* [BRANWYN].

Whether carried or worn or implanted, the various appendices are of two types - those which expand the body as an energy system (bicycle and skateboard) and those which expand the body as an information system (book, boom-box, goggles-and-gloves). The former are of little theoretical interest. The bicycle and the skateboard are means of getting the person from point A to point B. If the trip is uneventful, the person is essentially unchanged at the destination. The latter are more interesting, since the person is changed by the acts of reading the book, listening to the music, exploring cyberspace. Let us focus, therefore, on the latter - on systems involving bits rather than atoms [NEGROPONTE].

If we turn for inspiration to the fictional characters in cyberpunk novels and in the films mentioned above, we note that they have **POSITIVE prosthetics**. That is, whereas they may replace missing organic parts, they are superior to those parts and, in some cases, they are added to a perfectly functioning body.   For example, whereas our eye-glasses merely return our failing sight to normal, the goggles, worn by Hiro, the hero of *Snow Crash*, expand his sight beyond the visual spectrum [STEPHENSON 1992]. We have now all seen such goggles in action in the recent Operation Iraqi Liberation (OIL).

The prosthetics may be positive but they are not necessarily used in positive ways. The characters in the *Matrix Trilogy* (*Neuromancer, Count Zero, Mona Lisa Overdrive*) by William Gibson have positive prosthetics which are usually weapons necessary to survive in his apocalyptic vision of the near future [GIBSON W 1984, 1987, 1988]. Eve, the eponymous heroine in *Eve of Destruction*, has a nuclear bomb in place of a womb and must therefore be treated very carefully. Let us focus on prosthetics which are positive in both senses - constructive rather than destructive tools.

The decision to focus on positive prosthetics which extend us as information systems leads to a consideration of media - the 'machines' which store and transmit information. In Chapter 1, I argued that the co-evolution of the person and media is the Big Story of historical time. The conception-day gift of memory and speech is adequate only for a hunter-gatherer society.   Over historical time, we had to extend our nervous systems by storing and transmitting information outside our bodies to manage the transitions to agricultural, industrial, and now information societies. That is, history is the story of the cyborgization of the person. How do you plan to use those extragenetic and extrasomatic tools?

Each of those generations of media extends us as information systems, since they enable us to share information with other people. The fourth generation - in which information is stored electronically in disks and transmitted electronically through the informatics infrastructure of computers interlinked by telecommunications - is, however, particularly powerful, because it is more integrative and interactive. Since numbers, text, images, sounds can all be reduced to a lowest common denominator of 0s and 1s, the products of the generations can be integrated in electronic storage. Since the person can interact intimately with this electronic information, the person and the machine can be tightly coupled. This rich feedback between person and machine creates a cybernetic organism (cyborg) as the term was originally intended. We now have a positive prosthetic which is a perfect fit. Here then are four different answers to the question: *What kind of cyborg do you plan to be?*

11.2 THE EXTENDED PERSON
- W. LAMBERT GARDINER

Many scholars have got excited about the fourth generation of media as a means of solving the perennial problem of organizing the vast amount of information we accumulate during our academic lives. It promises to integrate all our favorite books and articles, our own books and articles, notes and talks, and to enable us to interact with those extrasomatic stores of information. This was the inspiration for the Memex of Vannevar Bush [BUSH] for the Xanadu Project of Ted Nelson [NELSON 1973, 1984], and for the many innovations of Douglas

Engelbart in his crusade to augment human intellect [BARDINI], during those heady early days in which the emphasis was on enlightenment rather than on entertainment. My contribution to this tradition is the Siliclone - that is, a silicon clone of myself.

The first version (see Figure 11-1 VERSION 1.0) was a collection of files in a variety of programs, available for my first computer - the first Macintosh with 128 K of memory - bought for $3,000 in 1984.[1]   Since the programs were incompatible, I had to search each file in turn for whatever concept I was interested in. Plagiarizing myself (every scholar does it. We recycle our ideas. We are good environmentalists!) was an elaborate search and cut-and-paste operation.

The second version (see Figure 11-1 VERSION 2.0) was a more integrated version, since all the files, whether text or image, were within the same program - HyperCard - released by the Apple Corporation on 11 August 1987. This first generally available authoring program was interactive as well as integrative, since each card could contain not only text and/or images but buttons linking it to any other card. The metaphor was a filing cabinet for each category of information with an in-box and an out-box to enter and extract information from the files.

The third version (see Figure 11-1 VERSION 3.0) overcomes some of the limitations of that first authoring system. There was no way in which a person with my limited programming skills could search the entire database rather than look in each drawer in turn. Nor was there any way for anyone, regardless of their programming skills, to upload this information on to the internet. This current version is written in HTML (one of the more sophisticated authoring programs since the pioneering HyperCard) and uploaded to the internet at

---

[1]   Twenty years later, in a visit to B Mac in Montreal, I noticed that they were using two of them as bookends!

www.siliclone.com. The elegant design is by Trisha Santa, the brains behind the screen.

Each of us fortunate enough to have a few thousand dollars to spare has, at our fingertips, the power available only to multinationals for millions of dollars only 50 years ago. One way to realize this power is to use this fourth generation of media to create a conceptual self-portrait, a sort of expert system of oneself. The Siliclone is a primitive prototype. Person-machine synergy can be explored as the appropriate division of labor between your natural intelligence and the artificial intelligence in this satellite brain, or, more precisely in my case, between Scot and Siliclone. As in any partnership, the division of labor is based on the competences of each partner.

One view of the division of labor is that Siliclone deals with content, setting Scot free to deal with context. That is, data is placed in context to yield information, information in context to yield knowledge, knowledge in context to yield understanding, understanding in context to yield - God forbid - wisdom. This is how value will be added to raw data to generate wealth in our information society.

A second view is in terms of clutter and complexity. Information overload is often described as *the* basic problem of the post-industrial society. In the industrial society, we had too little energy; in the post-industrial society, we have too MUCH information. However, this is like surveying a huge smörgåsbord and complaining about overload because we can not eat it all. In our outside-in education, in which being educated is viewed as stuffing oneself full of facts, we are overwhelmed by the fact that we could not even assimilate the contents of our local library in our lifetime.

DATABASE	VERSION 1.0	PROGRAM
01 NOTES		FACTFINDER
02 QUOTES		FACTFINDER
03 SOURCES		FILE
04 RESOURCES		FILE
05 IMAGES		MACPAINT
06 STORIES		FACTFINDER
07 LISTEN		FACTFINDER
08 READ		FACTFINDER
09 SPEAK		MACWRITE
10 WRITE		MACWRITE

FIGURE 11-1   EVOLUTION OF THE SILICLONE

The inside-out teacher, who views education as growing from the inside out, welcomes our enriched environment.   One of the few conclusions we psychologists have reached is that so-called stupid people grow up in impoverished environments and so-called smart people grow up in enriched environments. Beneath the pseudo-problem of information overload, however, there lurks a real problem of management of complexity. (Strategies for managing complexity will be discussed in Section 15.4.) Our enriched objective world enables us to build a subtle, sophisticated subjective map of it.

However, true complexity must be distinguished from mere clutter. The siliclone can be viewed as a means of removing the clutter of content so that one can see more clearly. Thus memorizing lists - lists of favorite quotes and anecdotes, lists of books read and films seen, lists of lists - is subcontracted out to siliclone. Scot prefers to be listless. The brain is not designed to play trivial pursuits - it is designed to select a nutritious, balanced diet from the smörgäsbord of information and to integrate that information into a full and accurate subjective map of the objective world.[2]

A third view is in terms of means and ends. The 'sili' in 'siliclone' was originally seen as referring, of course, to silicon. However, it is beginning to carry an additional 'meaning'. We are all familiar with people who are not so much stupid as silly. Silliness refers to ends whereas stupidity refers to means. Silly people use perfectly good means to trivial ends. The Siliclone is 'silly' in this sense. It has powerful means but no worthy ends. The capacity for meaningful ends is the domain of natural intelligence. We should subsume means to ends by sub-contracting out means to our respective siliclones, and focusing on worthy ends.

---

2   I recently heard of someone who prided himself on having seen every Seinfeld episode many times and being able to recite the dialogue. Such information is already available on the internet - all I need is the URL to find it when necessary and the judgment to evaluate its worth.

The idea of the siliclone is part of the zeitgeist - the spirit of our times. Various writers, using various very different languages, propose such an innovation (see Figure 11-2 for some examples). Most of the major scholars who have inspired me while writing this book have websites, whether provided by their university, created by themselves, or by their "fans". A sample of their URLs is provided later in Figure 15-4. More and more people are creating "Blogs" informing us about their day-by-day lives and commenting on the news and cultural products (reviews of books and films). Such Personal Pages will become more and more numerous as people recognize the need to establish a web presence by uploading their minds on to the internet.

11.3 THE ENHANCED PERSON
- ANDY CLARK

Andy Clark (1957-   ) argues that our human destiny is, paradoxically, to become a cyborg [CLARK]. Our very plastic brains are designed to merge with media. The really important media mergers are thus not AOL with Warner but the merger of the mind with media. We think quite literally outside the box. The system which does the thinking is not the brain, as most cognitive psychologists have assumed, but the integrated system of the brain and its various extensions. (This is why I never note any half hour period devoted to "pure" thinking when I keep a record of time spent communicating. There is always some accompanying communication act. This is why I don't know what I think until I hear what I say or read what I write. This is why my true education began when I started teaching rather than when I was "*learning*".)

As soon as the little girl picks it (A Young Lady's Illustrated Primer) up and opens the front cover for the first time, it will imprint that child's face and voice into its memory --
Bonding with her. Yes, I see.
And therefore it will see all events and persons in relation to that girl, using her as a datum from which to chart a psychological terrain, as it were. Maintenance of that terrain is one of the book's primary processes. Whenever the child uses the book, then, it will perform a sort of dynamic mapping from the database on to her particular terrain.

Neal Stephenson, THE DIAMOND AGE, Page 106

--- there'll be so much material about my life, they could make a virtual replica of me, indistinguishable from the real thing.
Josh Harris, **We Live in Public** quoted in Charles Platt, *Streaming video*. **Wired**, 8(11), November 2000, Page 166

--the complete causa-sui project: to create all by oneself a spiritually, intellectually, and physically similar replica of oneself: the perfectly individualized self-perpetuation or immortality symbol.

Ernest Becker, **The Denial of Death**, Page 232

Bill Gates' software engineers are working on ways to load every photo you take, every letter you write -- in fact, your every memory and experience -- into a surrogate brain that never forgets anything.

Quote from **New Scientist** in
Globe and Mail, 27 December 2002, Page A18

It is called a penseive, said Dumbledore. I sometimes find, and I'm sure you know the feeling, that I have simply too many thoughts and memories crammed in to my mind.
Er, said Harry, who couldn't truthfully say that he had ever felt anything of the sort.
At these times, said Dumbledore, indicating the stone basin, *I use the penseive. One simply siphons the excess thoughts from one's mind, pours them into the basin, and examines them at one's leisure. It becomes easier to spot patterns and links, you understand, when they are in this form.*

J. K. Rowling, **Harry Potter and the Goblet of Fire**, Pages 518-519

FIGURE 11-2   SIGHTINGS OF THE SILICLONE

Merlin Donald argues that the mind is assumed not only to be empty (tabula rasa) but to be isolated (**tabula isola**). That is, we tend to think of thinking as the function of a single mind [DONALD]. However, whether language and thought evolved because we were hunters or because we were hunted, it evolved in a social context. Language and thought evolved to serve the group. It evolved for cooperation not conflict. Our cognition subsequently was adapted to serve the individual, and to fuel conflict between individuals. However, we must recognize its positive social origins.

Andy Clark challenges the tabula isola assumption in another sense. Over historical time, we have invented extrasomatic tools to extend the nervous system by storing and transmitting information outside our bodies. Thus, the cultural evolution which has recently supplemented the biological evolution involves the mind "thinking" with its extensions. The brain is relatively inept on its own. When confronted with a problem as simple as multiplying two two-digit numbers, we find ourselves reaching for pen and paper.[3]   Clark would thus agree that the Big Story of historical time, as told in chapters 1 through 8, is the co-evolution of the person and media as extensions.

However, whereas I view this process as the piggy-backing of cultural evolution on biological evolution and thus we do not differ essentially from our hunter-gatherer ancestors, Clark suggests that we are different from them. During the long period of infant dependency, our prefrontal cortex is molded by the media available to us. Our minds are not hunter-gatherer minds in new technological clothing, but are primed to merge with what media they find and what media they themselves create. Media do not simply extend minds but they

---

[3]   Albert Einstein once stated that his pencil was smarter than he was. Andy Clark once lost his laptop and experienced his loss as an amputation. Our favorite example of trapped intelligence is Steven Hawking. Without his extrasomatic devices, he would be in a nursing home cared for like a baby rather than an author of influential books [HAWKING]. ALL our intelligences would be trapped, according to Clark, without our various extrasomatic extensions.

change minds.

William Calvin wondered why brain damage affected the reading ability of his father. Surely reading, unlike speaking, is acquired culturally rather than biologically, and thus could not be affected by damage to a particular area of the brain? He concluded that "-- *reading abilities are wired up on the fly during childhood -- as we say, they are 'soft-wired' during development rather than hard-wired in the manner of instincts*" [CALVIN, Page 141]. Perhaps the various extrasomatic tools we have acquired over historical time have been so "soft-wired" into our nervous systems as extragenetic tools. They thus become part of the processing system rather than just part of the content which is processed. We learn to read and then we read to learn.

Clark proceeds to document some interesting features of the latest element in this integrated person-media cognitive system - what I have presented as the fourth generation of media, Multimedia and Internet. The internet is traditionally viewed as an anarchist system which works amazingly well despite the fact that there is no central control. Clark points out that it works well BECAUSE there is

Select one of those five cards
Stare at it for 30 seconds
Turn to the next page
You will see that I have made it disappear

no central control. And thus it is free to organize itself. It thus joins the self-organizing systems designed by Mother Nature rather than by our limited selves.

Google works better than the search engines which preceded it because it is based on this self-organization rather than by our clumsy key-word system superimposed on it. It is based on the trails left by the millions of surfers on the internet. Thus it takes you to where the best information on your topic is located, based on the fact that other people interested in this topic voted with their fingers for the best websites.

Andy Clark uses the card experiment depicted in Figure 11-3, and many other experiments, to demonstrate that our perceptual system just picks up a rough sketch of a situation. Detail is filled in only with much subsequent effort. In this case, we simply register 5 face cards and are surprised when the card we have chosen is not among the four remaining cards, which we assume are the other four cards in the original set.

FIGURE 11-3
CARD EXPERIMENT - ANDY CLARK

11.4 THE GOGGLED PERSON
- STEVE MANN

My ten top reasons why the real world is inferior to the virtual world are listed in Figure 10-1. I was just joking. Steve Mann (1962-) is serious. He has lived in the virtual world for 20 years [MANN & NIEDZVECKI]. Every morning he dons his wearable computer (**wearcomp**) apparatus before he opens his eyes and takes it off again in the evening after he closes his eyes. After graduating from MIT, he came home again to Canada, where he is a professor at the University of Toronto. His apparatus has got less and less cumbersome over those 20 years and his wife Betty has joined him in cyberspace.

He would add a number of other reasons to my top 10. One is that the virtual world is relatively less explored than the real world and he can thus, as a scientist, be a pioneer in learning about it. In described the mobile movie-studio-cum-theatre of the mind (see Section 4.3), I said that the movie theater has only one seat. I therefore have to learn to write to tell you about my home movie. Steve's theater is not as limited. His wife can watch his home movie along with him. He can show as well as tell. Betty can see the world as Steve sees it. Advantages range from the trivial - they can shop together when she remains at home - to the profound - she can empathize with him as they share experiences. Another limitation of Steve's unaided nervous system is that the record of his experience is accessible only to himself. Wearcomp can record what Steve sees and Betty can relive his experience later.[4] This record is more accurate than the record previously available to the natural brain, which is subsequently "edited" to tell a better story.

We are all participant observers in our own lives. There's a need for

---

[4]   Philippe Ramsay-Lemieux, one of my students, went to Boston to interview him. Later, Steve showed Philippe the interview from his point of view on his computer - he had been recording Philippe as Philippe was recording him.

balance between being too much a participant (*The unexamined life is not worth living*) and being too much an observer (*The unlived life is not worth examining*). Does Steve's strategy push him into the latter extreme? He is watching his own life as if it were a movie? Is he volunteering to be the eponymous hero of *The Truman Show*? Or does he gain MORE autonomy, as he claims, by being able to edit and annotate his environment, being able to survey the surveillers, and being able to learn by being as well as by doing?

Howard Rheingold points out that Steve Mann paradoxically uses his wearable technology to *reduce* the information he is exposed to [RHEINGOLD 2003]. Upset by the pollution of our environment by advertisements, Mann arranges to wear technology which will remove them. The management of complexity once again involves the elimination of clutter.

11.5 THE IMPLANTED PERSON - KEVIN WARWICK

Kevin Warwick (1954-   ) is a cyborg. On 20 April 1998, he had a silicon chip inserted into his arm. It is contained in a glass capsule 23 millimeters long and 3 millimeters wide. In conjunction with some equipment built into his office, the chip greets him as it opens his door, turns on lights when he enters a room and turns off lights when he leaves it, and keeps a tally of the mail in his e-mail box [WARWICK].

Before that date, Kevin Warwick was relatively obscure, despite the fact that, as a professor of cybernetics at the University of Reading, England, he had acquired over 4 million dollars in grants and had written over 400 papers. He is now famous. Many of his academic colleagues are critical of his fame. It's okay perhaps for a scholar to be a visionary but he is suspected of becoming also a missionary. Scholars don't like the missionary position.

On 14 March 2002 at 8:30 a. m., Warwick moved into the next phase of his research (code-named Cyborg 2.0). This time the chip is not only implanted but linked to his nervous system. This time, his wife Irena will be similarly equipped. This time, they want to explore various questions previously considered only in scifi novels. Can emotions such as intoxication, anger and lust be read by the computer in terms of patterns of nervous excitement? Can states like intoxication and sexual arousal also be read? Can these recorded emotions and states be beamed back to the chip in the body and experienced all over again? Can those emotions be communicable between two people? Warwick plans to go to New York to see if the desire he experiences in New York will be felt by his wife back home in London? Will they be able to read one another's mind and communicate by telepathy? Will the dream of direct communication with no mediation even by the first generation of speech be realized? Will it change forever what it means to be human? Will this spell the end of the faked orgasm?

It is difficult to find out what answers are emerging from this research. We would assume that Kevin Warwick has a huge presence on the internet. However, his official web site - *www.kevinwarwick.org.uk* - has disappeared into cyberspace, leaving no forwarding address. There is no shortage of places to go to read *about* him - *Kevin Warwick Watch* makes sighting forms available to keep track of his activities, *Register* documents the adventures of Captain Cyborg, and there are countless interviews of him and articles on him in the various hip magazines. They alas have axioms to grind. It's weird to be wired.

They have two children, neither of whom have as yet been fitted with a chip. However, a family in Florida has. A Verichip, designed by Applied Digital Solutions specifically for this purpose, has been implanted in the shoulders of Derek and Leslie Jacobs and their son Jeffrey [GROSSMAN]. The chip contains their medical records so that appropriate medical procedures can be used in an emergency. A device called the Digital Angel can trace them and read their vital signs. Pets have been fitted with chips, so that their owners can avoid quarantine by demonstrating that the pets have had the required shots. The implanted chips also help find them if lost. The next obvious step is to have chips inserted in children, so that they can be found if lost or kidnapped. This is the thin edge of the chip which could lead to implanted chips being more acceptable.

11.6   IS THIS THE FIFTH GENERATION?

Those four visions of the cyborg represent four more and more "intimate" mergers of the person and the machine, or alternatively more and more invasive uses of technology. The first - my vision - is the least invasive, and the last - Warwick's vision - is the most invasive.

Warwick's vision, in which chips are implanted in the body, is what many of my students have in mind when they talk about a fifth generation of media. They interpret my resistance to this vision as due to a certain squeamishness about implanted chips. They are right. I plan to leave the planet with the same number of holes in my body as I came in with. Many of my students are tattooed and pierced and don't share my concern about the invasiveness of implanting.

However, I do not concede that this is a fifth generation of media. Whereas the chip is technically inside the body, it is still essentially extrasomatic. This is certainly not the next step in evolution as many people imagine. Evolution is a slow, dignified process from the inside out. It is not affected by ramming in a chip from the outside in. The children of Kevin and Irena Warwick will not be born with implanted chips any more than the children of Steve and Betty Mann will be born with wearcom helmets.

I can still deal with this vision - however reluctantly - within my 2x2 matrix of four generations of media. Whereas the vision of direct communion between people is, as discussed in the previous chapter, best considered as a return to the first generation in a lo-tech future, this vision is best discussed as the ultimate extension of the fourth generation in a hi-tech future. There is, however, a third vision that some students have in mind when claiming that there is a fifth generation. This is a vision in which the machines we create are able, by accident or intent, to get beyond our control. They are no longer extensions of our selves but entities in their own right. They have escaped my 2x2 box and may indeed constitute a fifth generation of media. Let us turn to this vision in the next chapter.

CHAPTER 12
ETERNAL FUTURES

12.1 THE QUEST FOR ETERNAL LIFE

12.2 BIOTECHNOLOGY

12.3 NANOTECHNOLOGY

12.4 CRYONICS

12.5 ARTIFICIAL LIFE

12.6 FROM IMMORTALITY TO OBSOLESCENCE

I can visualize a time in the future when we will be to robots as dogs are to humans.
Claude Shannon
THE MATHEMATICAL THEORY OF COMMUNICATION, 1949

The aim of this book is to argue that Huxley was right; that the most significant threat posed by contemporary biotechnology is the possibility that it will alter human nature and thereby move us into a "posthuman" stage of history. This is important, I will argue, because human nature exists, is a meaningful concept, and has provided a stable continuity to our experience as a species.
Francis Fukuyama, THE POSTHUMAN FUTURE, Page 7

Within fifty to a hundred years, a new class of organisms is likely to emerge. These organisms will be artificial in the sense that they will originally have been designed by humans. However they will reproduce and "evolve" into something other than their original form; they will be "alive" under any reasonable definition of the word. These organisms will evolve in a fundamentally different manner --- the pace --- will be extremely rapid --- The impact on humanity and the biosphere could be enormous, larger than the industrial revolution, nuclear weapons, or environmental pollution. We must take steps now to shape the emergence of artificial organisms.
Dayne Farmer & Alletta Bellin, 1992

12.1 THE QUEST FOR ETERNAL LIFE

The futures in the previous chapter were based on information technology. Let us look now at futures based on **biotechnology**. The extensions of the person proposed in the previous chapter were based on the fact that, when we cross the digital divide, we can consider the merger of the person and the machine, because we both use the same type of energy. With the third and fourth generations of media, the energy is no longer physical but electrical, as is the energy of the human body. The shift from infotechnology to biotechnology takes this a step further. It proposes that our machines may be constructed out of the same material - genes.

The shift from atoms to bits is controversial but this further shift from bits to genes is much more controversial. Indeed, my students are so comfortable at their side of the digital divide that I can't even get a debate going, as I used to a decade ago, between the **technophiles**, who love new information technology, and the **technophobes**, who hate it. Gradually those concerns abated, until now the most I can manage is a debate between advocates of the one-button mouse and the two-button mouse or between the Mac and the Windows platforms.[1] Now they are all largely technophiles. Or, at least, they all accept infotechnology as inevitable. However, they do not accept biotechnology as inevitable - they are still divided between **biophiles** and **biophobes**. They are smart enough to recognize that implanting electrodes is mere tinkering and has nothing to do with the next step in evolution. The children of Kevin Warwick and his wife will not be born with electrodes attached to their brains. However, biotechnology threatens to affect the evolutionary process (the basic theory in this book), and

---

[1]   Even this debate is petering out as the two platforms become almost indistinguishable. This is due to the blatant copying of the Mac interface by Microsoft in their Windows interface (This betrays where I stand on this issue!)

thus to change human nature (the basic constant in this book).

The arena has shifted from information technology to gene technology. Here the threats of the biophobes are louder than the opportunities of the biophiles who emphasize the positive potential of gene technology. Why have we strayed into this new arena? What has this to do with media studies? The discovery of the DNA molecule in the 1950s taught us that we are written in a code of four letters and the completion of the Human Genome Project in the 1990s has taught us the sequence of those letters. We not only store and transmit information, we ARE information.

In Chapter 1, I provided a happy beginning in compensation for the fact that life does not have a happy ending. Some people are arguing, however, that life need not have an unhappy ending. They are trying to write a life script with a happy ending. Or, rather, no ending - that you and I will live for ever. This chapter will explore whether such a script is possible or whether they have just seen too many Hollywood movies.

The Human Genome Project has been identified with all the great human quests - for the Holy Grail (the cup Jesus drank from at the Last Supper), the Philosopher's Stone (that will turn base metals into gold), the Elixir of Life (that will provide eternal life), and so on. Of those quests, the most relentlessly pursued by our species throughout our history is this search for eternal life. The Holy Grail and the Philosopher's Stone would be tossed aside as useless trinkets if they were discovered in the Fountain of Youth containing the Elixir of Life.

We are the only species that knows it is mortal and thus the only species which aspires to immortality. This is a central feature of human nature. The search for immortality has been with our species ever since we realized that we were mortal. This desire for immortality is so powerful that Ernest Becker argues, in his Pulitzer Prize book, that much of human psychology is based on the denial of death [BECKER]. The search has been conducted within the context of religion.   Much of the motivation for religion, which plays a large role in human psychology, is the promise of eternal life. We want to avoid the epitaph *"Here lies Joe Blow, all dressed up with nowhere to go."*[2]   Recently the focus for some people has shifted to science and technology, A number of disciplines - biotechnology, nanotechnology, cryonics, and artificial life - hold out some promise of extending life and, perhaps, even extending it indefinitely. Let us look at each of those disciplines in turn.

12.2 BIOTECHNOLOGY

The big breakthrough in biotechnology was, of course, the breaking of the genetic code by Watson, Crick, and Franklin in 1953 [WATSON JA]. They told us that we are written in four letters - ACGT - arranged in pairs around a double helix. This discovery triggered the Human Genome Project to write the sequence of those pairs. This project was completed in record time - partly because of the improvement in technology in the interval, and partly because of the race between public and private teams. The Human Genome Project to write our code was touted like the project to land one of us on the moon as a *"great leap for mankind"*. The lay-person tends to experience a great anti-climax. S/he was

---

[2]   Perhaps our fascination with vampires (*Buffy the Vampire-Slayer* lasted for seven seasons and became the focus of much scholarly research) may be largely due to the fact that they were reputed to be immortal. Scholars argue that Buffy fascinates as a blonde teenager who is not the victim in the horror movie. However, Buffy the Badguy-Slayer would not have penetrated our consciousness so fully if she was slaying those with only a mortal life to lose.

encouraged by the media to have unrealistic expectations and subsequently abandoned by the media when the exciting race was over and the hard detailed work began.

The genetic code is a language. A language is a hierarchy of units plus rules for combining units at one level to create meaningful units at the next level. That is, there are rules of vocabulary to combine phonemes (roughly corresponding to letters) into morphemes (roughly corresponding to words); rules of grammar to combine morphemes into sentences; and rules of logic to combine sentences into discourses (see Figure 6-1). So far, we have simply identified the letters and the order in which they appear. We have not learned the rules of vocabulary, grammar, and logic, and thus do not know which biological morphemes, sentences, and discourses make sense.

Primitive as our knowledge is, we have already had a number of surprises. We have surprisingly few genes - 30,000 to 40,000. Some varieties of rice by contrast have 65,000 genes. Unlike us, rice can't move around to avoid their enemies and must develop chemical strategies. There is a surprisingly little difference between our set of genes and those of our closest biological neighbors - we share 95% with the chimpanzee. Even more surprizing is the finding that we share certain genes with very primitive forms of life. The function of most genes is to create proteins. .However, some genes, called **homeobox genes**, which regulate the behavior of other genes, are common to all forms of life [RIDLEY]. The discovery of those genes forces us to reconsider the nature of the mind and of evolution. In *How the Mind Works*, Steven Pinker anchors mind in the brain [PINKER 1997]; in *The Birth of the Mind*, Gary Marcus now anchors the brain in the genes [MARCUS]. Darwin's principle of natural selection implies that evolution is a gradual process (*evolution by creeps*) as opposed to a series of sudden changes (*evolution by jerks*). A slight change in one of those homeobox genes can cause a dramatic cascade of effects which could result in a new species with no "missing links" as would be implied by gradual evolution [SCHWARTZ J].

Much of the discussion so far in the popular press about biotechnology has focused on **cloning**. Although the suddenness of the announcement of the cloning of a mammal - Dolly, the Scottish sheep - was alarming (we didn't know that things had gone so far so quickly), cloning is not our major concern with respect to biotechnology. Dolly is simply a delayed twin of her "mother". Twins we can deal with. A mother could raise her clone as her child and no one would notice (some argue that it is already happening).

In her sophisticated and sensitive exploration of the ethical issues raised by biotechnology, Margaret Somerville points out, however, that cloning raises problems for the person cloned [SOMERVILLE].   Much of the trauma of adolescence is based on the need to differentiate oneself from one's parents.[3] This will be much more difficult when the child is NOT differentiated genetically from one of the parents. This differentiation is complicated by the fact that parents often have, consciously or unconsciously, certain expectations for their children. Adolescence is a process of throwing away the various life scripts written by parents and writing one's own script. Imagine a script in which you are expected to relive the life of a parent and this time do it right. If you are cloned to replace a beloved child who has died, then the script would be even more constraining.

Cloning also poses other identity problems for the clone.   I recently saw my birth certificate for the first time. Unlike those other pieces of paper - my diplomas, someone finally asked to see it. It was a relief to see that there were

---

[3]   Summer camps are viewed by some people as a first step towards what they call an "adultectomy". Many camps ban cell phones, laptops with internet access, and even visiting days to facilitate the child's early steps towards autonomy.

two names on it that I recognized as the two people I have always assumed are my parents and I'm also reasonably sure, given the times and the state of human knowledge, that I was created in the old-fashioned way. However, our new technologies may create some identity problems for people in the future. In the case of the clone, there would be only one name on that birth certificate (assuming that the test-tube is not mentioned). In some cases, as Preston Manning pointed out in his campaign against funding for some aspects of biotechnology, there could be five names - sperm donor, egg donor, surrogate mother, adoptive mother, and adoptive father.[4]

There are also certain possible medical problems. Dolly had arthritis and died at a very early age - even for sheep. Perhaps we have to learn how to reset the biological clock so that clones are not born as adults. The prospect of creating chimera - part human, part animal - is another concern of passing genes back and forth between species. Such freakish developments are due to our failure to totally understand the complex code we are written in. However horrendous those problems, they remain problems simply for that single person.

However, there are aspects of biotechnology research which threaten not the individual but the species. Stem-cell research promises the possibility of growing organs to replace those which have failed. Since stem-cells have not yet decided what they are going to be when they grow up, it is possible to persuade them to grow up as a liver or a heart or whatever is currently in demand. Some fear that an error in replicating stem cells could be introduced into the human gene pool. This would affect our species as a whole rather than simply an individual member of our species. Some scientists argue that we should indeed do so. However, after seeing how our species has screwed up nature, we should

---

[4]   No doubt, parents in the future will reassure their children that they were carefully planned, whereas most people were mere accidents. Just as now adopted children are assured that they were chosen whereas natural parents had to take whatever came along.

be very apprehensive about any proposal to tamper with human nature.

The argument is tempting. Biotechnology is providing us with a more precise knowledge of the relative contributions of nature and nurture. It is opening up that conception-day gift and telling us more precisely what it contains. It warns us that this gift may contain a bomb. It may be a time bomb set to go off at a particular time regardless of what happens, or may go off if you live long enough (new diseases are emerging due to increased longevity), or it could go off only if jostled (some suggest that the Parkinson's disease in Michael J. Fox was triggered by some environmental event, since other members of a cast also got Parkinson's). The relationship between the language-acquisition device (LAD) and language-acquisition support system (LASS) was discussed above in Section 2.2. The Lads and Lasses continue dancing, but now we are beginning to know the tune.

Since the mutant gene which "causes" Lou Gehrig disease (ALS - Anyotropic Lateral Sclerosis) has been identified, some argue that we should cut it out or, more dramatically, abort children with it. There goes Lou Gehrig disease but, oops, there goes Lou Gehrig.[5] Not to mention Morrie Schwartz and Stephen Hawking. Eliminate Parkinson's and there goes - not Parkinson, he's the physician who described it - but Muhammed Ali, Michael J. Fox, and Pope John Paul 11. Fox is working hard to eliminate it and retroactively himself. The issue is further complicated by the fact that there is very seldom a single gene-disease correspondence. We don't know what else is being removed since the gene could be an element in a complex system.

The assumption that there is a direct one-to-one correspondence between gene and disease is extended to include other phenomena. Thus people talk about

---

[5]   Between 1925 -1939, in his career as first baseman for the New York Giants, He hit 493 home runs - a record for a first baseman. He was the first athlete to have his jersey retired.

genes for homosexuality, for leadership, for obesity, for violence - or whatever the person is trying to explain. (There has been an attempt to explain the tragic history of the Kennedy family to a risk-taking gene which runs in the family.) This enables critics to take a cheap shot of dismissing genetic research as a process not of explanation but of explaining away phenomena by postulating a gene for it. The instinct theory of William McDougall, which was away ahead of its times, was dismissed on the grounds that he explained away human behaviors by postulating instincts for each of them.   His promising line of research was thus cut off.

The breaking of the human genome raises the prospect of controlling our own evolution. If we can find and control the genes which are responsible for aging, then we may be able to slow down or even stop the process.   Already, we know how to coax stem cells to become human organs. By replacing failing organs with those manufactured spare parts, we can theoretically live for ever. Ray Kurzweil argues that before the year 2099 *"Life expectancy is no longer a viable term in relation to intelligent beings"* [KURZWEIL, Page 280}.

12.3 NANOTECHNOLOGY

An alternative strategy to growing spare parts is to repair them. This has the advantage of saving the trauma of an operation in which the defective organ is torn out and another one is inserted. One simply repairs the defective organ in situ.   Hope for such a scenario is offered by the emerging techniques of **nanotechnology**. This technology was inspired by a speech by Richard

Feynman, a Nobel-Prize-winning physicist, in 1959, entitled *There's plenty of room at the bottom* [FEYNMAN]. Feynman encouraged us to consider the ultimate in biomimicry, the building of molecules out of atoms, the basic building blocks of nature. Less than 30 years later, K. Eric Drexler introduced the scientific community to nanotechnology [DREXLER] and Grant Fjermedal, a journalist, introduced the general public to the discipline by interviewing Drexler and his various colleagues and published *The Tomorrow Makers: A Brave New World of Living-Brain Machines* [FJERMEDAL]. They invited us into a world of very very small machines, which were small enough to travel through the body and intelligent enough collectively to fix it.

After the initial excitement, the book was largely dismissed as alarmist. The *"Tomorrow"* of the title was far in the future and may never ever arrive. However, it's baaack.[6] Vast resources of public and private organizations are being poured into research on nanotechnology. If we can mimic nature using her basic materials, then we can create anything which nature creates - precious metals, powerful computers, human organs, and human beings. Such molecular manufacturing can be based on arrangements of atoms which have been demonstrated to work over thousands of years. Those mini-machines would perform their functions collectively rather than individually, like swarms of bees or colonies of ants. Intelligent functions would emerge as unintelligent elements worked together. Herds of animals, flocks of birds, and schools of fish have

---

[6]   One sure sign is that Michael Crichton has written a book about it. He invariably writes a techno-thriller around each new technology which may possibly get out of control. *Jurassic Park* is his take on cloning getting out of control - what if dinosaurs could be resurrected from genes preserved in amber? *Prey* is his more recent techno-thriller based on nanotechnology getting out of control - what if those nanotechnology entities get out of control? [CRICHTON]. The concern is based on exponential growth. Nature uses exponential growth - the single cell with which we all started splits in two, each of which splits in two again, each of which splits in two, and so on. However, nature knows when to stop. We may not know how to tell self-replicating organisms we create when to stop.

intelligent strategies for survival which are far beyond the competence of individual animals, birds, and fish.

12.4 CRYONICS

The promise of eternal life offered by biotechnology and nanotechnology may be realized for our children or our grandchildren. However, it may be too late for you and me. Unless, that is, we can preserve our selves until their potential is realized. Such a possibility is raised by **cryonics** - the process of freezing the body and re-activating it later, presumably after the cure for the disease it was just about to die of had been discovered.

This process has taken place successfully in a number of movies – in *Demolition Man*, the hero (Sylvester Stallone) and the villian (Wesley Snipes) have been cryonically frozen and revived to fight again, and in *Austin Powers: International Man of Mystery*, Mike Myers and HIS rival, Dr. Evil, have also been frozen and dethawed. - but probably not yet in real life. Many people however still aspire to eternal life by this method. The extropians (based in California, of course) plan to preserve only their heads - it's cheaper and, after all, that's the only important part. The body is just an appendix to keep the brain from dragging on the ground. Some of them have a dotted line tattooed around their necks with instructions *cut here*.

Cryonics certainly is alive and well as a plot device. Roald Dahl has a short story in which an abusive husband dies and has his head cryonically preserved by his long-suffering wife. She is thus able to verbally abuse him without any danger of retaliation. Dennis Potter, the English script-writer who has had a long series of brilliant plays on BBC - *The Singing Detective*, *Lipstick on my Collar*, etc. - ended his career with *Cold Lazarus*. A script-writer has his mind uploaded on to a computer, his head cryonically frozen, and his mind downloaded back into his brain when it is revived a few hundred years later. Some sleazy producer decides that his memories would make an interesting and lucrative TV series. Anyone who has seen *The Singing Detective* can imagine how annoyed the head would be at being powerless (since bodiless) to do anything to stop that.

Cryonics appears in the news from time to time. There was a recent debate among the children of Ted Williams about the plan to have him cryonically preserved as a source for cloned baseball sluggers. A documentary about Timothy Leary in which Tim ostensibly has his head frozen and ends with Tim smiling out at us from a glass refrigerator, enjoying what some say is Tim's Last Laugh. There are recurring rumors about the resurrection of Walt Disney whose whole body is reputed to have been frozen. However, you should not count on staying around forever by this means.

The major problem is that, whereas the body may survive freezing and thawing, the mind would not. One proposed solution is to upload the mind to a computer before freezing and download the mind from the computer after thawing.[7] In this metaphor of person as computer, the body is the hardware and the mind is the software. This transferring a mind from one body to another or to the same body at a later date is like uploading and downloading the contents of a hard disk from one computer to another. Body and mind are however more intimately entangled than hardware and software. The body is not simply a

---

[7]   Note that, whereas I hope to upload only a distillation of my mind at www.siliclone.com, they hope to upload the whole mind. Their project is more impressive. However, I wonder if it is a more worthwhile project. He's uploading the oats whereas I'm providing the liqueur.

container which can be emptied and filled at will. Indeed, they were separated only conceptually by René Descartes. Some have suggested that he did this - not because he believed they could be separated - but simply to avoid attack by the Church. He could say that his comments were not sacrilegious, because he was simply talking about the body and not about the mind (soul, spirit, whatever) which was the domain of the church.

This divorce has been a disaster for both the mind and the body. The body is looked down at - literally and metaphorically - as a lesser partner by the conning tower of the mind.[8] It can be abused and misused, disregarded and discarded. Many respondents to a poll conducted by the Whole Earth Review answered "*yes*" to the question "*Is the body Obsolete?*" [WHOLE EARTH REVIEW]. I was surprised the question was even asked far less answered in the affirmative. The mind, on the other hand, is viewed as sacred and beyond the reach of science. It's only recently that we have been able to look mind straight in the eye.

12.5 ARTIFICIAL LIFE

The results of the very promising artificial intelligence movement have been disappointing. There are some success stories. Big Blue did indeed defeat the world champion in chess. Diagnostic programs have - by distilling the

---

[8]   When I decided after fifteen years of intensive academic study to get out of my mind and back to my senses, I went to Esalen Institute, the first Growth Center. I was involved in a session in which we were talking through our feet all together in a circle. My feet were complaining "*So neglected - walked on all day - so far away*". Another member of the group said "*So far away from where? You academics think you live in your heads. The body is just a device to keep your mind from dragging on the ground.*"

expertise of a number of doctors - outperformed any single doctor. However, this success is within a limited domain - the simple worlds of an 8 x8 board and of a set of if-then statements. Artificial intelligence is notoriously dumb when dealing with simple real-life situations like ordering a meal in a restaurant. Emphasis has shifted from artificial intelligence (AI) to intelligence amplification (IA) as exemplified above in Chapter 11 with the various cyborg futures.

The artificial intelligentsia has had more success however in shifting their strategy from building intelligence from the outside in to growing intelligence from the inside out. Or rather they set the initial conditions and rules and let it grow itself. Biological systems, unlike physical systems, are self-organizing. Neither you nor they need to know what their goal is at the beginning. Kevin Kelly, in summarizing this research on **artificial life**, calls his book ominously *Out of Control* [KELLY].

Stephen Wolfram bought a decade of time off from the university by writing a brilliant program called *Mathematica* and thus becoming a dot.com millionaire. He devoted the time to doing research which he summarized in a huge book entitled *A New Kind of Science* [WOLFRAM]. In that book, he demonstrated that the most complex systems in nature can be generated from applying a few simple rules to a simple initial situation. The only catch is - was - that those rules must be applied over thousands of iterations. We could not - until recently - plagiarize nature by replicating those thousands of generations of evolution. The computer has now finally become powerful enough to do so.[9]

He entitles his book *A New Kind of Science* because traditional science makes a mathematical model of complex phenomena in the hope of understanding

---

[9]   Just as the microscope makes the too-small large enough to study and the telescope brings the too-far near enough to study, so the computer makes the too-complex simple enough to study.

it.[10]   He proposes that we instead represent our theory as initial simple conditions and rules and let the computer "evolve" the complex system. In passing control over to the computer, however, things can get *"out of control"*. Biological systems are self-organizing and they could very well organize a self that we do not want to share our planet with. However, it would be too late - you can't stuff the Genie back into the bottle.

---

[10]   This has caused at least one scientist to say: *This phenomena is too complex for us to understand it. Let's make a model of it. Now we have TWO things we don't understand!*

12.6 FROM IMMORTALITY TO OBSOLESCENCE

In pursuing this goal of immortality, we should remain aware of the various cautionary tales in our mythology. Icarus in his search for flight, Prometheus in his search for fire, and Midas in his search for gold, were all warned to be careful about what they wished for. They were all punished for their hubris in playing God. Icarus fell when he flew too close to the sun, Prometheus was chained to a rock and had his liver pecked out daily, Midas starved to death because he could not *eat* gold. Those stories have been updated for our times. *Frankenstein* was subtitled *Prometheus Unbound.* In the film *Bedazzled,* the hero offered wishes by the Devil gets more than he wished for, because he failed to be precise. The message is invariably "*whether you are looking for God or for gold, when offered a wish, read the small print; when you make a wish, hire a lawyer to write the small print*" There are a long series of wish jokes with similar outcomes. Here is my personal favorite:

Three men - an Englishman, a Frenchman, and a Scotsman - are crawling through the desert, on the verge of dying of thirst. A Genie suddenly appears, saying "*Normally, I grant three wishes. However, since there are three of you, I'll grant you one wish each.*"

The Englishman says "*I wish I was back in a London pub with a beautiful brunette by my side and a pint of beer in front of me.*" With a whoosh, he was gone back home to London.

The Frenchman says "*I wish I was back in a Paris sidewalk café with a beautiful blonde by my side and a carafe of wine in front of me.*" With a whoosh, he was gone back home to Paris.

The Scotsman looks sadly from side to side, and says "*I wish I had my friends back.*" Whoosh. Whoosh.

The means of attaining immortality are further off than we think. However, we may also want to consider the end. The added years will be added on at the end and they may not be the best years. As our facilities decline, we may welcome the opportunity to get out of here. There is no point in solving dying if you don't also solve aging. Everlasting life is not equivalent to eternal youth. We may opt for the short happy life over the long miserable life. Quality of life may trump quantity of life. Since we can die only by accident, we may lead excessively careful lives. A long miserable careful life, walking on eggs, may not be what we had in mind during our quest for eternal life.

At a social level too, it could be something of a disaster. The option of eternal life would, no doubt, not be universally available. It would of course be available initially to the rich and powerful. The poor and powerless could very well be farmed for spare parts. The urban myth of the person waking up after a sexual encounter with a prostitute missing an organ persists because of such a fear. Decay and Death are the great levelers. Who has not taken some delight in the fact that some fabulously rich man is bald (with all his power and money he is no more able to control this than me) or some heiress dies (she can't inherit immortality). The planet is over-crowded already. It will be standing-room only if no one dies but others continue to be born.

Ironically, our pursuit of immortality could result in our obsolescence. Many members of the artificial intelligentsia - for example, Marvin Minsky, Hans Moravec, Ray Kurzweil - have made statements like that at the beginning of the chapter by Claude Shannon. We will be succeeded by superior entities which we created and which may condescend to keep us as pets. No doubt (I hope) they are talking tongue-in-cheek, while still secretly rejoicing in the fact that they have tongues and cheeks. However, if so many so-brilliant people have this vision of our future, we cannot dismiss it as a possibility. We certainly can't say that we have not been warned. My students who insist on talking of a fifth generation (the most persistent was Kieran Crilly, who persisted in the argument well after the course was over) are indeed right. This is very definitely a fifth generation, this is beyond my 2x2 box representing the co-evolution of the person and media as extensions. The artificial intelligentsia is thinking outside my box.

Whether our species will become obsolete is open to debate. However, one thing we know for sure is that each of us individually will become obsolete. In the film - *What to do in Denver when Dead* - the protagonist is offered Afterlife Advice. Here is some Beforedeath Advice. Forget about the afterlife (If you want a happy ending, go to the movies). Focus on this life. That you know for sure. No point in being distracted by the dim prospect of an afterlife into killing time in this life in your hurry to get to that life. This is just suicide on the installment plan. One thing you know almost for sure is that you will become obsolete. Plan your obsolescence. Try to leave something behind which is your contribution (however small) to the accumulated wisdom of our species.

CHAPTER 13
DYSTOPIA AND UTOPIA

13.1 BETWEEN DYSTOPIA AND UTOPIA

13.2 HUXLEY'S CARROT AND ORWELL'S STICK

13.3 THE MATRIX - HUXLEY MEETS ORWELL?

13.4 DEMOCRATIC SOCIETY - PERSONAL POWER

13.5 LEISURE SOCIETY - PLAY

13.6 ABUNDANT SOCIETY - PLENTY

What if everything is an illusion and nothing exists?
In that case, I definitely overpaid for my carpet.
Woody Allen

I tell them I'm doing fine
Watching shadows on the wall.
John Lennon

We're interested in mythology, theology, and to a certain extend, higher-level
mathematics. All are ways human beings try to answer bigger questions, as well
as The Big Question. If you are going to do epic stories, you should concern
yourself with those issues. People might not understand all the allusions in the
movie, but they understand the important ideas. We wanted to make people think,
engage their minds a bit.
Larry and Andy Wachowski
(Directors of *The Matrix*, *Matrix Reloaded*, and *Matrix Revolutions*)

Literacy remains even now the basis and model of all programs of industrial
mechanization: but, at the same time, locks the minds and senses of its users in
the mechanical and fragmentary matrix that is so necessary to the maintenance of
mechanized society.
Marshall McLuhan
UNDERSTANDING MEDIA, 1964

13.1 BETWEEN DYSTOPIA AND UTOPIA

The Big Story of historical time, told in Chapters 1-8, is the "invention" of the agricultural society, the industrial society, the information society and their corresponding generations of media. We have also imagined other societies - bad societies (**dystopias**) and good societies (**utopias**). They are based, respectively, on the two major human emotions with respect to the future - fear and hope. Those emotions will play a significant role in the determination of our individual and collective futures.

The two most famous dystopias are described by Aldous Huxley in *Brave New World* [HUXLEY 1932] and George Orwell in *1984* [ORWELL]. We will discuss those two alternative visions of a grim future (Section 13.2) and a more modern dystopia, presented in the *Matrix* movie trilogy, which could be considered as Huxley meets Orwell in Cyberspace (Section 13.3).

Whereas there are many dystopian novels, there are few utopian novels. In a perfect society, there is no conflict and thus no story. However, there have been many attempts to create utopian societies in the real world. There were two basic strategies - go back to a pre-industrial society and go forward to a post-industrial society. The beatniks of the 1950s dropped out of the industrial society; the hippies of the 1960s created alternative places to drop in. The former strategy is not of much interest here. Our species has been there, done that.

I spent a decade as a hippie in the Gatineau pursuing the pre-industrial option. We soon found out why the agricultural society yielded to the industrial society, why people moved from the country to the city. The simple life on the farm was back-breaking, frustrating and boring.[1]   Many utopian hippie

---

[1]   On my latest visit, the few remaining members of our idyllic community were exhausted because they had worked all day slaughtering, de-feathering, and dis-emboweling 125 chickens. They would like to have done more but a fox had done it for them. Later in the evening, they

communities foundered on the failure to realize the great human capacity for boredom. After a (very short) while, the planting of crops and the raising of livestock gets boring. Escape-from-boredom contortions - going to city for entertainment, sleeping around, etc. - lead to the disintegration of the community. The world was not brave enough or new enough. T. C. Boyle describes the disintegration of such a community in his recent novel *Drop City* [BOYLE].

People drifted back into the city and on to the post-industrial option. Stewart Brand, editor of the back-to-the-land bible - the *Whole Earth Catalog*, went on to write a book about the Media Lab at MIT [BRAND]. Timothy Leary, a hippie guru (*tune in, turn on, drop out*) shifted from better living through chemistry to better living through technology. Some promises of the utopian vision of such post-industrial gurus were personal power, play, and plenty. They were embodied in utopian visions of the Democratic Society - Personal Power (Section 13.4), the Leisure Society - Play (Section 13.5) and the Abundant Society – Plenty (Section 13.6).

Aldous Huxley wrote a utopia - *Island* [HUXLEY 1962] – as well as his famous dystopia. He makes the point that a dystopia is often simply a utopia that went sour. They go sour because of some aspect of human nature which had not been considered in the design of the utopia. Indeed, the whole idea of *designing* a society may be contrary to human nature. A recent film - *Vanilla Sky* - explores how dreams can become nightmares. Certain circumstances arouse the sleeping giant of the unconscious and it creates its havoc just on the edge of our awareness. In *Humanity:A Moral History of the Twentieth Century*, Jonathan Glover describes our most recent century as the bloodiest of all [GLOVER]. A major contribution has been the utopian visions of Russian, Chinese, and Cambodian

---

found that a bear had wiped out three of their hives. They had no energy left for conversation, beyond *"What have you been doing?"* *"I wrote a book."* *"But you've already written books!"* *"At least I'm writing different books - you've been ploughing the same field!"*

leaders who killed millions of their own citizens in pursuit of their dream society. Human nature could not deal with the absence of private property, constraint on human autonomy, and allegiance to a group larger than family or tribe.

The utopians are dreaming. They must be asleep. So also are the dystopians. Those who have nightmares rather than dreams are also sleeping. Both the dreams and the nightmares are unrealistic because they don't take into consideration the reality of human nature. An attempt at describing this reality was made in Chapter 9 as a biological and psychological framework was created for the remainder of the book. The remaining chapters have looked at various visions of the future of media and evaluated them in the light of this framework.

The emphasis up till now has been on individual futures. In Chapter 10, readers are invited to consider where they prefer to place themselves along a dimension from lo-tech to hi-tech futures. In Chapter 11, readers can chose to consider what kind of cyborg they plan to be. In Chapter 12, readers can consider the extent to which they choose to take advantage of the life-extending prospects of gene technology.

Here we look at society as a whole. The balance between fear and hope in each of us influences our individual futures. We tend to be self-fulfilling prophets. However, the collective atmosphere of fear or hope will also influence society as a whole. The collective future that will emerge will fall somewhere between the two poles of dystopias and utopias presented here. There are no societies which are all bad (dystopias) or all good (utopias) because they consist of people and there are no people who are all bad or all good. However, it is useful to look at the end-points to see where real societies fall along this dimension.

13.2 HUXLEY'S CARROT AND ORWELL'S STICK

A mule can be moved by dangling a carrot in front or applying a stick from behind. The various dystopias can be considered as falling along a dimension in terms of their emphasis on the carrot or the stick. Aldous Huxley's *Brave New World* [HUXLEY 1932] emphasizes the carrot whereas George Orwell's *1984* [ORWELL] emphasizes the stick. The two major emotions with respect to the future are hope and fear. Huxley focuses on hope and Orwell focuses on fear. In our exploration of the future of media, we must realize that we can be trapped as much by hope as by fear. As many lives are ruined by what the person loves as by what the person hates. The two tragedies in life are to get what you want and not to get what you want. As argued in the previous chapter, we must be careful of what we wish for.

Both Huxley and Orwell had the foresight that media would play an important role in the future. In our current information society, the future of media IS the future of society. They also both had the insight that television - in its infancy when Orwell was writing and not yet born when Huxley was writing - would be the most important medium. Huxley however saw its role as entertaining the public whereas Orwell saw its role as threatening the public. The telephone is not a contender. A central government agency could not lull or scare the public into complacency by means of the telephone. Big Brother couldn't call us all individually.

Neil Postman argues that the carrot is more powerful than the stick [POSTMAN 1986]. It is more subtle and slips below our radar screen set up to detect autonomy-eroding influences. We don't need to be abused to death by someone else - we can amuse *ourselves* to death. Television is a latter-day soma, lulling the public into somnambulant conformity. It is the *bread and circuses* designed to distract us while the current Roman Empire is being built by the rich and powerful and non-addicted. They are weapons of mass distraction. So far, television has not gone as far as providing Christians vs Lions for "entertainment". However, reality shows like *Fear Factor* and *Dog Eats Dog* are moving in that direction. Various dystopias published since Huxley - e.g. *Rollerball, Running Man* - anticipated this trend when they imagined television shows which lured the attention of a depraved public with the prospect of the injury and death of the protagonists.

Television is autocratic (a few sources with many destinations) whereas telephone is democratic (everyone is source as well as destination). We see the same distinction with respect to the second generation of media - Print and Film. The newspaper is autocratic (a few sources with many destinations) whereas the Post Office is democratic (everyone is source as well as destination). What about the fourth generation - Multimedia and Internet? Since the internet piggy-backs on the telephone system, it is intrinsically democratic. However, as we saw in Section 7.3, there are some disturbing current signs that the autocratic forces are moving in.

In chapter 9, I argued that autonomy is a basic characteristic of the person. The above dystopias, in their different ways, limit the autonomy of the public. We can be terrorized by democratic media. The Unibomber case and the anthrax scare demonstrate that even the friendly old snail mail can be turned to malicious ends. However, it's the autocratic media which pose the major threat to human autonomy. Since the fourth generation of media - Multimedia and Internet - will play a progressively larger and larger role in the future, we must be sensitive to the attempts to piggy-back an autocratic agenda on to an essentially democratic structure.

The stick strategy persists in some recent dystopias - *Gattica*, *Handmaiden's Tale*, *Oryx and Crake*. They introduce some new themes - biotechnology in *Gattica*, feminism in *Handmaiden's Tale*, the creation of chimera in *Onyx and Crake*. However, the basic theme of human autonomy being constrained by terror and threat remains. Let us focus, however, on *The Matrix*, which introduces many new elements.

13.3 THE MATRIX - HUXLEY MEETS ORWELL?

The Matrix trilogy envisions a future in which the public is lulled into a false sense of security by machines which project virtual worlds that people mistake for reality. A number of scholarly books explore the religious, political, and technical ramifications of those movies. [e. g. IRWIN, YEFFETH]. Plato's Cave, Baudrillard's Simulcra, and other philosophical devices are enlisted to make sense of the movies. Those books are published by two small, obscure publishing companies - Benbella Books in Dallas, Texas and Open Court in LaSalle, Illinois - which have recently started publishing collections of scholarly papers on popular culture. Open Court has published collections on *Seinfeld and Philosophy*, *The Simpsons and Philosophy*, and are planning similar volumes on *Buffy, The Vampire-Slayer*, *Lord of the Rings*, and *Woody Allen*. Benbella Books has one on *Buffy, the Vampire-Slayer* in production. Such books are greeted with hoots of derision from many people in both the media and the university.

However, media studies should not dismiss them as casually. They are worthy of consideration even if only for motivational and heuristic reasons.

Consider the two collections of scholarly articles on *The Matrix* mentioned above - *Taking the Red Pill: Science, Philosophy, and Religion in The Matrix* [YEFFETH] and *The Matrix and Philosophy: Welcome to the Desert of the Real* {IRWIN}. The movie raises genuine scholarly issues, which the student would be more likely to engage in the context of the movie than if those issues were presented in a journal article. The Wachowski brothers, who wrote and directed the Matrix trilogy, are sincerely involved with those issues. They could have written articles in journals to be read by a few scholars or they could explore those issues on the screen in the guise of an action movie which will be seen (and discussed) by millions of viewers. I can, in turn, piggy-back on their work by capitalizing on the interest of the students generated by the movies.

The Matrix Trilogy could be considered as Huxley meets Orwell in cyberspace. As long as people are content to "live" in the virtual world created for their amusement by the machines, there is no problem. This is the Huxley scenario. However, if they escape from this virtual world and fight the machines in the real world, then they are hunted down and killed. This is the Orwell scenario. However, there is a new element beyond Huxley and Orwell. The forces which control us are not other members of our species but our own creations allowed to get out of control. This story has been around since Frankenstein but is updated for our times, when the scientist may still be mad but is also bad and is much more dangerous to be with.

The Matrix goes beyond the dystopian visions of Huxley and Orwell. Both Orwell and Huxley, like Pogo, argue "*We have met the enemy and it is us.*" Big Brother and the faceless creators of the "brave, new world" are other people. The enemy in *The Matrix* are machines, which we have created and allowed to get out of control. Our enemy is not us but our creations. This is the fifth generation of media my students have been warning me about. *The Matrix* is not just the same old story, as I argue in class and in Section 4.4 of this book. A new fear has emerged to haunt us.

Virtual reality/cyberspace introduces new issues into the discipline of communication studies, which make the old issues, published only a decade ago, look quite quaint [JOURNAL OF COMMUNICATION]. *The Ferment in the Field* was a Tempest in a Teapot. The central issue could be whimsically reduced to the question of whether communication studies should be a branch of political science (critical studies) or of business administration (administrative studies). The threat of dissolving into another discipline, which has always haunted the field, is now replaced by the opportunity to be the central discipline in the academy. The shift in emphasis from media to hypermedia is part of a system of correlated shifts - from a modern, industrial society, based on energy, to a post-modern, post-industrial society, based on information; from physics, a study of energy systems, to biology, a study of information systems, as the basic discipline; from a behavioristic concept of the person to a humanistic concept of the person, and so on. This paradigmatic shift also shifts communication studies from a peripheral to a central role in the university. If the argument of this book that the Big Story of historical time is the co-evolution of the person and media as extensions, then the basic project of education is for each of us to recapitulate this story in our individual lives, to acquire those tools, which are the subject matter of media studies.

13.4 DEMOCRATIC SOCIETY - PERSONAL POWER

The Canadian vision of the future (embodied in the Toronto School of Harold Innis, Marshall McLuhan, and their students, which has been used as a theoretical framework for this book) could be considered as a balance between the utopian vision of the United States and the dystopian vision of the various European schools of media studies. It seeks a balance between the gee-whiz of the United States and the oh-my-God of Europe. The optimistic attitude of the United States is best embodied in The Media Lab at MIT and *Wired* magazine, which had replaced *The Whole Earth Catalog* as the Bible of the counter-culture. They promised power to the person. As computers got smaller and smaller, faster and faster, cheaper and cheaper, people would use them to extend their nervous systems and thus enhance their personal power. This was the attitude I advocated during my short career as Superman [GARDINER 1987]. Wherever it came from, it involved using Yuppie means to Hippie ends.

As the computers merged with telecommunications to create the internet, the promise now was that personal power could be further enhanced since each person had potentially access to *all* computers. The real falls far short of this ideal. One needs a computer and an internet service provider to have access to this information. Most people on our planet don't have the means of access. Thus we move from the haves and the havenots of the industrial society to the knows and knownots of the information society. In general, it is the havenots who become the knownots because one thing they havenot is the resources to gain access.

When I met Ted Nelson in 1981, he was advocating his **Xanadu Project** [NELSON 1974, 1983]. The vision was of a large database of information to which everyone has access as source as well as destination. Let us say, I submit a recipe and you submit a short story. I access your story. Whatever, I choose to do with it - read it on the screen, save it to my hard disk to read later, print it out to read on paper - takes time. I'm charged for that time and you are paid royalties based on the time other people spend with your information. Meanwhile, I'm collecting royalties on my recipe. Even this simple, limited version of the democratic ideal - a sort of eBay for knowledge - has not yet become reality.

A number of insidious new trends raise the specter of an Orwellian future once again. The Chinese government is clamping down on internet cafes, which they see as the lairs of dissidents and anarchists. Some have argued that the Soviet Union fell apart because they could not deal with the liberating potential of the new media. More crude methods are used in developing countries. Tyrants control the public by having them inform on one another. The surveillance by neighbors is aided by surveillance by technology. Monitoring centers were discovered in Iraq. They did not have the eagerly-sought *"weapons of mass destruction"* - they were too busy making war on their own people. The Orwellian dystopia is here and now in many Third World countries.

However, it is also threatening the so-called democracies. In the wake of 9/11 comes the prospect of 24/7 surveillance. The Homeland Security Department has a huge budget to keep America safe. It's a gigantic protection racket with no limit in time as well as budget - the "war" against terrorism never ends. The vast resources of this department can be used to set up a national I. D. card system. Eighty per cent of the public agreed that the carrying of such cards should be mandatory. People are willing to sacrifice freedom for security. No one protests any more about being searched as they board a plane. This invasion of privacy is worthwhile to ensure that the plane is not flown into a high-rise building. However, this insidious process can continue to a point at which people sacrifice freedom so that freedom can be safe. *We had to destroy the village to save it*, said one U. S. officer in Vietnam. Will autonomy be destroyed by the means to protect autonomy? When does fighting for freedom shade into fighting against freedom?

Terrorism can destroy freedom directly (the dead have no freedom and the maimed have less), or it can destroy freedom indirectly by triggering an over-reaction which in turn destroys freedom. As computers become more and more powerful, they can be used to monitor telephone calls more and more fully. Thus Homeland Security funds are being directed to monitoring calls. Key words are picked up to alert the authorities to terrorist attacks. The monitoring of a citizen's private calls is, of course, illegal. However, if the U. S. government is monitoring Australian citizens and vice versa, then it slips through a legal loophole. Once again, many citizens say: monitor away, if it helps you catch the bad guys who threaten to blow up me and my family.

In Section 11.4, we met Kevin Warwick, who has had a chip implanted into his nervous system. The chip "knows" when he is entering and leaving his office. It has to know this in order to say hello when he arrives and cheerio when he leaves. Warwick is keenly aware that some central authority could use this technology to know where he is at all times. Pet owners already have such chips implanted in their pets. Thus they can be found if lost. It is a small step towards convincing parents that they should have such chips implanted in their children so that they can find them if they are lost or rescue them if they are kidnapped. Pets and kids usually want to be found. However, a criminal who can choose between imprisonment and the wearing of an implanted chip may choose the latter as the lesser of two evils. Victims of Parkinson's disease have already accepted implants which enable them to live normal lives. They don't want to be found but are willing to be found to be outside prison and the prison of Parkinson's. If the identification card does not work, it's a small step towards mandatory implants (for security, of course). Those of us who don't use a cell phone because they do not want to have an electronic leash are very apprehensive about the prospect of a built-in phone carrying calls that you can't refuse.

13.5 LEISURE SOCIETY - PLAY

Another element in the utopian vision was the idea of the leisure society. Our new electronic colleagues were not only going to provide access to information but were going to take over the work of manipulating this information. We were moving into a new Athens in which the computers were the slaves. The machines were to take over the mechanical work to set us free from mundane maintenance matters and thus free for lives of leisure, pleasure, and contemplation. I remember shocking audiences by saying: *Anyone who could be replaced by a machine should be replaced by a machine. Machines, by definition, do mechanical things. People should not be doing mechanical things.* Forty years later, we seem to be working harder than ever. What happened?

Later (Section 14.3), we will see how that vision was clouded by the hi-jacking of artificial intelligence by the corporate culture. Artificial intelligence was used to replace natural intelligence. The process of automation - simulating human functions with machines - got hijacked by the corporate culture. Emphasis shifted from labor-saving to labor-replacing. Emphasis in research on artificial intelligence (AI) shifted from understanding to control. Corporations discovered that they could save money by replacing employees with machines. Everyday, we read in the business section of the newspaper that x thousand employees lost their jobs because of such down-sizing. Unemployment was not what we had in mind when we talked about the leisure society.

We were going back to the cottage industry, which preceded the industrial society, in which people were herded into factories. However, now it would be an electronic cottage, since we were processing information rather than goods. We would be able to move back to the country, since the information can be as accessible from darkest Hudson as from London, New York, or Cupertino, California. We would be going back not just to the agricultural society but to the hunter-gatherer society. However, now we would be hunters and gatherers of information. We would be able to move back to our caves. However, now we would not even need to leave our caves to hunt and gather.

This vision failed to take into consideration that we are social animals. We want to leave our caves. In this new Athens, we want to go to the new Agora - the market-place is the meeting-place. The electronic cottage turned into the enclave - a sort of womb for two (or a few) connected to a dangerous outside world by the umbilical cord of the cable over which was supplied information and goods. This utopia-turned-sour is grimly depicted by novelist E. M. Forster in his short story *The Machine Stops* [FORSTER] and by film-maker Rick Hancox in his short film *Nester*. The theme of the former is obvious from the title; of the latter is that the delivery system continues mechanically long after the protagonist is dead.

We are limited in our capacity to play. Few of us can imagine anything much beyond hitting a ball into a hole with a stick. Thorstein Veblen argued in his *Theory of the Leisure Class* that we would spend most of our time on conspicuous consumption [VEBLEN]. The Parti Quebecoise proposal of a four-day week was resisted largely on the grounds that we could not afford the double whammy of one day less to earn and one day more to spend. Disneyland is regarded by many people as a utopia. Las Vegas is seen as Disneyland for adults. Few of us could imagine ourselves being happy there much beyond a two-week vacation. Switzerland and Singapore are often touted as utopias, since they are so clean and safe. Yet Singapore is dismissed by William Gibson as *Disneyland with the Death Penalty*; and Switzerland is whimsically dismissed by Oscar Wilde: *In Italy, for thirty years under the Borgias, they had warfare, terror, murder, and bloodshed, but they produced Michelangelo, Leonardo da Vinci, and the Renaissance. In Switzerland, they had brotherly love,* === *they had 500 years of democracy and peace, and what did they produce? The cuckoo clock.* Our species is not entirely motivated by the pursuit of pleasure and the avoidance of pain. As we saw in Chapter 9, we have better models of the person than behaviorism. We seem to need some chaos to be creative.

13.6 THE ABUNDANT SOCIETY - PLENTY

As we move from an industrial society, based on energy, into a post-industrial society, based on information, we move from a psychology of scarcity to a psychology of abundance. The basic problem of the industrial society is that we have too little energy, the basic problem of the post-industrial society is that we have too *much* information. Information overload is often described as the problem of our times. You can give away information and still keep it. You can be a Robin Hood of information, taking from the rich and giving to the poor, without impoverishing the rich and enriching yourself in the process. Having the only Mona Lisa painting in the industrial society makes you envied; having the only telephone in the information society makes you pitied. The more other people who also have a telephone, the more valuable yours becomes.

The slogan shifted from *"power to the person"* to *"all information for all people in all places at all times."* [GODFREY & PARKHILL]. There are some quibbles. If the information is about me, then I should have some control over who has access to it. If the information is *by* me, I should be able to charge for it so that I can continue generating information. The ideal of all information for all people in all places at all times was associated with the idea of an information utility. Just as we had an energy utility to deliver energy to our home in the industrial society, we would have an information utility to deliver information to our home in the post-industrial society. I've had an account with Bell Canada for my telephone service for decades. In anticipation of the information utility, I have recently arranged for a television service (Bell ExpressVu) and a computer service (Bell Sympatico). However, they still send me three separate bills. Hydro Quebec, my energy utility, does not send me different bills for the kitchen, the bathroom, and the living-room.

Why should Bell Canada, my information utility, send me separate bills for my telephone, my television set, and my computer? It turns out that it is illegal - at least, according to cable television companies, which are trying to do the same thing starting with television service. Jean Monty, lately CEO of the parent company for Bell Canada and its affiliates, unsuccessfully pursued a strategy of convergence. It has turned out to be more difficult than anticipated. Indeed, it has not been possible to even "converge" the bills.

CHAPTER 14
MEDIA AND THE CORPORATION

14.1   CORPORATION AS COG OF CAPITALISM

14.2   YOU AS CAPITALIST

14.3   YOU AS WORKER

14.4   YOU AS CONSUMER

14.5   YOU AS COMMODITY

14.6   YOU AS PERSON

If we want a stable and secure world, we must build a more just and equitable world.

Luiz Inacio Lula da Silva, President of Brazil

The $200 billion culture industry - now America's biggest export - needs an ever-changing, uninterrupted supply of street styles, edgy music videos and rainbows of colors. And the radical critic of the media clamoring to be "represented" in the early nineties virtually handed over their colorful identities to the brandmasters to be shrink-wrapped.

Naomi Klein, NO LOGO, Page 115

14.1   CORPORATION AS COG OF CAPITALISM

The corporation is the central cog of the capitalist system. Capitalism has proven itself as a powerful device for the generation of wealth. With the recent fall of the Soviet Empire, Francis Fukuwaya declares the end of history with the triumph of capitalism over its major rival - socialism [FUKUYAMA 1992]. He fails, however, to point out that this is a sort of Pyrrhic victory. It has demonstrated that certain negative aspects of human nature - power and greed - are stronger than certain positive aspects - brotherhood and empathy.[1]

Capitalism can not be dismissed as a conspiracy of evil people (or even *stupid white men*). It involves people like you and I (with our usual mixture of good and evil) operating within the logic of a system. This system involves buying raw materials and labor at as low a cost as possible, selling finished goods at as high a price as possible, and distributing the difference - the profit or the loss - among the shareholders in the corporation.

My own earliest experience of capitalism was the career of my brother-in-law who, with the help of my sister, built up a huge industry from nothing. He provided jobs for many of the less enterprising people in my village. Since he had taken the initiative and the risk, he justly reaped more of the rewards, lived in the biggest house in the neighborhood, and had the most expensive toys. His career was certainly more commendable than that of the upper-class twits - born on third base who thought they had hit a triple - who frowned down on him as "*nouveau riche*".

A second relevant experience was during a visit to Syncrude Oil with two

---

[1]   Phillipe Gigantes entitled his recent book - *Power and Greed: A Short History of the World* [GIGANTES]. A companion book - *Brotherhood and Empathy* - would be a VERY short history of the world. It would describe the many failed attempts to build a society based on the more positive aspects of human nature.

of my colleagues at the GAMMA think tank, while we were working on the conserver society project. Three of us were giving talks to a group of top executives of Syncrude Oil, who were under attack from conservationists for exploiting workers squeezing oil out of tar sands in Northern Alberta. Graham Smith, Dean of Business Studies at McGill University, sitting symbolically at the right of Kimon Valaskakis, the President and Founder of GAMMA, was speaking. The audience was highly critical of his argument for full-cost accounting, that business should pay for social costs of their operations. Kimon whispered to me that perhaps we had finally found the bad guys. I, sitting symbolically on his left, was apprehensive about their reaction to me.

It turned out that my leftish views were so far out that I was just comic relief. However, at a cocktail party afterwards, two Vice-Presidents sidled over to me and asked essentially if there was a place to drop in if they dropped out. Both of them had bought small country properties and were poised to lead a life outside the capitalist system. If either of them had found the courage to drop out, someone else would have been slotted into their position in the system, and it would continue as before, following the logic of the capitalist system.

Within this system, you can choose some combination of three roles - capitalist, worker, and consumer. Let's look at each of them in turn.

14.2   YOU AS CAPITALIST

You have the right to set up a business and, if you manage it well so that your income exceeds your costs, to make a profit. If your business grows large enough, you can sell shares in it on the stock market. Or, if you prefer, you can simply buy such shares on the stock market and have your money working for you to generate an income. You worked for your money - now let it work for you. Capitalists would claim that you live in a democracy - you have an equal opportunity to create a business and earn a profit.

However, if you happen to have been born in a Third World country, this option is not open to you. Hermando de Soto tells why in his book *The Mystery of Capitalism: Why Capitalism Triumphs in the West but Fails Everywhere Else* [DE SOTO]. You can't become a capitalist without capital and your country lacks the institutions to enable you to generate capital. You can't go to a bank with a piece of paper which states that you own your parcel of land and/or the house you built on it and use this to get a loan to start a company to generate more property to get a bigger loan to extend the company, and so on. The start of most corporations were such boot-strap operations, but in developing countries there are no boot-straps.

The stock market is another important cog in the capitalist system. It provides the capital to conduct a business by inviting the public to become partners by buying shares. Initially, those junior partners were rewarded by quarterly dividends as their share in the profit. However, the emphasis shifted more and more to using the profit to expand the company and the reward of the shareholder was the increase in the value of the shares as a result of this expansion. Thus, buying shares became a bet that the company would grow. The partner has become a gambler and the stock market has become a casino. This has worked as long as the market was expanding. In a strong wind, even turkeys can fly. However, as the market has slowed down, some of those turkeys have come home to roost. Many of those turkeys were high-tech companies whose expansion was based not on real assets but on virtual promises. As they collapsed, the Chief Executive Officers of Enron, Nortel, etc. left with million-dollar severance packages while the stock-holders lost their nest eggs. *The buck stops here* acquires a whole new meaning.

14.3   YOU AS WORKER

The demise of the Leisure Society was discussed above (see Section 13.5). The process of automation - simulating human functions with machines - got hijacked by the corporate culture. Emphasis shifted from labor-saving to labor-replacing. Emphasis in research on artificial intelligence (AI) shifted from understanding to control. Corporations discovered that they could save money by replacing employees with machines. Everyday, we read in the business section of the newspaper that x thousand employees lost their jobs because of such down-sizing.

Where do those people go? They can't become bank tellers, who are being replaced by the **automatic teller machine (ATM)**.[2] They can't become travel agents, who are being bypassed by the internet.[3] Soon they won't even be able to work at the checkout counters in the grocery store. That too is being

---

[2]   I had learned how to use the ATM in the city. Scotsmen like to be able to visit their money at any time. However, when I moved to the country, I decided to deal with a live teller in the spirit of neighborliness in a small village. She took me over to the ATM and showed me - in that condescending tone reserved for the young and the old - how I could save time and trouble by using the machine. She is no longer there.

[3]   I had planned a recent trip on the internet and was poised to click one last button to order my plane ticket when I decided to deal with the travel agent in the village. She told me that I would have to pay a fee of 60 dollars for the purchase of the plane ticket since Air Canada no longer gives travel agents a commission. I asked if I could use my air miles towards the payment. Another fee of 60 dollars. At this point, I said I'd have to think about it, went home, called the air miles number and five minutes later the ticket was on its way to my mail box.

automated. So they enter the leisure society. But unemployment was not what we had in mind.

Arthur Cordell anticipated this when he talked about the Boeing Effect. Imagine the Boeing Jet with its hi-status, hi-paid pilots in the cockpit and its lo-status, lo-paid stewardesses in the body. He argued that automation was driving a wedge between the hi-paid jobs which can't be automated and the lo-paid jobs which won't be automated because it is cheaper to hire people at low wages.[4] It's the middle jobs that are disappearing - and along with it the middle class. Middle-management positions in the corporation are shrinking since upper management can control people in the lower-level jobs through the informatics infrastructure. The discrepancy between the rich and the poor is increasing. The ratio of the top salary and the bottom salary in a corporation, which was about 40-1 in 1960, soared to 400-1 in 2000. Income tax averaged 10% and corporate tax averaged 35% in 1960; those figures were reversed by the year 2000 [PHILLIPS].

Henry Ford refused to automate his production lines because robots don't buy cars. Are those corporations which are now automating their production process cutting their own throats by removing the means of buying their products?[5] One solution is for the military-industrial complex to sell to itself. Preferably expensive things which go boom and thus have to be frequently replaced - like million-dollar smart bombs. One of the many motivations for war

---

[4]   The Boeing was perhaps an unfortunate choice of metaphor, since it's the hi-paid pilots who have been automated. Those large planes are essentially on automatic pilot with the pilot there only to over-ride the system if something goes wrong and to assure the passengers that someone not something is in charge. That's why he has to be a large male with a deep voice. The stewardess, on the other hand, can't be replaced by a machine, since her job involves empathy. It is comforting for an old lady on her first flight to have someone like her daughter reassure her. I've retained the male pilot and the female stewardess to make the point that the human jobs, which are held largely by women, are the ones which should have hi-status, hi-pay.

[5]   Some wit described the factory of the future as "manned" by a number of robots, a man, and a dog. The dog is there to prevent people from damaging the robots and the man is there to feed the dog.

is such planned obsolescence.

Meanwhile at the other end of the pay scale, people have to work at two MacJobs to support a family. The problem is compounded by the fact that such service people can't afford to live in the same area as those they serve, and thus long commutes are added to their work day. Whether raised by one very tired parent or two parents with one such job each, children suffer neglect. The long litany of social problems begins at such a home. Barbara Ehrenreich worked at various such MacJobs and described how difficult it was to carve out a decent life in her book *Nickel and Dimed: How (Not) to Get By in America* [EHRENREICH].

As the agricultural society was automated, farm workers moved into the factories and the offices of the industrial society. Industrialists were the prime movers in advocating universal schooling. My university motto is *Real Education for the Real World*. This means roughly *Learn to Earn*.[6] The motto of the industrialists was *You Learn, We Earn*. Farm workers could be trained to fit as cogs into the industrial machine. As the industrial society is, in turn, being informationised, there is no similar motivation to take care of those who are displaced. Unless, they can become information workers, there is no place for them to go.

Government in a democracy is supposed to ensure a fair distribution of the wealth generated by industry. However, it has been hijacked by the military-industrial complex, which General Eisenhower warned about while he was President of the United States. The media and the academy have also largely been swept up by this juggernaut. We have then essentially a plutocracy - government by the rich for the rich. Canada is doing a better job of protecting those squeezed out of the system. However, when was the last time you heard

---

[6]   Later we will look at the advertising industry whose motto is *Learn to Yearn*.

any mention of the guaranteed annual wage? The job is just one local and recent means of distributing wealth. When everyone walked, there were no pedestrians. There was no unemployment in hunter-gatherer societies. Jobs create unemployment. Creating jobs is easy - if 1 man with a grader can replace 100 men with shovels, then 1 man with a shovel is replacing 100 men with teaspoons. Important social functions, like raising children, has no status, since it is not a job.

Michael Moore, a fleshier and flashier version of Noam Chomsky, focuses on this job-creating and then life-destroying role of the corporation. His home town in Michigan was essentially closed down by General Motors when they closed down the plant in which most of the townspeople worked. His first film - *Roger and Me* - followed his attempts to interview the President of General Motors to have him take responsibility for the town population. He never did get to meet Roger, who could argue that within the logic of capitalism, he had no allegiance to his former employees, he was not responsible for their lives. Indeed, within the capitalist system, when you lose your role as worker, you also lose the other roles as capitalist and as consumer, since you now lack the means to participate in those roles. Moore has since raised his sights to focus on the entire government-military-industrial complex in his more recent films - *Bowling for Columbine* and *Fahrenheit 9/11*.

14.4   YOU AS CONSUMER

Advertising is another important cog within the capitalist system. If the finished goods can not be sold, then there will be no profit, and if people don't know about the finished goods, then they will not be sold. Few of us would complain about ads which inform us *"Here it is. If you want it, come and get it"*, or even *"you better hurry - it's going fast"*. We all share in the wealth generated by the capitalist system, and can't complain about the need to inform us about the goods whose sales create the wealth.

However, critics like Naomi Klein and Carl Lasn have a legitimate complaint when this process goes so far that our environments are polluted by such advertisements [KLEIN, LASN].[7] Klein complains mainly about the public relations departments of corporations which cover the world with their logos whereas Lasn complains mainly about the advertising departments of corporations which pave our world with ads for their products. Corporations have now moved into the internet where they are erecting bill-boards on the electronic superhighway. Hackers deface those bill-boards because of their ethic that information wants to be free, as opposed to the corporate ethic that information is merely a commodity to be bought and sold on the market.

There are also legitimate criticisms when advertising strikes us below the belt. Evolutionary psychology raises again the prospect that subliminal advertising can be effective. Three authors point to the implication of their emerging view of consciousness for subliminal perception. *Indeed, the literature*

---

[7]   They should visit my village Hudson for momentary relief. By-laws prohibit corporations from building their franchises, erecting their logo signs and exhibiting their wares. The contrast with neighboring villages of Dorion and Rigaud is striking. The wooden signs of local merchants are a pleasant contrast to the neon signs of corporate chains. Some residents take this exclusion policy a bit far. They protest the signs for Hudson on the nearby highway are an invasion of privacy!

on subliminal perception indicates that for each sensory modality there is a level of stimulation below which experience fails to occur but in which information about stimuli is received and processed. For example, emotionally threatening words presented below the experiential visual threshold cause changes in auditory sensitivity and vice versa. [DIXON, quote from FLANAGAN, Page 331]. *Not only are minds accessible to outsiders; some mental activities are more accessible to outsiders than to the very 'owners' of those minds* [DENNETT 1987, Page 162]. Norretranders quotes Dennett and adds *Which is disturbing in general and is particularly so in a society where many people's jobs consist of enticing the rest of us to do things we cannot afford to do* [NORRETRANDERS, Page 165].

Another low blow is the targeting of younger and younger children. Tweens - that is, pre-teens - are a massive and essentially captive market. Under the influence of advertising, those children are becoming caricatures of adults as they ape their allegiance to brand names and current fashions. An even lower blow is targeting pre-schoolers. Pre-schoolers are not wealthy but their parents often are - advertisers depend on the whining factor to have the children wheedle money out of their parents to buy the toys they see advertised.

As the public gets more and more resistant to advertising, it must become more sophisticated (translated as subtle or sneaky, as you prefer). Product placement is one such technique. The product is casually included in films. Sometimes it is not so subtle, as demonstrated in the ubiquity of Fedex in *Cast Away*, the update of Robinson Crusoe with Tom Hanks, .and spoofed in *Jose and the Pussycats*. Product placement is, of course, not possible in period pieces. You can't have Hector drinking a refreshing Coca Cola after his skirmish with Achilles. Some people seriously consider the demise of such period pieces as a result.

Another more sophisticated technique is to have *"cool-hunters"* identify the Next Big Thing so that relevant products can be manufactured and sold to the huge youth market. The hero of *Pattern Recognition* is such a **cool-hunter** [GIBSON 2003]. Even cool-hunters, however, balk at the process of short-circuiting this process by creating - rather than simply identifying - the Next Big Thing. People are hired to casually praise a product in the hope of generating word-of-mouth advertising, which is powerful and free. However, it is based on trust, which is very important for we social animals. Hiring people to be sincere undermines trust.

14.5   YOU AS COMMODITY

The title of this chapter is MEDIA AND THE CORPORATION. However, in a sense, media IS a corporation. Most mass media is owned by major corporations. For example, ninety per cent of all books published are now published by six multinational corporations [TOSCHES]. The two remaining North American ones - AOL/Time-Warner and Viacom - are multimedia corporations with only about 1% of their incomes generated by books. Their major interest is in other media - film, television, etc.

What do they sell to make their profit? We would assume offhand that they sell information. However, on deeper consideration, we realize that they are actually selling time to advertisers, and on even deeper consideration, that they are delivering audiences to other corporations. Advertisers have little interest in information and would have no interest in buying time unless people were staring at the screen. The more eyeballs staring at the screen, the more expensive the time. The media corporation is thus selling us to advertisers. Media corporations thus offer you another role - you as commodity.

This is why media focuses more on entertainment than on enlightenment. The former is more popular[8] - that is, it delivers more eyeballs to the advertisers. We are mesmerized by the programs but they are just fillers between the ads. Neil Postman bemoans our capture by television and later by computer screens [POSTMAN 1986, 1993]. We went to bed dreaming about strolling in the Agora in a New Athens with Socrates and wake up imprisoned in Plato's Cave convinced that the shadows on the walls are reality.

That is why the corporate point of view is favored. Media is a corporation. It allows SOME criticism. This diffuses the opposition by letting off some steam. Even critics like Naomi Klein and Michael Moore are imprisoned in this corporate cave. To do their "jobs" as critics of the corporate culture they must distribute their books and their documentaries through the media corporations. They are subsumed within the system. However, if critics threatened the system seriously, they would be yanked from the stage.

14.6   YOU AS PERSON

The capitalist system is a valuable wealth-generating device. However, the limited roles it offers fail to satisfy the needs of the person as described above in chapter 9. It should be part of the social system but not the entire social

---

[8]   A program called *Enlightenment Tonight* would not have continued on prime-time television for 30 years. Nor would a rival media corporation create an alternative program - *Inside Harvard.*

system.

There is the harsh capitalism of **social Darwinism**, in which Francis Galton misapplied the theory of his cousin Charles Darwin to suggest that society should be based on the survival of the fittest. We should not concern ourselves with the "losers" in the struggle for survival, since they must be weeded out to improve the species. Few today would advocate this today, though its adoption in the past has tarnished the reputation of the theory of evolution.[9]

There is a compassionate capitalism, which concerns itself with the distribution of wealth as well as with the generation of wealth. It is a noblesse oblige attitude which takes care of those squeezed out of the capitalist system. However, this is a paternalistic attitude, in which we should be grateful for the largess of the capitalists for social services. It still sees the corporation as central and every other institution in society as peripheral. Thus Henry Ford is applauded for providing homes for his employees. However, unless they live teetotalling, Christian lives, they can no longer remain employed and housed by Ford. Andrew Carnegie is applauded for his contribution to education by providing libraries and money for research. However, enlightenment is at the mercy of the goodwill of such capitalists.

Life could be considered as just so much time. If most of your time is devoted to working for a corporation, then your life is essentially controlled by that corporation. You are permitted a little spare time at the end of the day, at the end of the week, at the end of the year, and at the end of your life. I once noticed a well-dressed businessman addressing a young man going past in the street. He was probably just asking directions, but I flashed on the thought that he was saying : *Say, brother, can you spare some time?* He had devoted most of his life

---

[9]   Many of us share this experience of being blamed for something done by a cousin.

"time" to making money and had realized that he was running out of time. Money without time is just as bad as time without money. If you have money left over when you die, you have miscalculated; if you have a lot of money, then you have really screwed up.

Corporate culture has become dominant in industrialized countries. Now, globalization threatens that it would become dominant throughout the world. Multinational corporations are footloose. They have no allegiance to a particular country. Swiss Air for example has its accounting done in India and its maintenance done in Eastern Europe. They are simply once again applying the logic of capitalism. It's cheaper than in Switzerland, and thus more profit can be generated for the share-holders. They have work havens, where they employ cheap labor, pollution havens where they can pollute without any penalty, and tax havens, where they can pay a minimum tax. If a national government complains about pollution, for example, they will simply pick up their plant and transplant it somewhere else where the country is too poor to be particular about pollution. National governments, by contrast, are not footloose. They have feet of clay. Kimon Valaskakis argues that we need global governance to deal with this cultural lag between economic globalization and political globalization [VALASKAKIS K 2001].

The corporation is an important element of the social system. However, it should not be the only element, and not even the element which defines the other elements at its periphery. To say that there are only two categories of people in the world - those who are wealthy and those who want to be wealthy - is as silly as saying that there are only Scots and those who want to be Scots. It denies the rich diversity of human beings and human values. A world in which everything is a commodity including ourselves, and in which we know the price of everything and the value of nothing is a very grim and limited world. It is a world of many means to the limited end of making a profit. It is a world in which the GNP gets grosser and grosser while the QOL gets grimmer and grimmer.

Kimon Valaskakis gave a talk in which he predicted that those who are not included in the sharing of the wealth generated by capitalism will start smashing things. This was just before the Attacks on the Acronyms, as massive protests were organized against the various institutions advocating globalization. This was way before 9/11. Such protests and terrorist acts are the tip of an iceberg of resentment.of the rich by the poor. The Third World War has started. That is, the War in the Third World. It is a war between the Haves and the Havenots, the Greedies and the Needies. The Titanic is sailing towards this iceberg.

CHAPTER 15
MEDIA AND THE UNIVERSITY

15.1 A TALE OF TWO INSTITUTIONS

15.2 STUCK IN SECOND GENERATION

15.3 OPTIMAL ORCHESTRATION OF FOUR GENERATIONS

15.4 TURNING TEACHING INSIDE-OUT

Education is a technology that tries to make up for what the human mind is innately bad at. Children don't have to go to school to learn to walk, talk, recognize objects, or remember the personalities of their friends, even though those tasks are much harder than reading, adding, or remembering dates in history. They do have to go to school to learn written language, arithmetic, and science, because those bodies of knowledge and skill were invented too recently for any species-wide knack for them to evolve.
Steven Pinker, 2002

*A wise man learns from his experience,
a wiser man learns from the experience of others.*
Confucius

We must learn from the mistakes of others. You can't possibly live long enough to make them all yourself.
Sam Levenson
(Quoted in Globe and Mail, 3 May 2004)

Imagine a classroom with a window on all the world's knowledge. Imagine a teacher with the capability to bring to life any image, any sound, any event. Imagine a student with the power to visit any place on earth at any time in history. Imagine a screen that can display in vivid color the inner workings of a cell, the birth and death of stars, the clashes of armies, and the triumphs of art. And then imagine that you have access to all of this and more by exerting little more effort than simply asking that it appear
John Sculley in
[SueAnn Ambron & Kristina Hooper,
INTERACTIVE MULTIMEDIA, Page vii].

15.1 A TALE OF TWO INSTITUTIONS

Charles Dickens begins *A Tale of Two Cities* with *"It was the best of times, it was the worst of times -- "*. This chapter is a tale of two institutions - Media and University. Why is this the best of times for the media and the worst of times for the university? It should be the best of times for both. We are - it is generally acknowledged - in transition from an industrial society, based on energy, to a post-industrial society, based on information. Since both those institutions focus on information, they should both be thriving.

The University, an institution founded in Europe during the Middle Ages, has devoted itself to the acquisition, preservation, and transmission of knowledge, throughout the intervening centuries. During that period, it has - with a few minor setbacks - been growing rapidly. However, it is currently in crisis. The budgets and enrollments of many universities have stopped growing and, in many cases, are actually shrinking. The Academy is being attacked from the right [e.g. BLOOM A] and from the left [e.g. SMITH], from outside [e.g. NEWMAN] and from inside [e.g. READINGS]. Post-modern critics within the institution are questioning its very core value - the preservation of Western civilization - as documented in *Impostors in the Temple* [ANDERSON] and *Tenured Radicals* [KIMBALL].

At the same time, Media - another institution of about equal antiquity, if arbitrarily dated from the invention of the printing press - is thriving. The convergence of the computer and telecommunication industry, the broadcast and motion picture industry, and the print and publishing industry, predicted by Nicholas Negroponte, is happening even more rapidly than he anticipated [BRAND]. Huge corporations within each of those industries are merging into mega-corporations in anticipation of the vast fortunes to be made in the emerging multimedia industry, represented by the triple overlap of those three industries (see Figure 8-6). It was argued in Chapter 8 that corporations have been unsuccessful so far in exploiting this generation of media but with their vast resources, it is only a matter of time before they do so.

Whereas the emphasis in the University is on enlightenment, the emphasis in the Media is on entertainment. This would appear to explain the relative popularity of the Media over the University. It is difficult to imagine a program called *Enlightenment Today* surviving for 20 years on prime time television, or a rival network challenging it with *Inside Harvard*, or Metro-Goldwyn-Meyer producing a popular series called *That's Enlightenment!*. It is estimated that a billion people watching the 30th Oscar Awards on television. If it were televised live, what audience could we anticipate for the handing out of the Nobel Prizes - the equivalent awards for enlightenment? Indeed, entertainment is so much more popular than enlightenment, that even when Media is involved in enlightenment - for example, in presenting the news - it tends to present it as entertainment rather than enlightenment. In order to compete in the ratings race, the networks have to make the news *"entertaining"*. News anchors are chosen because they are attractive rather than because they are well-informed.

By setting up entertainment and enlightenment as two mutually exclusive categories, I am, of course, illustrating the principle I am condemning. Conflict implies drama implies entertainment. There is no necessary conflict between entertainment and enlightenment, as the various hybrid terms - infotainment, edutainment, etc. - imply. All the four generations of media can be used for both entertainment and enlightenment. Entertainment is not intrinsically more interesting than enlightenment. I argued above in Section 9.3 that there is an organic basis to the need to know and understand. Aristotle opens his *Metaphysics* with the statement *"All men, by nature, desire to know"*. Evolutionary psychologists and molecular biologists are currently documenting the empirical evidence for this insight. Enlightenment is built into the biology of our species, whereas entertainment is simply a cultural diversion to compensate for unfulfilled lives. Media has simply done a better job of interesting the general public in entertainment than the University has of interesting them in enlightenment.

The fourth generation of media promised to restore some balance between entertainment and enlightenment. In the early 1990s, I produced the *"edutainment"* section of the CD-ROM to accompany the movie *Rob Roy*. That section was a short history of Scotland to place Rob Roy in historical perspective. We had visions of a future in which each movie is accompanied, when appropriate, by a CD-ROM, just as each movie is now, when appropriate, accompanied by a CD-audio sound track. There were CD-ROMs focusing on the work of Marshall McLuhan, Alexander Graham Bell, and Marvin Minsky. There were CD-ROMs exploring Greenwich Village with Bob Dylan (*Highway 61 Interactive*), traveling across Australia (*From Alice to Ocean*), and wandering all over our planet to meet animals in danger of extinction (*Last Chance to See*).

The DVD, which largely replaced the CD-ROM, was even more promising because of its much larger capacity. However, that larger capacity has been used to include the movie itself The information supplementing the movie in a DVD is mostly about the making of the movie. This is of value to students of film-making. However, we had hoped that supplementary material would be available which was of value to students in other disciplines. For example, period films would contain some history of that period. Thus, someone who got interested in the American Civil War after watching *The Patriot* would find some information about the true story of the Civil War in the DVD version of the movie. There are a few gestures in this direction. The DVD accompanying a movie *Blow* about the drug trade between Columbia and the United States contains a documentary about the impact of the cocaine industry on the economy of Columbia and an interview in prison with George Jung, the person on whom the movie is based (He offered to trade places with Johnny Depp who portrayed him in the movie!). Citizen Kane is accompanied by a documentary, *The Battle over 'Citizen Kane'* about the attempt by Hearst, the inspiration for Kane, to destroy the movie. However, the DVDs still largely lean to the entertainment side.

Many scholars are advocating that we do not continue to depend on piggy-backing on entertainment under embarrassing headings such as *"edutainment"*. We can use multimedia and the internet directly for enlightenment. The CD-ROM industry, once so promising, has petered out. One major reason is that CD-ROMs are so easy to copy. It became impossible to earn a living making CD-ROMs since there were 10 pirated disks for each disk sold. However, scholars did not need to make a living selling CD-ROMs. Most have an adequate salary as professors in some university. They do not need to worry about pirates - indeed, they would welcome pirates since their major motivation is for their ideas to be widely distributed. Their problem is that the hundreds of hours required to create a CD-ROM or a website (a website is to a CD-ROM as a book in the university library is to a book in a personal library) is not acknowledged as legitimate work by their university. Stuck in the second generation, the university recognizes only print projects as scholarship.

15.2 STUCK IN SECOND GENERATION

The Big Story of historical time, it is argued in chapters 1 through 8, is the co-evolution of the person and media as extensions. Media has moved through the four generations as we moved from a hunter-gatherer to an agricultural to an industrial to an information society (see Figure 1-2). One of the reasons why the university has failed to "sell" enlightenment is that has got stuck in the second generation.

A few universities - e.g. Oxford and Cambridge - were founded so early that the second generation of print had not yet become firmly established. They thus emphasized the first generation of speech and memory. The focus is on face-to-face tutorials with students talking to professors one on one.

Most universities were founded during the agricultural society and thus emphasize the corresponding media of print. They have retained only vestiges of the oral tradition with that peculiar hybrid of first and second generation, the lecture, in which the professor speaks and the student writes, and in the oral defense of the thesis for graduate degrees. They have not been able to go back to the first generation - the tutorial tradition of Oxbridge. Paul Piehler tried throughout his career as a Professor of English at McGill University to interest the administration on the tutorial system (which he had found so effective in his own education at Oxford University) with no success. Alex Duke presents the history of the many failed attempts to introduce the Oxbridge system in North America [DUKE].

Nor have they been able to go forward to the third and fourth generations of media. Media had to adjust to each new social system in order to survive, whereas the university did not need to adjust. It is so valued, appropriately, by society that it has "tenure" as an institution.

Although some classrooms are finally being equipped with electronic equipment, most professors continue to use talk (first generation) and chalk (second generation). Those who use the technology tend to use it within the traditional outside-in framework. I myself in the early 1990s developed a talk entitled *How to Turn Teaching Inside-out in Ten Easy Steps,* which I finally abandoned when I realized that I was still in show business and was simply using the technology to put on a better show. The technology did help somewhat since the students were provided with HyperCard and subsequently PowerPoint handouts containing outlines, figures, and references for each lecture. Thus, they were less secretaries, mechanically copying this information, and more scholars, listening and reacting to the content of the lectures.[1] It is more important to get the technology into the heads of the student than into the hands of the professor.

In the meantime, students have moved into video-based media (third generation) and computer-based media (fourth generation) as their major source of information.[2] The two solitudes of professors and students are lined up at opposite sides of the digital divide. The excrement will really impinge on the ventilation device when a generation of students who have been acquiring computer culture from the inside-out since infancy arrive at university. Marshall McLuhan argued that there is so much more information outside school than inside that children interrupt their education by going to school. Steve Jobs and Steve Wozniak who founded Apple, and Bill Gates, who founded Microsoft, are all university dropouts. They were ahead of their times.

---

[1]   One hears horror stories of professors reading their lectures off PowerPoint slides while the students write their copies of the slides. At least, when reading directly from their notes, the pre-PowerPoint professors were facing the class.

[2]   The e-mail addresses of most of my colleagues are those issued free by the university for an antiquated text-only system, whereas only a few of the students have retained them.

It made sense in an agricultural society to have people come to a certain place and sit in rows to receive information. There was little information available outside the classroom. However, it makes little sense for my current classroom to have long "pews" nailed to the floor for the students with a raised "pulpit" for me to preach - oops, teach. I'm tempted to intone in my best Presbyterian voice, "*we shall commence reading from the book of Gardiner, Chapter 1, Verse 1.*" No doubt, I will - the best way to deal with temptation is to succumb to it.

One trivial but telling illustration of the fact that the educational system is designed for an agricultural society is the long Summer vacation. I asked one class how many of them needed it to help with the harvest. One student raised his hand, saying "*I'm from Saskatchewan*". John later told me that he was putting me on. So no students need the long Summer vacation. Yet we still have it. If we could haul our minds out of the agricultural society into our current information society, we could have a trimester system, which would enable us to use the university facilities all year and a third of us could get out of Canada during the Winter. But we have to tote those bales.

The familiar qwerty keyboard was designed to slow typists down, because the keys stuck when they typed too fast. The keys don't stick anymore (especially in the computer keyboard) but we are stuck with the keyboard. The educational system is a gigantic qwerty phenomenon.

Another reason why the university has failed to interest the general public in enlightenment is the emphasis on research over teaching (using whatever generation of media). This emphasis is understandable. It is the creation of new information, rather than the transmission of old information, which is the distinctive function of the university. However, it is teaching which the student is exposed to, and it's the bad teaching which has turned most students off enlightenment. If you asked a script-writer to write six hours of new material a week or an actor to present six hours of new material a week, they would be horrified. However, a professor with neither of their skills is required to do both. The result is the familiar dull reading of the same notes year after year. Here are two small incidents to illustrate how little teaching is regarded.[3]

In a meeting to give input on the design of a new building for our department, I said that we should make sure the doors are at the back of the classrooms. In all our current classrooms, the doors are at the front. Students arriving late either miss the first half of the class because they are too polite or nervous to disrupt the class or -- they disrupt the class. Our chairman said that he preferred the door at the front for surveillance. He was joking, of course. However, the discussion shifted to our department policy about tardiness, and a committee was formed to draft the policy. I was invited to join the committee but declined on the grounds that it would be easier to put the door at the back of the classroom. The university looks down on the church as a less enlightened institution, but they are at least smart enough to put the door at the back of the church. When I asked an architect why they did this, she said that she just provides a rectangular room. It's the person who puts up the blackboard who determines whether the door is at the back or the front. I asked one of the university employees who puts up the blackboard. He said he just follows the instructions of an administrator. Administrators tend to be professors who didn't like to teach and thus moved into administration.

Twice I went to attend lectures by Noam Chomsky and Alan Ginsberg respectively at my university. On both occasions, I arrived to find that the 700-seat auditorium was full. As I milled around outside with the hundreds of disappointed people who could not get in, we were instructed over a loudspeaker

---

[3] Both those incidents are at my own university. It is no stupider than any other university. I'm very fond of it. It just happens to be the one I know best. Similar horror stories can be told of any university.

to go away since the auditorium was full. If they had the means to tell us to go away, they had the means to let us hear the lecture. Not many of us came to see Chomsky or Ginsberg (though it would have been nice), we came to hear them. When Richard Feynman came to Cornell in the early 1960s, the overflow crowd was directed to another auditorium where we could both hear and see him on a video monitor. Surely, the technology has not regressed in the intervening 30 years so that that is no longer possible.

15.3 OPTIMAL ORCHESTRATION OF FOUR GENERATIONS

If, as argued above, the Big Story of historical time is the co-evolution of the person and media as extensions, then the educational process should recapitulate this history. Each generation of media brings out different aspects of the human potential. We should acquire as many of the communication tools and skills as possible to bring out more and more of our human potential.

Much debate about communication, both inside and outside my class, is about the relative merits of the four generations of media (Figure 15-1). This debate is about as futile as arguments about the relative merits of four generations of transportation. I walk to the village to get my mail, I cycle to the Willow Inn for a drink, I take the train to Montreal to teach my classes, and I fly to Scotland to see my family. No generation is any better than any other. You use whatever is appropriate in the circumstances. As many communication tools and skills as possible should be acquired to be prepared for the various situations we find ourselves in. Each tool could be considered like a club in our golf-bag. You would not argue that your putter is better than your driver, nor would you throw away your driver on acquiring a putter.

The computer will never replace the book.
For example, you can't take a computer to bed.
Actually you can take a laptop computer to bed
and project the image on the ceiling for easy reading.
But you still miss the smell of the leather binding and texture of the paper.
You sound pretty depraved - sniffing and fondling books in bed!

FIGURE 15-1   WHICH GENERATION IS BEST?

Traditional education focuses on content. However, we now have lots of content. Indeed, some scholars argue that information overload is THE problem of our times. Whereas the industrial society, based on energy, experiences an energy crisis, the information society, based on information, experiences an information crisis.   However, the energy crisis is that there is too *little* information; whereas the information crisis is that there is too *much* information.

As we have seen in Section 3.1, there is some evidence of a limitation in the rate of processing information. George Miller has compiled this evidence in his article *The magical number seven, plus or minus two: some limits on our capacity for processing information* [MILLER]. However, there is no evidence that anyone has reached the limit to the memory capacity of the human brain. The argument that senility is nature's way of of saying "*disk full*" is vitiated by the fact that it is the creative people (whose brains are fuller) who are most resistant to senility.

It may well be that the *problem* of information overload is a pseudo-problem; yet another illustration of our human capacity to turn solutions into problems. One consistent finding in years of research on intelligence is that intelligence is a function of the richness of the environment of the organism. Smart people grow up in enriched environments and stupid people in impoverished environment. The traditional outside-in teaching was appropriate in impoverished environments, where the tell-'em-and-test-'em sessions with a teacher provided at least some enrichment. However, we now have incredibly rich environments which can help pull out the human potential. We turn this solution of a rich environment into a problem of information overload. A magnificent smorgasbord of food is a problem only if you think you must eat it all. Perhaps, people raised within an outside-in educational system tend to think that they must assimilate everything in that rich smorgasbord of information in our modern environment. The inside-out teacher - whose concept of the person is of someone growing from the inside out rather than being conditioned from the outside in - welcomes the richness.

The information overload *problem* may perhaps best be rephrased as one of the management of complexity.[4] Our information-rich modern environment permits us to build complex, subtle subjective maps of the objective world. The challenge is to organize the diverse information pouring in from the wide variety of sources into a coherent and comprehensive subjective map. It is not a quantitative matter of too much content but rather a qualitative matter of putting content into context. We must learn how to put data into context to yield information, information into context to yield knowledge, knowledge into context to yield understanding, and understanding into context to yield wisdom, as we move up that data-wisdom hierarchy, which is the means of adding value to the raw material of the information society.

For most people complexity is not a problem. They deal with it by simply refusing to assimilate any information which does not fit within whatever subjective map of the objective world they have settled for as satisfactory. The Jehovah Witness looks around nonplused at all my books. He has one book which contains all the answers. The retiree (in body and in mind) has no need to learn anything more. He will devote his last few years to hitting a ball into a hole with a stick. The 'philosopher' in the local pub learns nothing because he already knows everything. His wife has returned the encyclopedia. The specialist in the university sacrifices breadth at the altar of depth. Complexity can perhaps be contained within a narrow domain. Much of the popularity of Ronald Reagan may be due to the fact that he was, not so much the *Great Communicator* as the

---

[4]   In the 1980s, when information overload was considered as *the* problem of the information society, Dr. Arthur Cordell of the Science Council of Canada asked me to think about it. *How hard should I think? $5,000. How long should I think? Eighteen months - I have to incorporate it into a report due 2 years from now.* I thought about it and, fifteen months later, realized that it was a pseudo-problem. That was obviously not worth $5,000. However, I realized that this pseudo-problem masked the real problem of the management of complexity and wrote the report on that. Everything I've done since is related somehow to the management of complexity. Arthur had set the agenda for the rest of my scholarly career.

Great Simplifier. Bernard Berelson and Gary Steiner, in compiling an inventory of scientific findings about human behavior, concluded that the human being is a *"creature who adapts reality to his own ends, who transforms reality into congenial form, who makes his own reality"* [BERELSON & STEINER].

For those of us who still regard it as a problem, one constructive response to the challenge is to develop skills for managing complexity. Those skills go beyond the traditional information-processing skills of speaking and listening, reading and writing. We can add to the explaining skills of speaking and writing the skills which I will call **heuristics** (the set of skills for organizing information at the source for effective transmission), and we can add to the traditional understanding skills of listening and reading the skills which I will call **mnemonics** (the set of skills for organizing information at the destination for effective reception) (Figure 15-2).

We have already looked at a number of tools for the management of complexity. The Triad Model (see Figure 3-2) helps organize vast amounts of information within an optimal seven categories. The Four Generations of Media model (see Figure 1-2) helps organize information within the technosphere, once again within an optimal seven categories, and serves as a structure for this book. The siliclone (see Figure 11-1) is a device for removing the clutter of content, which is often mistaken for complexity. Idea processors and authoring languages (see Figure 8-2) help us organize information in two dimensions of hierarchical structures and three dimensions of networks of interlinked nodes.

Earlier books on this issue - e.g. Alvin Toffler's warning about *Future Shock* [TOFFLER 1971] and David Shenk's warning about *Data Smog* [SHENK] - are phrased in terms of information overload, but later books - e.g. Kevin Kelly's warning about being *Out of Control* [KELLY] and Thomas Homer-Dixon's warning about being being faced with *The Ingenuity Gap* [HOMER-DIXON] - are phrased in terms of the management of complexity.

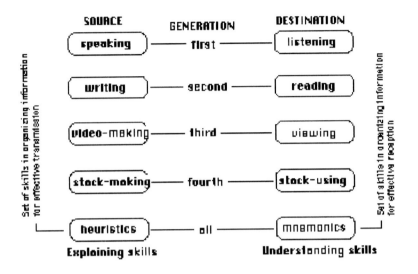

FIGURE 15-2
EXPLAINING AND UNDERSTANDING SKILLS

All I am adding here is the argument that complexity has always been a feature of the objective world - what is new is the recognition that it must therefore become a feature of our subjective maps. Complexity was here in the ecosphere before we arrived. We have added to that complexity in the sociosphere and the technosphere and the super-complexity of the interactions among those three great spheres, and we have been arrogantly assuming that we can manage this complexity by extrapolations from our various "toys" in the technosphere. What is new is the recent recognition that we must turn from the mechanism to the organism as our model, from physics to biology as our basic discipline, from simple to complex systems as our focus. This is not rocket science. Rocket science is easy.

Media no doubt contributes to this complexity. However, it can also contribute to the management of complexity. The Big Story of the co-evolution of the person and media told here could be considered as the story of how our species extended our nervous systems to manage the increasing complexity as we moved from a hunter-gatherer to an agricultural to an industrial and now to an information society.

Although both Media and University are concerned with information-processing - albeit with very different visions, values and goals - they have had surprisingly little to do with one another. There is, of course, some sniping back and forth between the two trenches - accusations of elitism and obscurantism from one camp and of superficiality and sensationalism from the other, snide remarks about popcorn concessions when a professor shows a video in class, and stereotypes of pedantic scholars in the popular press.

The discipline of Media Studies occupies a peculiar position in the no person's land between the two trenches. Unlike the more established disciplines, Media Studies is represented in only a minority of universities, usually in a peripheral role. The discipline often gets static from both camps - from the academy, under its banner of rigor, and from media, under its banner of relevance. We tend to lean towards the former, even while suspecting that the academy is sometimes so rigorous that rigor mortis sets in. Convinced that rigor times relevance is a constant - that is, if either goes to zero, the product is zero - we strive to keep our constant up.

Perhaps we can serve a positive role as a bridge between those *"two solitudes"*. As a scholar within this discipline, I will argue here that education could best be considered in terms of the *acquisition, preservation and transmission of knowledge* by means of four generations of media - speech, print, video, and multimedia. We scholars can survive our current crisis - and even thrive in it - by using the realistic means of the Media to attain the idealistic ends of the University. If we shift, as suggested here, from an emphasis on content to an emphasis on process, then Media Studies shifts from the periphery to the center of the new university.

The Toronto School of Media Studies falls within the intelligence amplification (IA) tradition of the history of computing. This whole IA tradition, documented brilliantly by Howard Rheingold, could be considered as the story of the management of complexity [RHEINGOLD 1985]. Just as the microscope makes the too-small large enough to study, and the telescope brings the too-far near enough to study; the computer makes the too-complex simple enough to study. Thierry Bardini documents the life of Douglas Engelbart which has been devoted to the management of complexity [BARDINI]. His strategy is not the traditional one of simulating the organism with a mechanism - artificial intelligence (AI), but the alternative strategy of supplementing the organism with a mechanism - intelligence amplification (IA). The management of complexity requires the optimal orchestration of natural intelligence and artificial intelligence, the partnership of the organism and the mechanism.

15.4 TURNING TEACHING INSIDE-OUT

In 1970, I retired after teaching *Introduction to Psychology* to classes of 700 for five years. A decade later, I published a book entitled *The Psychology of Teaching*, in which I advocated that teaching be turned inside out - that is, from an outside-in process in which information is transported from professor to passive students (as I had been doing for those five years) to an inside-out process where students actively transform themselves with the professor creating a congenial climate for their growth [GARDINER 1980].. At that time, I didn't know how to do it but that, as you know, doesn't prevent an academic from publishing.

However, I was kindly invited back into our university by the Department of Communication Studies, and, after 20 years in this discipline, have some idea now how to turn teaching inside-out. The short answer is that we subcontract out the outside-in information-providing aspects of teaching to our new electronic colleague, the computer, setting us free for the inside-out inspiration-creating aspect of teaching. The long answer is contained in my forth-coming book - *Turning Teaching Inside-out* [GARDINER 2005]. In this book, I detail how information-providing can be subcontracted out to the computer. Here is the "Goldilocks" answer - neither too short nor too long.

Turning teaching inside-out shifts the focus of education from the teacher to the student. The Shannon-Weaver model of communication was presented in Chapter 2 as a source and destination linked by a channel. Whereas it was argued there that this model is more useful for describing communication between machines rather than between people, it does provide a useful taxonomy of communication settings. Forgetting the various channels for a moment, we could classify communication settings in terms of the number of sources and destinations. Distinguishing between one and many sources and destinations yields four communication settings, as depicted in Figure 15-3.

In the academy, we are familiar with the one-to-many setting (lecture), the many-to-many setting (seminar), and one-to-one setting (tutorial). However, the fourth setting - many-to-one is largely neglected. However, this is the real-life situation in which the students find themselves. Each student is one destination confronted by many sources - teachers and coaches, family and friends, print and electronic journalists. Let us focus on this much-neglected fourth setting.

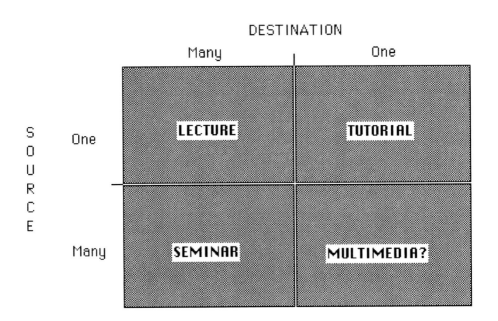

FIGURE 15-3
FOUR COMMUNICATION SETTINGS
IN UNIVERSITY

Obviously, one can not simply send the student off into cyberspace with a few keywords corresponding to each "course". We have all experienced that lost-in-cyberspace feeling as we search for a needle in a field of haystacks. Tools have to be created which make the relevant information available in an integrated and interactive form. My Virtual Village project, which will be discussed in Section 16.1, is a prototype of such tools. The technology is already available to create such tools. However, it is currently being used to satisfy our hunger for entertainment. The computer games industry, which generates more money than the film industry, is at the leading edge in using the computer for simulation. It can equally well simulate the real world for enlightenment as a fantasy world for entertainment.[5]

There are movements towards the legitimation of the production of websites and CD-ROMs in the academy. Many scholars have their own websites. Figure 15-4 lists those for a number of scholars I have consulted in writing this book. MY website is at www.siliclone.com (since I am too modest to include it with those distinguished scholars!). Many of those sites contain generous extracts from books written by those scholars and sometimes even the whole book. There is also a growing movement to bypass the corporations which publish scholarly journals by publishing the journals on-line on-demand. The community of scholars can thus talk to one another directly rather than through the mediation of expensive commercial organizations.

---

[5]   Robert de Jong, one of my students, showed me a fantasy game called *Medieval*. It is based on the real history of those times. He showed me how he, taking the side of the English against the Scots, had won the Battle of Bannockburn in 1314. I protested that actually the Scots had won - indeed, that was the last one they won except for an occasional soccer game - and asked if it could be played as it actually happened. No problem, he said, the difficult thing is to program the game so that there can be various alternative outcomes.

Jerome H. BARKOW	www.dal.ca/~barkow/home.htm
Janine BENYUS	www.biomimicry.org
Stewart BRAND	www.well.com/user/sb
William CALVIN	www.williamcalvin.com/index.html
Noam CHOMSKY	www.chomsky.info/
Andy CLARK	www.cogs.indiana.edu/people/ homepages/clark.html
Arthur & Marilouise KROKER	www.ctheory.concordia.ca/krokers
Daniel DENNETT	ase.tufts.edu/cogstud/~ddennett.htm
Umberto ECO	www.themodernword.com/eco/
Francis FUKUYAMA	www.sais-jhu.edu/faculty/fukuyama
William GIBSON	www.williamgibsonbooks.com/ index.isp
Stephen Jay GOULD	www.stephenjaygould.org/
Donna HARAWAY	www.asahi-net.or.jp/ ~rf6t-tyfk/haraway.html
Katherine HAYLES	englishwww.humnet.ucla.edu/ faculty/hayles/
Thomas HOMER-DIXON	www.homerdixon.com
Kevin KELLY	www.kk.org
Naomi KLEIN	www.nologo.org
Ray KURZWEIL	www.kurzweilai.net
Brenda LAUREL	www.tauzero.com/brenda.laurel/
Paul LEVINSON	www.sff.net/people/paullevinson/
Steve MANN	www.eecg.toronto.edu/~mann/
Marshall MCLUHAN	www.marshallmcluhan.com
Nicholas NEGROPONTE	web.media.mit.edu/~nicholas/
Ted NELSON	xanadu.com.au/ted/
Steven PINKER	pinker.wjh.harvard.edu/
Neil POSTMAN	www.preservenet.com/theory/ Postman.html
Neal STEPHENSON	www.nealstephenson.com
Sandy STONE	www.sandystone.com
Don TAPSCOTT	www.nplc.com
Sherry TURKLE	web.mit.edu/sturkle/www/
Kevin WARWICK	www.kevinwarwick.com
Stephen WOLFRAM	www.stephenwolfram.com

FIGURE 15-4   SOME SCHOLARS AND THEIR URLS

CHAPTER 16
ALL OF OUR FUTURES

16.1 MY FUTURE

16.2 YOUR FUTURE

16.3 A DETOUR INTO SEX

16.4 THEIR FUTURES

So often times it happens that we live our lives in chains
And we never even know we have the key.
The Eagles

It's very hard to predict things - especially the future.
Yogi Berra

Only now are we beginning to sense a hinge in history, a time when the earth is
beginning to move beneath our feet. In the near term (of an exponential increase
in technology affecting human capabilities), the world could divide up into three
types of humans. One would be enhanced, who embrace those opportunities. A
second would be the naturals, who have the technology available but who, like
today's vegetarians, choose not to indulge for moral or aesthetic reasons.
Finally, there would be The Rest - those without access to those technologies for
financial or geographical reasons, lagging behind, envying or despising those
with ever-increasing choices. Especially if the Enhanced can easily be
recognized because of the way they look, or what they can do, this is a recipe for
conflict that would make racial or religious differences quaintly obsolete.
Joel Garreau, 2003

Most current computer users do not realize that they have more computer power
at their fingertips than NASA had to send a man to the moon.
Thierry Bardini, BOOTSTRAPPING, Page xii

16.1 MY FUTURE

I've been leading my life in neat, multiple-of-five-year, volume-sized installments for the convenience of biographers:

VOLUME 1   00-20   GROWING UP IN SCOTLAND
Flunked out of elementary school, High School, and Glasgow University.
The only residue of this volume is a peculiar speech aberration.

VOLUME 2   20-25   STUDYING IN CANADA
Worked by day and studied by night, Script by Horatio Alger.
B.A. (Psychology) from Sir George Williams University and High School Teaching Diploma from McGill University.
Taught High School for two years.

VOLUME 3   25-30   STUDYING IN UNITED STATES
Got Ph. D. (Psychology) from Cornell University.
Nothing else happened.

VOLUME 4   30-35   TEACHING PSYCHOLOGY IN CANADA
Returned to Sir George Williams University to teach introductory psychology to 700 day students in the matinee and 700 evening students in the late show.
Planned my obsolescence by writing down all I knew in two books - *Psychology: A Story of a Search* [GARDINER 1970] *and An Invitation to Cognitive Psychology* [GARDINER 1973].
Quit show business and retired. Freedom 35.

VOLUME 5   35-45   WANDERING AROUND THE PLANET

Divided my time between being a hippie in the Gatineau Hills near Ottawa in the Summer and an author-in-residence at a California publishing company in the Winter.

Made many detours to visit counter-cultural communities exploring alternative ways of living and learning (and hence teaching) - Esalen Institute and Tassajara Zen Mountain Center in California (*"the edge of history"*), Naropa Institute in Boulder Colorado, Findhorn in Scotland, and Auroville in India.

Condensed the experience of this decade into a book - *The Psychology of Teaching* [GARDINER 1980], advocating that teaching be turned inside out - that is, from an outside-in process in which information is transported from professor to passive students (as I had been doing for those five years) to an inside-out process where students actively transform themselves with the professor creating a congenial climate for their growth.

VOLUME 6   45-50   THINKING IN CANADA

On one foray through Montreal, I got trapped by a think tank called GAMMA which was studying the conserver society and the information society concepts. Summarized this experience in *The Ubiquitous Chip: The Human Impact of Electronic Technology* [GARDINER 1987].

VOLUME 7   50-70   TEACHING MEDIA STUDIES IN CANADA

So many students were coming from Communication Studies at what was now Concordia University that they finally got embarrassed and hired me.

One of my courses has evolved into a book - *A History of Media* [GARDINER 2002]. When my two other courses - *The Futures of Media* and *The Psychology of Communication* - evolve into books, I'll have planned my obsolescence once again. This book is a synthesis of all three courses, and another step towards obsolescence.

VOLUME 8   70-??   TYING UP SOME LOOSE ENDS?

So how should I spend the next (and final) volume? Should I simply return to my Scottish roots and devote my last volume to hitting a ball into a hole with a stick? Alas, I'm still too Presbyterian to devote my time to having fun. As the volumes above indicate, I like to lead a tidy life. There are three loose ends to tie up before it ends. The first has to do with *The Psychology of Teaching* - the book which rounded out Volume 5; the second has to do with *A History of Media*, the book which is a beginning towards rounding out volume 7, and the third loose end is a general loose end which affects us all. Let's look at each in turn.

The first loose end is the project of turning teaching inside out. When I argue for this in my 1980 book, *The Psychology of Teaching*, I didn't know how to do it.   But that, as you know, doesn't prevent an academic from publishing. However, I was kindly invited back into our university by the Department of Communication Studies, and, after 20 years in this discipline, have some idea now how to turn teaching inside-out. The short answer is that we subcontract out the outside-in information-providing aspects of teaching to our new electronic colleague, the computer, setting us free for the inside-out inspiration-creating aspect of teaching.

The long answer is contained in my forthcoming book - *Turning Teaching Inside-out*. In this book, I detail how information-providing can be subcontracted out to the computer. Obviously, one can not simply send the student off into cyberspace with a few keywords and URLs corresponding to each "course". Tools have to be created which make the relevant information available in an integrated and interactive form. You have to create integrated structures of information so that the student can - by exploring it - become at home in the domain of interest.

A website entitled *The Virtual Village* will be created as a prototype of the bodies of integrated and interactive information I have in mind. Some small steps towards the **Virtual Village** have been taken. Trisha Santa and I published a book *Main Road, Hudson: Then and Now* which is essentially a walking tour of our village. It is spiral-bound - on the top there is an old picture of the various houses along the Main Road which are of historical interest and on the bottom is a current picture of the house with a paragraph of historical information. You can read it at www.siliclone.com.

This book will be the skeleton of the Virtual Village website. All the information that can be gathered about the village will be organized around those existing buildings and later others off the Main Road. Thus, the archives of the local newspaper will be found in the Hudson Gazette offices, official documents will be found at the Town Hall, clips of movies set in Hudson will be found at Jim's Video, and clips of local performers will be found in the Village Theater. Visitors to the Virtual Village will be able to wander around it and become at home in it rather than simply reading facts about it. In the future, our Global Village, the internet, will contain many such Virtual Villages.

The Siliclone (see Section 11.2) also contributes to turning teaching inside out. Instead of sitting passively in rows listening to what Scot happens to have to say from 8:45 till 11:30 a.m. on Monday mornings, the student can go to Siliclone from any place at any time and actively explore whatever s/he is interested in and come to Scot for a face-to-face chat about matters of mutual interest. However, it also contributes to tying up the second loose end.

That second loose end of my life to be tied up concerns *A History of Media*. The argument repeated throughout this book is that the Big Story of historical time is the co-evolution of the person and media as extensions. Our conception-day gift contains a means of storing information (memory) and a means of transmitting information (speech). This first generation of media

(Memory and Speech) is adequate only for a hunter-gatherer society. We have to extend our nervous system by storing and transmitting information outside our nervous system. Such extrasomatic storing (Print and Film - second generation) is correlated with the shift to an agricultural society; transmission (Telephone and Television - third generation) with the shift to an industrial society; storage and transmission (Multimedia and Internet) with the shift to an information society. Those three shifts are different stages of the unfolding of the human potential.

As argued above in Section 8.3, the completion of this process is somewhat anti-climatic. No one seems to know what to do with this magnificent informatics infrastructure of computers interlinked by telecommunications. It's a solution in search of a problem, it's the can-opener before the can. Huge media corporations have lost billions trying to decide what the problem is. The only success stories are electronic solutions to problems which have already been solved - how to use the internet to sell stuff (www.amazon.com) and how to organize a garage sale to sell stuff (www.ebay.com). All the myriad proposed killer apps so far have been simply means of doing things we could do before but faster and on a global scale. This is functionally useful but not intellectually interesting.

Here, then, is my candidate for killer app. We could consider a medium as mediating not just between you and me but also between our various subjective maps and our common objective world. With this fourth generation of media, we finally have a medium which is isomorphic with the subjective map and the objective world. It can thus be used to simulate the subjective map and the objective world. Or, to change the metaphor, it can be used as a mirror of the subjective map or as a window on to the objective world (see Figure 16-2). Siliclone is a mirror simulation and the Virtual Village is a window simulation.

The third loose thread is one we all share. One of the few things that all parents and teachers know is that they are going to become obsolete. It's important that we plan our obsolescence. Each of the previous volumes have been rounded out by writing a book, which essentially made me obsolete and forced me on to the next volume. At the moment, Scot and Siliclone are partners. As in any partnership, there is a division of labor. Each of us does what we are good at. Siliclone is good at memorizing content. He loves lists. Since Scot wants to be listless, he subcontracts out content to Siliclone, setting him free for what he is good at - putting content into context. When Scot goes off to the final Volume in the Sky, Siliclone will shift from satellite to surrogate. I have to go but I now can leave my mind behind. You can visit my mind at my website rather than my body at my gravesite. Now I've *really* planned my obsolescence! While I'm still here, do you have any questions?

16.2 YOUR FUTURE

If you are reading this book, then you are no doubt a member of species homo sapiens with the most powerful brain nature has evolved over hundreds of thousands of years. Did you get the operating manual for it? When you got your car, you got an operating manual. When you got your computer, you got an operating manual. I thought my manual had been issued by another department and lost by British Post. Halfway through my life, I started writing my own manual. When all else fails, write the manual.

The first version of my **operating manual for species homo sapiens** was largely about the isolated brain. It involved meditation to reduce the noise from the central nervous system and biofeedback to enhance the signal from the autonomic nervous system so that I could listen to the very local news from my body. The mind is assumed not only to be empty (tabula rasa) but to be isolated (tabula isola). Now I realize that a very large part of the operating manual is the acquisition of the skills of the four generations of media. In 1990, I started keeping a record of the time spent communicating with the first three generations of media to see the impact on this pattern as I got involved in the fourth generation. Figure 16-2 shows the results for the first 6 months. The most startling finding was the sheer amount of time spent communicating - typically over 70 hours a week, that is over 10 hours a day. Since most of my waking life involves the use of those four generations, that is what I should get good at. The only other activities which came close were the mundane maintenance matters of sleeping and eating. Those I have pretty well mastered.

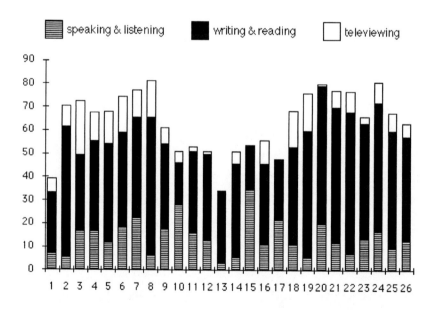

FIGURE 16-1 TIME SPENT COMMUNICATING

In Chapter 2, we looked at the emerging fourth generation of media - Multimedia and Internet - at a sociological level, and concluded that there was not much new. Turning to the psychological level of analysis, we find also that there is little new. Most of us use it as a typewriter. Those who venture beyond do things which could be done before - creating slide shows using PowerPoint, making movies using Premiere, communicating with friends using e-mail. Those are all valuable functions. However, as McLuhan argues, we are driving into the future looking through the rear-view mirror. One indication that we are mired in the past is the terminology that is used. The internet consists of *folders* containing *documents* consisting of *pages* which can be *bookmarked* and sent by *mail* to other people, listed in our *address book*. If the page is too long (as often happens since the page is portrait=shaped whereas the screen is landscape-shaped) then we *scroll* down the page. This takes us way back in technology.

There is some heuristic value in using second-generation terminology within fourth-generation media. The unfamiliar can be best understood by analogy with the familiar. However, analogies are most interesting when they break down. Then what is essentially new is revealed. It would be interesting to use this powerful new tool to do things that we could not do before. At the psychological level, you can do something about it. Here are some suggestions.

The subjective map could be considered as composed of a perceptual map and a conceptual map, corresponding roughly to the thing and the word in the objective world and to text- and image-based media (see Figure 16-2). It is a useful metaphor to consider the perceptual map as a function of the right hemisphere and the conceptual map as a function of the left hemisphere. Within this metaphor, the computer could be consider as the corpus callosum. This captures the two basic characteristics of computer-based media - integration and interactivity. The corpus callosum links the two hemispheres, as the computer integrates text and image, and it links the cerebral cortex with the rest of the body, as the computer provides interactivity between thought and action. We finally have a medium which represents the whole nervous system, a positive prosthetic which fits, a three-dimensional tool which mediates between our three-dimensional brain and our three-dimensional world.

We have to reconsider our current dependence on one- and two-dimensional tools, and our continuing use of the computer as a box to bury old one- and two-dimensional media. We typically use the computer as a typewriter to do one-dimensional word-processing. It is necessary to proceed to two-dimensional idea-processing, in which the computer is used to generate the hierarchical structure of thought underlying the sequential presentation of language, and to three-dimensional multimedia, in which it is used to nest more nodes within any node and to link any two nodes within the hierarchy (see Figure 8-2). This three-dimensional structure is isomorphic with the cognitive structure of the subjective map, viewed as concepts with relationships between them, and with the informatics infrastructure of the objective world, viewed as computers interlinked with telecommunications (see Figure 8-3).

The computer, used as a typewriter, produces a linear string of words. Thus, a one-dimensional medium mediates between your three-dimensional brain and our three-dimensional world. As a typewriter, the computer can tell stories about our world. We all love to tell stories, we all love to hear stories. This is a very important function. However, the computer can go beyond one-dimensional word-processing to two-dimensional idea-processing. Idea-processing programs enable us to explore the hierarchical structure of thought underlying the sequential presentation of language. I start every writing project using an idea-processor (*Think Tank*, later called *More*) rather than a word-processor. Alas, the company which distributed the program is no longer in business. Fortunately, Dave Winer, who wrote the program, has a web site where he gives it away - *www.outliners.com* - and maintains a lively dialogue among those who hav

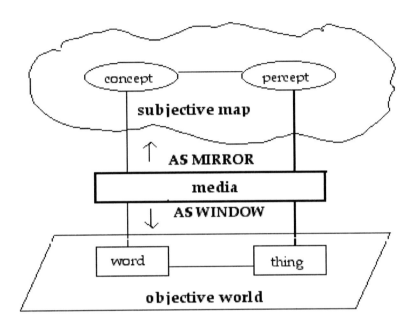

FIGURE 16-2   MEDIA AS WINDOW AND AS MIRROR

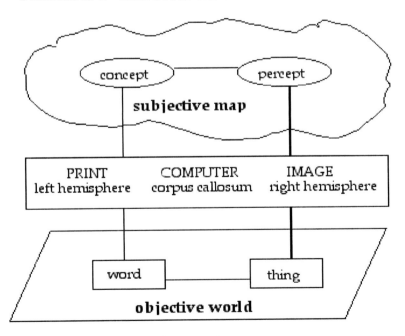

FIGURE 16-3   COMPUTER AS CORPUS CALLOSUM

moved into the two-dimensional use of the computer

The universe changed on 11 August 1987. On that day, Apple Computer Company launched the first publicly available authoring program - *HyperCard*. It enabled us to create a stack of cards (landscape-shaped) rather than a book of pages (portrait-shaped). Thus cards fitted on the computer screen. The cards could contain text or images or text-and-images - thus taking advantage of the integrative power of the computer. The cards could also contain buttons to link to other cards - thus taking advantage of the interactive power of the computer. Bill Atkinson, who wrote the program, insisted that it be given away with each Macintosh computer sold. Thus people began using the computer as a computer. When Atkinson resigned, the Apple Computer Company stopped giving it away and reverted to bundling their Macintosh computers with MacWrite and MacPaint. People returned to using the computer as a typewriter and as an easel.

HyperCard has been followed by a number of more sophisticated authoring programs, like, for example, *Director*, for creating integrative and interactive CD-ROMs and DVDs. Programs like *HTML* and its successors enable us to capitalize on the integrative and interactive power of the computer in creating web sites on the internet. The internet could be considered as a gigantic HyperCard stack. However, none of those programs have the simple elegance of the original - HyperCard. It has been abandoned by Apple Computer Company. However, enthusiasts keep it alive at www.members.aol.com/hcheaven.

HyperCard and its successors allow us to move into a three-dimensional use of the computer. Idea-processors enable us to build a hierarchy. However to get from one node to another, one has to climb the tree structure and go down another branch. *HyperCard* can link any card directly to any other card. It can also use one card as a footnote to another card, and a third card as a footnote to that footnote. Word-processing is represented by a line, idea-processing by a tree, and authoring by a network of nodes. . Media could be considered, not only as mediating between you and I, but as mediating between the objective world and each of our subjective maps of that world. Three-dimensional media consisting of a network of interlinked nodes is isomorphic with the objective world, consisting of computers interlinked by telecommunications, and the subjective map, consisting of interlinked concepts. Thus, it is a perfect tool for creating a full and accurate subjective map of the objective world.

16.3   A DETOUR INTO SEX

I argued in the previous section that human nature is universal, that we all receive the same conception-day gift. There is, however, one exception. We are all hunter-gatherers, but all we men are hunters and all we women are gatherers. Traditional history based on conflict is largely about men, as pointed out by feminists who argue whimsically for a parallel "herstory". In rewriting history as the story of communication rather than conflict, I find, to my embarrassment, that once again it focuses on men. The cast of characters tends to be the obsessive tinkerers - Johann Gutenberg, Alexander Graham Bell, Douglas Engelbart, to name just one from each generation - who have invented those extrasomatic tools.

This boys-with-their-toys emphasis is finally broken only with the fourth generation of media:

- The story of the extension of thought using computers begins with two teen-age girls - Mary Wollstonecraft Goodwin and Augustus Ada Byron (alas, still best known by their married names - Mary Shelley and Lady Lovelace).

• While wandering around the world exploring multimedia in the early 1990s, I was impressed by the fact that many of the most significant figures were women. The Apple Multimedia Laboratory was directed by Kristina Hooper-Woolsey and the experimental classroom in Marin County, generously supported by George Lucas of the nearby Skywalker Ranch and Industrial Light and Magic, was run by her sister.

• Principal speakers at the conference on Virtual Reality in San Francisco were Sherry Turkle and Brenda Laurel [TURKLE 1984, 1996, LAUREL].

• At that conference, Ted Nelson, the visionary behind the Xanadu Project and the hypertext concept, suggested I go to Glasgow to meet his European representative, Liz Davenport. Liz introduced me to two of her friends at Strathclyde University - Patricia Beard and Noreen Mac Morrow - who were publishing *Hypermedia*, the first scholarly journal of multimedia.

• While preparing a speech entitled *What kind of cyborg do you plan to be?* to be delivered to the International Cybernetics Association in Baden Baden, Germany, I found that two major figures in the area were women - Donna Haraway and Katherine Hayles [HARAWAY, HAYLES].

• While attending a conference on *Avatars in Virtual Worlds* at the Banff Center for the Arts, two of the major speakers were Sandy Stone and Janet Murray [STONE, MURRAY].

• Two of the best first-person accounts of life on the internet - *Confessions of an Infomaniac* by Elizabeth Ferrarini [FERRARINI] and *Cyberville: Clicks, Culture and the Creation of an Online Town* by Stacy Horn [HORN] - were written by women.

Some feminists have argued that women were best off in a hunter-gatherer society where they had an important, if under-appreciated, role of supplying 80% of the food [MILES]. The shift into the agricultural society (corresponding to our assimilation of the second generation of media) reduced the status of women.

Horticulture, the domain of women, was replaced by agriculture, the domain of men. Hence the familiar image of the man ploughing fields followed by the woman sowing seeds. The shift into the industrial society (corresponding to our assimilation of the third generation of media) further reduced the status of women. Production shifted from the home, the domain of women, to the factory, the domain of men. Hence the familiar image of the man supervising women laboring in a sweatshop. Perhaps the shift into the information society (corresponding to our assimilation of the fourth generation of media) may finally raise the status of women.

Leonard Shlain, in his book *The Alphabet Versus the Goddess*, has argued that, after a brief period during the early stages of the agricultural society when society was matriarchal and we worshipped Goddesses more than Gods, society suddenly turned patriarchal [SHLAIN]. A number of theories have been ventured to explain this shift.

The domestication of animals made hunting easier and the domestication of plants made gathering easier. Men, deprived of hunting other species as an outlet for the aggression they had accumulated over thousands of years, turned to fighting within our species.[1] In fights between neighboring tribes, the winners would carry off their spoils - the plants, the animals - and subsequently the women of the losers. Capturing women served the evolutionary function of breeding outside the group. However, as an unfortunate side-effect, it encouraged the attitude of thinking of women as property.

Another theory is that, at about that time, by extrapolating from our observation of the animals we had domesticated, our species finally realized the relationship between intercourse and birth. The concept of property extended

---

[1]   Some brave scholars have whimsically suggested that hunting evolved into fighting and gathering into shopping. Being "born to shop" may be demeaning but it is certainly more benign than being "born to fight".

then to one's children. This too contributed to evolution since it motivated men to devote resources to raise children. Once again, there is an unfortunate side-effect. It was important to ensure that the children you were devoting time and energy to raise were indeed your children. This contributed to the further oppression of women, since they had to be closely guarded to ensure that their "provider" was not being cuckolded.

Some permutation of those factors may have been involved. However, Shlain introduces a new factor into the mix. He suggests that the alphabet (or, in our terms, the assimilation of print which coincided with the shift from a hunter-gatherer to an agricultural society) introduced a communication system which was more congenial for men than for women. A hunter, who must focus on one thing in the environment, is more at home with a linear medium than a gatherer, who must scan the whole environment. Thus, men who already had more power because of their physical strength, were able to add further to this power because of this psychological advantage. Shlain surveys history and, time and again, finds that the shift to a patriarchal society coincided with the acquisition of print.

The theory of evolution has been the basic framework for this book. Evolution explains only how our species evolved to a hunter-gatherer society. Recent shifts to an agricultural society to an industrial society to an information society is too brief a time-frame for evolution. This book could be considered as the story of how a hunter-gatherer person acquired different extrasomatic tools to deal with those shifts into different societies.

We are thus all hunter-gatherers, regardless of how sophisticated our society has become. Or rather - to be more precise and more controversial - all we men are hunters and all we women are gatherers. That is, in the vast majority of cases, men tended to specialize in hunting and women tended to specialize in gathering [TOOBY & DE VORE]. Some scholars have suggested that our cognitive skills reflect this specialization.[2]

In a typical experiment, students learn how to walk from point A to point B on campus. They are then blind-folded. Men perform significantly better than women in now getting from A to B. The best explanation so far is that man-the-hunter must follow whatever erratic path the animal he is hunting leads them. To get back to his camp, he must depend on "dead reckoning" - that is, he must navigate by the polar coordinates. On the other hand, woman-the-gatherer can choose her own path to the plants which, unlike animals, remain in one place. To get back to her camp, she can depend on visual cues, picked up on the outward trip. Blind-folding a woman removes the visual cues and thus handicaps her in the navigation task.

In other experiments, however, women do significantly better than men. Irwin Silverman and Marion Eals have designed experiments in which women excel in spatial cognition [SILVERMAN & EALS].[3] In a typical experiment, subjects are in a room, ostensibly waiting to participate in an experiment. When they enter the experimental room, they discover that the experiment is to test how much they remembered about the nature and position of objects on a desk in the room in which they had been waiting. Women did significantly better than men in this task. The best explanation is that women must remember from season to season the relative locations of edible plants.

Further studies have demonstrated that women are better at multi-tasking, whereas men are better at concentrating on a single task. Women are scanning

---

[2]   This is treacherous territory to tread. Many people have used genetic differences as a rationalization for racism, sexism, etc. In broaching the possibility of genetic differences, you find yourself in bed with many people you would cross the street to avoid. However, if there are indeed genetic differences, then one must deal with them in order to understand our species. No matter how genuine differences turn out to be, they do not justify prejudice.

[3]   Note to Heritage Canada. Those experiments were conducted at York University in Toronto. Please consider this paragraph in assessing the Canadian content of this book.

the environment (as befits a gatherer), whereas men are staring straight ahead (as befits a hunter). Men are better at focusing on a single task, as required in hunting, and women are better at dealing with a number of tasks simultaneously, as is required in gathering.

Some would argue that there is not enough difference between men and women in genetic terms to transmit such wide differences in cognitive abilities. Men differ from women only in having a Y chromosome, which is a sort of stunted version of the corresponding X chromosome in women. However, there are many sex-linked traits. For example, color-blindness is largely the domain of men. One in ten men are color-blind whereas only one in a hundred women are color-blind.

Since plants are often color-coded, color perception is important in gatherers. On the other hand, color perception can be a drawback in hunters. Monty Roberts, the man who listens to horses, has remarkable visual acuity. He is said to be able to detect a gesture by a horse when others can't even see the horse [ROBERTS]. This acuity he attributes to his total color blindness. An artist friend wears dark glasses when sketching so that he is not distracted by color. In competitions to assemble jigsaws, participants are not allowed to turn all the pieces over, since it is easier to assemble it without the distraction of color.

Such studies are beginning to modify our conception of pre-history. Innovations in communication and cooperation have traditionally been attributed to the need for man the hunter to communicate and cooperate to outwit other animals which are stronger and faster than them. Perhaps the gatherer lifestyle resulted in innovations. The first tools may have been tools for digging, for carrying food, for carrying babies so that hands are free for gathering, and so on. Those tools may not have survived because they are made of more perishable materials than weapons.

The fact that women slung their babies over the left side so that they can continue to enjoy the comforting beating of the heart as in the womb may explain why we are right-handed. This is the hand which is free. This could in turn explain why the speech center would develop in the left hemisphere. As argued above, Leonard Shlain points out that man-the-hunter, with his single-task focus, find a linear tool more congenial than does woman-the-gatherer with her multi-tasking skills. Thus ironically this practice of women may have contributed to a male-dominated society. Is it possible that our fourth generation of media will lead to a more equitable balance of power?

Shlain argues that photography and film, in emphasizing the image, is creating a world in which women are more at home. Women have certainly had more access to the image industry, as attested by the success of Oprah Winfrey, Barbara Walters and others. However, even here, sexism prevails. A National Film Board (NFB) documentary, for example, focuses on the career of Alice Guy-Braché, the first film-maker, who has disappeared from the official history of film. A CD-ROM entitled *Reel Women*, narrated by Jodie Foster, document the undervalued contribution of women to film.

Shlain lines up Male and Female with a series of other dichotomies - e.g. Yang and Yin, left and right hemispheres, word and image, analysis and synthesis. While alert to the irony that he is writing a book bemoaning the emphasis on the word over the image and the further irony that the use of dichotomies is itself a left-brain, male activity as he pleads for a balance between left and right hemispheres, between male and female values. Perhaps we will move towards such a balance as we assimilate the fourth generation of media - Multimedia and Internet.

Parallel to this re-assessment of the relative power of men and women is the re-assessment of relative 'power' of the animals which men hunted and the plants which women gathered. Plants seem relatively powerless because they are immobile. Who has not get a secret thrill at the thought of a Venus fly-trap capturing and eating insects as the plant fights back? In Section 1.1, I used the example of giraffes eating leaves off tall trees. The eating of the leaves triggers a chemical reaction which makes the leaves bitter to taste. This reaction is communicated to nearby trees, so that the giraffes must move on to other clumps of trees before this clump is destroyed.[4]

In *The Botany of Desire: A Plant's-eye View of the World*, Michael Pollan describes how plants use us as much as we use them. He describes how the apple, the tulip, the marijuana plant, and the potato exploit, respectively, our desires for sweetness, beauty, intoxication, and control, in order to flourish [POLLAN]. We have co-evolved with our plants as well as with our media. The theory of evolution is a great leveler - the lowliest plant can be as well adapted to its environment as the most pompous animal. The fact that plants often have more genes than us deals yet another blow to our conceit. We are reminded that we are a part of nature and not apart from nature.

---

[4]   I'm indebted to Dr. Françoise Zurif for this insight.

16.4 THEIR FUTURES

You and I are among the fortunate few who have access to all those toys and tools. What about the vast majority of the people on our planet who do not have access?

There is much discussion, in industrialized countries, about moving into a post-industrial society. As described above, the transformation from an industrial to a post-industrial society is powered by innovations in electronic technology which have permitted the merger of the computer and the telecommunications industries. The emerging post-industrial society is generally viewed as based on information in contrast to the industrial society which is based on energy.

However, what about developing countries which are still largely pre-industrial societies? There are three options for such a developing country:

- It can remain a pre-industrial society. That is, an agricultural society.
- It can become an industrial society.
- It can "leap-frog" from a pre- to a post-industrial society. That is, to an information society.

The first option is unacceptable. Poor countries can not live any longer alongside rich countries without creating intolerable social tensions. This tension will be intensified in a "global village" where the media confronts the poor daily with the contrast. Terrorist attacks such as 9/11 are the tip of an iceberg of resentment of the rich by the poor. The Third World War has started. It is a war between the Third World, conducted until 9/11 largely IN the third world, and the First World. (The war between the second world (communism) and the first world (capitalism) has been declared over [FUKUYAMA 1992]). World War 3 will continue until the first world learns how to share the wealth.

The second option is unacceptable. Our planet could not sustain the industrialization of the developing countries. We are already pushing toward the limits to growth due to the industrialized of only a few countries [MEADOWS ET AL].

This leaves the third option. This option was actively pursued by Jean-Jacques Servan-Schreiber in the 1980s [SERVAN-SCHREIBER]. He had set up a center in Paris to help countries in French West Africa to leapfrog from pre- to post-industrial societies using Japanese capital, American expertise and French management. The attempt failed and the vision faded.[5] However, this **"leap-frog" strategy** is worth considering - even if only as the least of three evils.

This third option for the Third World is often dismissed with a number of arguments. It is a rationalization for depriving developing countries of the benefits of industrialization. Industrialized countries will not permit it since they wish to dump their obsolete technology on developing countries.[6] Developing countries WANT the old technologies since they associate them with the rich life-styles of developed countries.

Timing in the presentation of ideas is very important. If it is presented too soon, it is viewed as preposterous; if it is presented too late, it is viewed as obvious. One must hit the moment between the *what!* and the *so what?*. The "leap-frog" idea is still preposterous but, in our fast-moving times, may very soon become obvious. The aim of this section is to make a small contribution toward inhibiting the tongue-jerk response of dismissing the "leap-frog" hypothesis as

---

5

When I visited, Nicholas Negroponte, Seymour Papert, and other scholars from the Media Lab at MIT were there. Part of the problem may have been the conflict between the more authoritarian management style of the French as opposed to that of the United States. The Americas referred to Jean-Jacques Servan-Schreiber affectionately as J2S2.

6   Alvin Toffler argues that we are now dumping an entire obsolete society on them by recommending that they repeat our mistake by moving into an industrial society - that is, taking option 2 above [TOFFLER 1990]..

preposterous and, by presenting some arguments for it, however naive they may sound, helping it towards the obvious.

- ## PRE- AND POST-INDUSTRIAL SOCIETIES ARE ALIKE

Leaping industrial society with a single bound *sounds* as if it would cause great social upheaval. However, the "frog" may be smaller than we think. One desirable vision of the post-industrial information society has more in common with pre-industrial society than with industrial society. It emphasizes decentralization (trading telecommunications for transportation), living in small, intimate, rural communities, cottage industry (production by the masses rather than mass production). It is a global village and not a global metropolis.

It might, paradoxically, be easier to move to a post-industrial society from a pre-industrial society. There is less inertia to overcome from the established outmoded technology. The dramatic post-war recoveries of Japan and West Germany have been partly attributed to being "*bombed back into the Stone Age*". The war enabled them to start fresh by destroying their obsolete equipment. There is also less inertia to overcome from the established outmoded minds. The emphasis on images over words in a post industrial society is more congenial to pre-industrial peoples who have perceptual rather than conceptual-based cognitive systems. Anthropologists have often reported that pre-literate peoples have an incredible aptitude for working with modern technology.

- ## APPROPRIATE TECHNOLOGY MAY BE HIGH TECHNOLOGY

Those who question the value of high technology for the developing countries tend to couch their arguments in terms of appropriate technology. Who would dare argue against appropriate technology? However, high technology, in some cases, may be appropriate technology. This is such a case. As electronic memory gets smaller and smaller and smarter and smarter and cheaper and cheaper (to buy and to run), it gets appropriater and appropriater.

The "appropriate technology" argument tends to parallel the "hierarchy of needs" argument, based on the work of Abraham Maslow [MASLOW]. The former argues that one must first get low technology, then medium technology, and finally high technology; the latter argues that one must first satisfy biological needs, then sociological needs, and finally psychological needs. Both serve as a rationalization for keeping developing countries poor. Both are delaying tactics. Focus on the satisfaction of basic needs before continuing to the satisfaction of luxury needs (like human dignity and freedom, knowledge and understanding). Basic needs are, of course, never totally satisfied.

Just as the satisfaction of biological, sociological, and psychological needs has to be sought simultaneously, so low, medium, and high technologies have to be introduced simultaneously. There is an "appropriate" mix of the various technologies in each situation. The high technologies of the information society help satisfy the need to know and understand which are organically built into the human genes [see Section 9.3).

Another argument is that, whereas the electronic devices are getting cheaper, they require a very expensive infrastructure to support them. Satellite technology, however, promises to reduce the need for an elaborate infrastructure.[7] The Columbia spaceship, with the aid of Canadarm, is sowing satellites in the sky from which information can be picked up with inexpensive satellite dishes..

- ELECTRONIC TECHNOLOGY IS "FOOTLOOSE"

The technologies are "footloose". Those industries do not depend on any raw materials which anchor them in some geographical area. The gold-mining

---

[7]   The author and some colleagues visited Arthur C. Clarke in Sri Lanka. Clarke pointed out that a local lad had built a dish, pointed it toward a satellite (orbiting in Clarke's geostationary orbit) and all of Sri Lanka saw the Moscow Olympics.

industry has to be where the gold is and the timber industry where the trees are but the electronic industry can be anywhere. The basic raw material is silicon - second only to oxygen as the most widely-available element on our planet. Most developing countries have lots of sand. For certain psychocultural reasons, "silicon valley" is in California. So also is "silicon valley" (Broadway Street in the North Beach area where the first topless dancers performed). There are no technoeconomic reasons why either of them had to be there. Both commodities are equally available elsewhere. The ubiquitous chip is not only ubiquitous in terms of its use in so many devices, it is ubiquitous in terms of the sources with which it is constructed.

•   ELECTRONIC TECHNOLOGY IS FLUID

Like most powerful technologies, the new electronic technologies can be instruments of oppression or instruments of liberation. In their current volatile state, they consist mainly of vague threats and rosy promises. The potential can go either way. Intelligent intervention at this point can ensure that the good rather than the evil potential is realized.

Most discussion of electronic technology and developing countries is couched in a business-as-usual framework. Those new means will be used to old ends. The flavor of this discussion is contained in the titles of two major works within this tradition: *Media Imperialism Reconsidered* [CHIN-CHAUN] and *Electronic Colonialism* [MCPHAIL]. Such electronic exploitation is a distinct possibility. However, this outcome has not yet been determined. There is a positive alternative as well as this negative alternative.

Kimon Valaskakis has described two major scenarios for the information society - the **telematique** and the **privatique** [VALASKAKIS K 1979]. The former is modeled on the television system and the latter on the telephone system. In the former scenario, a few huge sources (like the three major television networks in the United States) beam information down a great electronic highway to millions of destinations at their terminals. In the latter scenario, the terminals are interconnected in a vast network, such that everyone can be a source as well as a destination.

No doubt, what will emerge will be some complex combination of both scenarios, complicated by the "pique" scenario in which some people reject some of the technology. However, those two "pure" scenarios help us evaluate which developments contribute toward oppression and which toward liberation. The telematique scenario is potentially more oppressive. Big Brother can not operate over a telephone network. On the other hand, as Hazel Henderson has demonstrated, grassroots movements can use it very effectively. It has been argued that a dictatorship can not thrive in a country where 20% of the population have access to a telephone.

• ELECTRONIC TECHNOLOGY IS ECOLOGICALLY BENIGN

It was argued above that developing countries could leapfrog from the first wave of the agriculture society to the third wave of the information society with only a cursory wave in passing to the second wave of industrial society. By-passing the industrial society means by-passing also the noxious by-products and the damaging side-effects of the process of industrialization. The means of doing so, electronic technology, is itself a clean industry. The raw materials are cheap and plentiful. There are no noxious by-products.

As argued above, the transportation-telecommunications trade-off, made possible by electronic technology, also contributes to conservation of our planet. Marshall McLuhan pointed out many years ago that executives drive to the office to answer the telephone. They are still doing so. However, more and more people are recognizing that they have a perfectly good phone at home. It is becoming increasingly possible to perform more and more job functions at home as that telephone trades its handset for a terminal. Cutting the cost of commuting makes good economic sense for the individual and good environmental sense for our society.

- ELECTRONIC TECHNOLOGY CAN HELP TURN DEVELOPMENT INSIDE OUT

There are two basic views of the teaching process [GARDINER 1980]. The traditional view is that it is an outside-in process in which the teacher passes on the accumulated wisdom of the culture to the next generation. It is a sort of psychic transplant operation. The alternative view is that it is an inside-out process in which the teacher arranges congenial environments to help draw out the intrinsic potential of the learner. Both views contain some of the truth. The student is learning from the outside in and growing from the inside out. The important issue is the optimal orchestration of outside-in learning with inside-out growing.

When traditional education was established, the outside-in view was perhaps appropriate. There was not much information available in the community and the teacher could view himself/ herself as a repository of useful information. Communities in developing countries often suffer from a paucity of information as in those early days of developed nations. Electronic technology can help solve this problem. With the Library of Congress quite literally at your fingertips, each small community need not stock up with expensive, immediately-obsolete books. They can all share a common databank which can be updated daily.

Those devices can not replace teachers. They can, however, perform the mechanical outside-in information-supplying function and thus free the teacher for the more human inside-out inspiration-creating function. Intelligence is a function not of innate ability but of information-rich environments in which we all share.

• CANADA CAN CONTRIBUTE TO THE 'LEAP- FROG'

Northrop Frye once said of Canada that it *"has passed from a pre-national to a post-national phase without ever having become a nation"*. Canada, it would seem, has applied the leap-frog strategy to nationhood. There are many ways in which it can contribute to the leap-frog strategy in the developing countries. Indeed, Canada has some Third World characteristics. More powerful industrialized nations tend to view it as a supplier of raw materials and a buyer of the finished products. In terms of the limited extent to which it has realized its vast potential, it could be considered one of the most underdeveloped countries in the world.

John A. Macdonald once described Canada as a country *"with too little history and too much geography"*. Because of this vast geography, it is held together with technology - first, with railway lines and, then, as telecommunications were traded for transportation, with telephone wires. Necessity has bred invention. We have what is probably the best communication infrastructure in the world. This technology and the expertise which developed it can be transferred to the developing countries.

The author had a what-am-I-doing-here? speech, which he delivered at technical conferences in electronics. The answer, of course, was that the introduction of new technology is not only a technical matter but also a psychological matter. This is especially important when it is being introduced to people of another culture. Our vast expertise in the social sciences (and reservoir of unemployed social scientists) can also contribute to the leap-frog strategy.

Canada is a unique laboratory for the study of the introduction of electronic technology in different cultures. We have an internal South-North situation which mirrors, in microcosm, the external North-South situation [VALASKAKIS G]. Our native peoples, Indians and Inuits, concentrated in the

North, tend to be living under poorer conditions than the immigrants in the South. Introduction of electronic technology into isolated Northern communities which request it could help us understand empirically what difficulties would be encountered in introducing it within the developing countries.

There will, of course, be incredible difficulties. However, it is imperative that we accept the challenge since, to return to the beginning of the argument, the "leap-frog" is the least of three evils. It may even turn out not to be an "evil" at all. Those who dismiss the leap-frog must come up with an alternative solution to the problem of the uneven distribution of wealth on our planet. This is the major problem of our brand-new twenty-first century.

This book opens with the promise to tell the story of communication rather than the traditional story of conflict. However, that traditional story continues. The Third World War - that is, a war in the "*third world*" - has started. This is a true world war rather than a couple of local skirmishes between developed countries. It is a war between the "greedies" and the "needies". Terrorism is the tip of an iceberg of resentment of the rich by the poor. Global media reminds the poor daily that household pets of the rich are better housed and fed than they are.

The alternative futures of media presented in this book are options only for the small, privileged minority which has access to those media to extend the nervous system. The majority of people in poor countries have never made a telephone call far less moved a cursor across a screen. This book focuses on a psychological level of analysis with only the previous two chapters - Chapter 14 *Media and the Corporation* and Chapter 15 *Media and the University* - rising to a brief consideration of the sociological level of analysis. However, the context of our various social institutions will play an important role in determining how we will each individually be able to use media to extend our nervous systems in the future.

APPENDIX A - CAST OF CHARACTERS

1400 GUTENBERG 1468

1791 MORSE 1872

1791 BABBAGE 1871
1797 GOODWIN 1851
1815 BYRON 1851

1809 DARWIN 1882
1823 WALLACE 1913

1819 SCOLES 1890

1830 MUGGERIDGE 1904

1847 BELL 1922

1888 BAIRD 1946
1889 ZWORYKIN 1985
1907 FARNSWORTH 1971

1896 PIAGET 1980

1894 INNIS 1952
1911 MCLUHAN M 1980
1939 LOGAN
1940 LEVINSON
1941 MCLUHAN E
1945 KROKER
1946 DE KERCKHOVE
1955 POWE

1912 TURING 1954
1925 ENGELBART

1928 CHOMSKY

1954 WARWICK
1957 CLARK
1962 MANN

APPENDIX B
LIST OF
RELEVANT FILMS

(There is a space after each
section to add the films I have
missed.)

ALL GENERATIONS

Cola Conquest, The
Connections
Day the Universe Changed, The
Marshall McLuhan: The Man and
   His Message
Manufacturing Consent

FIRST GENERATION -
MEMORY AND SPEECH

DOCUMENTARY

HISTORY OF ROCK 'N ROLL
Rock 'n Roll Explodes
Good Rocking Tonight
Britain Invades,
America Fights Back
Pluggin' In
The Sounds of Soul
My Generation
Guitar Heroes
The 70s: Have a Nice Decade
Punk
Up from the Underground

NATURE OF THINGS
Face Value
Memory
Mystery of the Mind

NOVA
In Search of the First Language
Private Life of Dolphins
Secret of the Wild Child

After Darwin:
Understanding Evolution
Dawn of Man
DNA: The Ultimate Test
Evolution
Gene Hunters
Inside the Animal's Mind
Something Hidden (Wilder Penfield)

DRAMA

Butterfly Effect
Cast Away
Children of a Lesser God
Fifty First Dates
Gossip
Heart is a Lonely Hunter
Horse Whisperer, The
Memento
Miracle Worker
Monday After the Miracle
Quest for Fire
Urban Legends: The Final Cut

SECOND GENERATION - PRINT AND FILM

DOCUMENTARY

AMERICAN CINEMA
The Hollywood Style
The Star
Romantic Comedy
Film Noir
The Studio System
Film in the TV Age
The Film School Generation
The Edge of Hollywood

American Splendor
Comic Book Confidential
Double Exposure: The Story of
    Margaret Bourke-White
8 mm
Embattled Shadows NFB
Frontline: Tabloid Truth
Future of the Book
Has Anyone Here Seen Canada?
History of Canadian Movies
Hollywoodism: Jews, Movies, and
    the American Dream
Lost Garden, The: The Life and
    Times of Alice Guy-Blaché
MGM: When the Lion Roars
National: Paper King (Conrad Black)
National: What Border? How We
    Lost it at the Movies
Visions of Light: The Art of
    Cinematography
Wonderful, Horrible Life of Leni
    Riefenstahl

DRAMA

Absence of Malice
All the President's Men
Cinema Paradisio
Citizen Kane
Day for Night
Defence of the Realm
Fahrenheit 451
F/X
Lotus-Eaters
Newsies
Paul Bartel's The Secret Cinema
Purple Rose of Cairo
State and Main
Truman Show
Zelig

THIRD GENERATION - TELEPHONE AND TELEVISION

DOCUMENTARY

American Experience:
Big Dream - Small Screen
CBS: The First 50 Years

DAWN OF THE EYE
Born Among Clowns
Embattled Witnesses
Eyes of the World
Inventing TV News
The Power and the Image

Dreamland: NFB
Edison Effect, The
Edison the Man
Empire of the Air: The Men Who
    Made Radio
Magic Time NFB
Media Literacy: The New Basics
Public Mind
Other Side of the Picture
Rogers' Cable, The
Signal to Noise: Life with TV
Sound and the Silence, The
TVTV
Vista: Revolution in a Box
Young Tom Edison

DRAMA

Alexander Graham Bell
Being There
Blade Runner
Brave New World
Broadcast News
Dear God
Dispatch from Reuters
EdTV
Max Headroom:

20 Minutes into the Future
Natural Born Killers
Network
Nineteen Eighty-Four
Pleasantville
Quiz Show
Radio Days
Rollerball
Running Man, The
Tron
Truman Show
Videodrome
Wag the Dog

FOURTH GENERATION - MULTIMEDIA AND INTERNET

DOCUMENTARY

Breaking the Code (Alan Turing)
Hackers: Computer Outlaws
Journal: Digital Dreams

MACHINE THAT CHANGED THE
WORLD
Giant Brains
Inventing the Future
Paperback Computer
The Thinking Machine
The World at Your Fingertips

Minerva's Machine:
Women and Computing

Nature of Things:
Highway to Cyberia
Nova: Decoding Nazi Secrets
Robots are Rising
Triumph of the Nerds
Nerds 2.0.1:
A Brief History of the Internet
Undercurrents: Wired Flesh
Using the Internet

Robocop
Rowing with the Wind
Short Circuit 1, 2
Smart House
Tank Girl
Total Recall
Tron
War Games
Wild Palms
You've Got Mail

DRAMA

AI
Antitrust
Beyond Human
Bionic Ever After
Blade Runner
Circuitry Man
Cold Lazarus
Computer Wore Tennis Shoes, The
Conceiving Ada
Cyberstalker
Cyborg
eXistenZ
Final Fantasy
Ghost in the Machine
Gothic
Hackers
Hardware
Harsh Realm
I, Robot
Johnny Mnemonic
Matrix, The
Net, The

GLOSSARY

Accommodation   Ontogenetic development (child to adult) has the same basic principle as phylogenetic development (animal to human) - adaptation. Adaptation involves the **assimilation** of information from the environment and the **accommodation,** if necessary, of the cognitive structure to this information (Jean Piaget).

Activation Theory   An emotion-arousing stimulus in the environment **(negative goal)** projects directly to the sensory reception area of the brain to provide the **cue function** and indirectly through the **amygdala** in the lower brain which acts diffusely on the brain to provide the **arousal function.** A psychological drive prepares the organism for appropriate action (fight, flight) by triggering the relevant physiological state **(rage, fear).**   see also **Theory of Evolution**

Aha phenomenon   see **Eureka Effect**

American Sign Language (ASL)   see **Code**

Amygdala   see **Activation Theory**

Anthropotropic Principle   The principle that technologies work better when they respect the nature of the human body and the human mind (Paul Levinson). Thus, for example, the mouse-qwerty keyboard combination does not respect the fact that humans have only two hands.

Arousal function   see **Activation theory**

Artificial life   Development of artificial intelligence from the inside out by simulating the evolution of life.

Artificial Intelligence (AI)   The attempt to simulate various conceptual and perceptual functions of the human brain. c.f. **Intelligence Amplification (IA).**   Using computers to supplement, rather than to simulate, natural intelligence.

Assimilation   see **Accommodation**

Asynchronous communication   see **Synchronous communication**

Automatic Teller Machine (ATM)   A machine to replace human tellers by simulating their functions.

Avatar   A digital representation of yourself which interacts with other avatars, representing other people, in a virtual world.

Biomimicry   A conscious strategy by designers to observe and learn principles of design from nature.

Biophile   see Biotechnology

Biophobe   see Biotechnology

Biotechnology   Technology which uses biological as opposed to mechanical and electronic systems. **Biophiles.** People who emphasize the opportunities offered by biotechnology. **Biophobes.** People who emphasize the threats posed by biotechnology.

Bit   A basic unit in measurement of information. Information from the source is measured in terms of **uncertainty** at the destination. One bit of information is information that cuts uncertainty in half.

Boustrophedon script   Script in which the text alternates between left-to-right and right-to-left. From the Egyptian word for "as the ox ploughs". It was used for large documents on walls so that the reader did not have to walk back to the beginning of the next line.

Braille   see **Code**

Camera obscurata   A pin-hole camera consisting of a light-tight box with a small hole. Used since the Middle Ages to create images by permitting light to shine through the small hole on to the surface at the opposite side of the box.

Chord keyset   A one-handed keyboard consisting of five keys (one for each finger). Letters are represented by a binary code consisting of some combination of those keys. Douglas Engelbart, the inventor of the mouse, recommended this chord keyset for the other hand.

Classical conditioning   A stimulus, previously neutral (**unconditioned stimulus**), can come to elicit a response (**conditioned reflex**) if paired with a stimulus (**unconditioned stimulus**) which already elicits this response (**unconditioned reflex**). (Ivan Pavlov).   c.f. **Instrumental Conditioning** A stimulus, previous neutral, can come to elicit a response if it is instrumental in gaining access to a stimulus which already elicits a desirable response. Also called **Trial-and-Error learning** (Edward Thorndike). Thorndike used a **puzzle box**, which was transformed by B. F. Skinner into a **Skinner Box**.

Cloning   The process of creating an exact biological replica of an existing organism from the genes of that organism.

Code   A system of communication which piggy-backs on language by creating a one-to-one relationship between the elements of the code and the letters of the alphabet. Used in situations where language can not be used. Examples are
- **Braille** for communication with the blind - a code in which patterns of raised dots represent the letters of the alphabet,
- **American Sign Language (ASL)** for communication with the deaf - a code in which hand signs represent the letters of the alphabet, and
- **Semaphore** for communication at a distance where there is visual contact but not auditory contact - a code in which the pattern of the positions of two flags represent the letters of the alphabet.
- **Morse code** for communication at a distance where there is neither auditory or visual contact, but there is a wire along which can be passed a series of short and long signals by interrupting the electric flow along the wire.

Cofigurative   A society in which young and old teach one another. c.f.
Prefigurative where the old teach the young and **postfigurative** where the
young teach the old (Margaret Mead).

Cognitive dissonance   The tendency to change one or the other of two
incompatible beliefs.

Conceptual map   see **Subjective map**

Conditioned stimulus   see **Classical Conditioning**

Conditioned reflex   see **Classical Conditioning**

Contractual relationship   A relationship based on a "contract", whether
explicit or implicit. I'll do this for you if you do that for me. c.f. An **intimate
relationship** which is based on the intrinsic worth of the two unique people
involved. They are not, as in the contractual relationship, interchangeable.

Cool-hunter   A person hired by a company to help anticipate the Next Big
Thing, so that they can exploit the trend commercially.

Craft literacy   Skills which are assimilated by the body rather than by the
mind and thus can not be transmitted to others through concepts and percepts.
Others must acquire those skills for themselves through practicing the skills.

Critical flicker frequency (CFF)   The number of still frames per second
necessary to create the illusion of motion. This illusion of motion is based on the
phi phenomenon (also called **persistence of vision**) - the fact that excitation of
the sensory neurons "persist" for a short time after the stimulus has gone.

Cryonics   The science of freezing a body (or head) and de-freezing it when
the cure is found for the disease from which the person is suffering.

Cue function   see **Activation theory**

Cultural determinism   see **Technological determinism**

Cyborg   Any entity which is part person and part machine.

Delayed response   The capacity to delay a response when presented with a stimulus. The length of delay possible is a useful rough index of phylogenetic development. It is significant since it indicates that there are internuncial neurons mediating between sensory and motor neurons. This permits the organism to say "no" to its environment. c.f. **Detour behavior** The capacity to detour around a barrier to reach a goal. It is significant because it indicates that the behavior of the organism is determined not by the **objective world** only but also by its **subjective map** of the objective world.

Deoxyribonucleic acid (DNA)   The code in which all organisms are written. Some researchers have argued that ontogenetic memory (that acquired during the individual life of an organism), is written in **ribonucleic acid (RNA)**, a biological cousin to DNA, in which phylogenetic memory (that acquired during the evolution of the species to which the organism belongs) is written.

Desktop Production (DTP)   Production of books, magazines and other print products on a computer. c.f. **Desktop Video Production (DTVP)** - now called **Digital Video (DV)**. Production of films, videos and other image products on a computer.

Desktop Video Production (DTVP)   see **Desktop Production (DTP)**

Detour behavior   see **Delayed response**

Digital Versatile Disk (DVD)   A disk the same size as CD Audio and CD-ROM but holding much more information. Since a full-length movie can be stored on the disk - with space left over for much supplementary material, the DVD is gradually replacing the videocassette in video stores. No one calls it Doubtful Very Doubtful any more.

Digital Video (DV)   see **Desktop Production (DTP)**

Drive   see **Need-Reduction Theory**

Dystopia   A pessimistic vision of a grim future.
c.f. Utopia   An optimistic vision of a bright future.

Echoic response   see **Verbal behavior**

Ecosphere   see **Triad Model**

Edutainment   Educational content embedded in an entertainment package.

Electronic superhighway   see **Informatics**

Equivocation   see **Transmitted information**

ETA Report   see **GAMMA**

Eureka Effect   The sudden realization of the solution to a problem. Such inspiration usually follows considerable perspiration. Also called the **aha phenomenon.**

Extragenetic information   Information which is outside the genetic code but still inside the body. c.f. **Extrasomatic information** - information which is stored outside the body (Carl Sagan).

Extrasomatic information   see **Extragenetic information**

Fear   see **Activation theory**

Fiber optics   Devices made of glass which can carry considerably more signals that the copper wires which they are replacing.

Fixed schedule   see **Total reinforcement**

GAMMA   Groupe Associé des Universitiés de Montréal et McGill pour l'Etude de l'Avenir (GAMMA) was an inter-university, inter-disciplinary think tank based in Montreal. Our Conserver Society Project culminated in a multi-volume report submitted to ten departments of the Federal Government of Canada and a popular book, entitled *The Conserver Society* [VALASKAKIS ET AL]. The major productions of our Information Society Project were the **ETA Report** and the **TAO Report** delivered to our various clients in government (municipal, provincial, and federal), in business, and in global non-government agencies (United Nations University, UNESCO, etc.). The ETA (environmental tracking analysis) Report was an account of the major processes of current change, and the TAO (Threats and Opportunities) Report was an assessment of the implications of those changes for each client.

Ganzfeld   German for "*total field*". A device for exploring the total visual field. The "pocket Ganzfeld", consisted of two half ping-pong balls placed over the two eyes, produced the same effect as the original Ganzfeld - a six-foot diameter hemisphere.

Geographical Positioning System (GPS)   Technology which enables you to tell where in the world you are in latitude and longitude. **Locative computing**   Various projects using computers and GPS.

Global Village   The world shrunk by communication technology to a village (Marshall McLuhan).

Goal   Goals may be positive - e.g. things you eat (see **Need-Reduction Theory**) or negative - e.g. things that eat you (see **Activation theory**).

Heuristics   The set of skills for organizing information at the source for effective transmission. c.f. **Mnemonics**   The set of skills for organizing information at the destination for effective reception.

Hierarchy of needs   Biological needs are more potent than sociological needs which, in turn, are more potent than psychological needs. As needs at one level are satisfied, the person can move up the hierarchy (Abraham Maslow).

High-definition Television (HDTV)   A long-awaited innovation in video technology providing a much better resolution than traditional television.

Homeobox genes   Genes which "supervise" the activities of other genes.

Homeostasis   see Need-Reduction Theory

Human Genome Project   The breaking of the code in which our species is written. It turned into a race between public and private organizations, with the private organizations winning, raising important moral and legal issues about the commercial spin-off from the resultant knowledge.

HyperCard   The first generally-available authoring program (Bill Atkinson). It has since been replaced by more sophisticated but less elegant programs like Director and HTML.

IMAX   A film technology, developed in Canada, but now exploited in the United States. Huge cameras shoot huge rolls of film to be projected on to huge screens. In the IMAX theaters, the film is high enough and wide enough to include the whole visual field of the viewer, thus making the experience closer to that of the "**mind movie**". In the **OMNIMAX** theaters, this effect is further enhanced by projecting the image on a semi-circular surface.

Imprinting   The process by which nature leaves a gap in the unfolding of the genetic program in the development of an organism to be filled in by the environment. Researchers have explored this phenomenon by interfering with nature's plans - for example, by substituting a person for a duck as the first large moving object seen by baby ducks (Konrad Lorenz). The acquisition of **language** could be considered as an imprinting process, in which nature leaves a large gap to be filled in by the particular language community in which the child is developing.

Informatics   The system created by the convergence of computer nodes and tele-communication links into a network. **Electronic superhighway** is a metaphorical term for informatics. It has gone out of fashion but should be retained to remind us that informatics is the infrastructure of the information society just as the transportation system was the infrastructure of the industrial society.

Inheritance of acquired characteristics   The erroneous idea that characteristics which an organism acquires in its life-time can be passed on to the next generation (Jean-Baptiste Lamarck).

Instrumental Conditioning   see **Classical Conditioning**

Intelligence Amplification (IA)   see **Artificial Intelligence (AI)**

Interval schedule   see **Total reinforcement**

Intimate relationship   see **Contractual relationship**

Killer application   A software function which encourages the sale of the faster and fuller hardware necessary to run it.

Language   A hierarchy of units plus rules for combining units at each level to make meaningful units at the next level. The smallest units are **phonemes** (sounds - corresponding roughly to the letters of the alphabet), which can be combined by the rules of vocabulary to create **morphemes** (smallest meaningful units - corresponding roughly to words). Those can, in turn, be combined by the rules of grammar into sentences, and those can, in turn, be combined by the rules of logic into discourses.

Language-acquisition device (LAD)   A hypothetical construct in the brain to explain the easy acquisition of language by children during a sensitive period (Noam Chomsky). It does not unfold in a vacuum. It needs a **Language-acquisition Support System (LASS)** (Jerome Bruner).

Language-acquisition Support System (LASS)   see **Language-acquisition device (LAD)**

Leap-frog strategy   A third option for the Third World, in which a country *"leap-frogs"* from a pre-industrial to a post-industrial society.

Localization   The theory that various psychological functions are precisely localized in certain areas of the central nervous system. c. f. **mass action**. The theory that, for certain functions, the central nervous system acts as a whole.

Locative computing   see **Global Positioning System (GPS)**

MACHO interface   see **User interface**

Mand   see **Verbal behavior**

Mass action   see **Localization**

Mind Movie   The mind could be considered as a magnificent movie studio which creates a "mind movie" running continuously throughout a lifetime. It also doubles as a movie theater where we can watch the show. Alas, it has only one seat and we need to become artists to show our home movies. see also **Visual field**.

Mnemonics   see **Heuristics**

Moore's Law   The law that computer memory will half in size and cost every 18 months. It has held for the last few decades and it is broadly assumed that it will continue to apply for some time (Gordon Moore).

More   see **Think Tank**

Morpheme   see **Language**

Morse Code   see **Code**

Nanotechnology   The building of various devices from the basic building blocks of nature - atoms and molecules.

Natural selection   see **Theory of Evolution**

Need   see **Need-Reduction Theory**

Need-Reduction Theory   An organism is jerked out of a steady state (**homeostatis**) by a state of deprivation called a **need** (hunger, thirst, etc.). In order to return to this steady state it must behave appropriately with respect to some environmental object called the **positive goal** (eating food, drinking water). The physiological need is transformed into a psychological **drive**, since only the nervous system knows the environment.
see also **Theory of Evolution**

Net Generation   The generation which has been raised with computers from infancy (Don Tapscott).

Noise   see **Transmitted information**

Objective world   see **Subjective map, Delayed response**

Observer effect   Since the person in the center is the element of the **sociosphere**, the social sciences must deal with the **observer effect**. That is, what is observed can be changed by the act of observing it, and by the attitudes of the observer. Since the person in the center is the source of the **technosphere**, in the sciences of the artificial we must deal with the **participant effect**. That is, the effect on the person can be influenced by the actions of the person.

OMNIMAX   see **IMAX**

Operating Manual for Species Homo Sapiens   A hypothetical manual which helps us operate our nervous systems. The author argues that all normal brains operate according to the same basic principles. Individual differences are a function of the extent to which a person learns those principles, which deal largely with the skills and tools of the four generations of media. The first generation could be considered as the conception-day gift and the other three generations as the unwrapping of this gift over historical time.

Partial reinforcement   see **Total reinforcement**

Participant effect   see **Observer effect**

Perceptual map   see **Subjective map**

Persistence of vision   see **Critical flicker frequency (CFF)**

Phi phenomenon   see **Critical flicker frequency (CFF)**

Phoneme   see **Language**

Phoneme-Grapheme correspondence   Correspondence between the set of elements of speaking (phonemes) and the set of elements of writing (graphemes). Perfect phoneme-grapheme correspondence would facilitate the learning of writing.

Physiological nystagmus   The fact that the eye is constantly moving up and down. This was seen by arrogant humans as a design flaw in nature's invention. However, it was subsequently found to be a useful design feature to ensure that the "film" in the eye "camera" is constantly refreshed.

Positive prosthetic   A device which enhances human functioning rather than simply replacing a function which is damaged.

Postfigurative   see **Cofigurative**

Prefigurative   see **Cofigurative**

Prestige   see **Self-esteem**

Privatique Scenario   A vision of the future of the information society based, like the telephone, on a network of nodes in which everyone can be source as well as destination. c.f. **Telematique Scenario**   A vision of the future of the information society based, like the television, in which a few sources beam information to millions of passive destinations (Kimon Valaskakis).

Puzzle Box   Device for studying learning in cats. The cat must learn to press a lever to get out of the box to earn *"fish, friends, and freedom"* (Edward Thorndike). c.f. **Skinner Box**   Upgraded puzzle box in which the dispensing of rewards and the recording of responses is automated (B. F. Skinner).

QWERTY Phenomenon   The traditional qwerty keyboard was originally designed to slow typists down because the keys would stick if one typed too fast. The keys don't stick any more (especially in a computer keyboard) but we are stuck with the keyboard because it has been mastered by so many people. Hence qwerty phenomenon refers to this human tendency to retain inefficient technology because there is a vested interest by those who are familiar with it and competent on it.

Rage   see **Activation theory**

Ratio schedule   see **Total reinforcement**

Redundancy   A feature of language in which the probability of an element is constrained by its context. e.e. the letter after Q in English must be a U and the next letter must be a vowel.

Ribonucleic acid (RNA)   see **Deoxyribonucleic acid (DNA)**

Sailboat Effect   Sailboat technology improved considerably when the sailboat was challenged by the steamship.   Hence sailboat effect refers to improvements in a technology as a result of the emergence of a competing technology.

Satellite   A person-made object orbiting the globe which is capable of relaying electrical signals back to earth.

Selective perception   The tendency to "select" from the vast array of sensory input those things which you have been set to see.

Self-esteem   Worth in one's own eyes. c.f. **Prestige**   Worth in the eyes of others.

Semaphore   see **Code**

Serendipity   The art of finding something by looking for something else.

Siliclone   A silicon clone of yourself. It consists of all your publications and presentations plus your favorite quotes and anecdotes, collected on a CD-ROM or in a web site. It serves as a satellite when you are alive and a surrogate when you are dead. People can visit your mind at your web site rather than your body at your grave site.

Skinner Box   see **Puzzle Box**

Social Darwinism   see **Theory of Evolution**

Sociosphere   see **Triad Model, Observer effect**

Standard Social Science Model (SSSM)   The typical model underlying much social science. It assumes that the mind is a "**tabula rasa**" on which the environment writes.

Staples theory   The theory that a country's economy can be best understood in terms of its raw materials - furs, fish, lumber, etc. in the case of Canada (Harold Innis).

Subjective map   The various maps each of us has of the **objective world**. The map can be composed of images (**perceptual map**) or of words (**conceptual map**). It is a useful heuristic to associate the conceptual map with the left hemisphere of the brain (where the speech center is located) and the perceptual map with the right hemisphere. see also **Delayed response**.

Symbolization   The representation of something by something else (e.g. an object may be represented by an image, a gesture, a word).

Synchronous communication   Communication when the sender and receiver are transmitting and receiving at the same time. c.f. **Asynchronous communication** when the transmission and reception of the message are at different times. With time-shifting devices, communication is becoming more asynchronous.

Tabula isola   see **Tabula rasa**

Tabula rasa   The mind is a "blank slate" on which experiences writes (John Locke). c.f. **Tabula isola** Cognitive functions take place within the single, isolated brain (Merlin Donald).

Tact   see **Verbal behavior**

Tally   A device for recording information. It showed only quantity without identifying what was being measured. c.f. **Token**. A device for recording information, which showed the measure plus what was being measured.

TAO Report   see **GAMMA**

Technological determinism   The argument that the major causal influence in society is technology. c.f. **Cultural determinism**   The argument that the major causal influence in society is culture.

Technophile   A person who emphasizes the opportunities offered by technology. c.f. **Technophobe** A person who emphasizes the threats posed by technology.

Technophobe   see **technophile**

Technosphere   see **Triad Model, Observer effect**

Telematique Scenario   see **Privatique Scenario**

Tetrad   A tool for exploring the impact of any new technology. It consists of a system of four questions you should ask of each such technology (Marshall & Eric McLuhan).

Theory of evolution   The theory that species evolved through the survival of the fittest - that is, of the members of the species who best "fitted" their environment (Charles Darwin). The basic principle of the theory is **natural selection** - organisms with a fitter characteristic will be better represented in the next generation. c.f. **Social Darwinism**   The use of the theory of evolution as a rationale (rationalization?) for certain social policies (Francis Galton).

Think Tank   A programme for the Macintosh computer. It permits a shift in focus from the sequential presentation of language (word-processing) to the underlying hierarchical structure of thought (idea-processing). A later version which contains more bells and whistles is called **More**.

Three Interfaces of Negroponte   Diagram representing the argument by Nicholas Negroponte that the informatics industry, the print industry, and the image industry would converge into one huge industry.

Token   see **Tally**

Toronto School   A group of scholars - Harold Innis, Marshall McLuhan, and various current *"new McLuhans"* - who argue that media are best understood as extensions of the person.

Total reinforcement   A situation in which every response is rewarded. c.f. **Partial reinforcement** - a situation in which only some responses are rewarded. Schedules of reinforcement can be a function of time - e.g. a pellet every ten seconds (**interval schedule**) or of responses - e.g. a pellet after every ten responses (**ratio schedule**). Interval and ratio schedules can be every ten seconds or every ten responses (**fixed schedule**) or, on the average, every ten seconds or every ten responses (**variable schedule**).

TOTE unit   The basic unit of the planning function (Miller, Galanter, and Pribram). Discrepancy between a desired state and a current state is removed by a feedback loop involved TEST-OPERATE-TEST-EXIT.

Transmitted information   Overlap between information transmitted by the source and information received by the destination.   c. f. **Noise** Information received by the destination but not transmitted by the source.   **Equivocation** Information transmitted by the source but not received by the destination.

Transportation-telecommunication trade-off (TTT)   Trading in you car for a computer, so that you can stay home and acquire information electronically rather than driving around to acquire it physically.

Transaction Theory of Communication   see **Transportation Theory of Communication**

Transformation Theory of Communication   see **Transportation Theory of Communication**

Transportation Theory of Communication   Information is transported from source to destination. Emphasis on input information, behavioristic concept of person. c. f. **Transformation Theory of Communication**   Information is transformed at the destination as a function of the information already stored there. Emphasis on stored information, humanistic concept of the person. **Transaction Theory of Communication**   Actions of destination provide fedback information which determines how input and stored information is processed. Emphasis on fedback information, interactionist concept of the person.

Triad Model   A model in which the person is represented as the triple overlap of three spheres - **ecosphere** (the natural world), **sociosphere** (the social world), and **technosphere** (the person-made world). Those are the domains, respectively, of the natural science, the social sciences, and the "sciences of the artificial" (Herbert Simon).

Trial-and-Error Learning   see **Classical Conditioning**

Turing Machine   An infinite loop of squares, containing either 0 or 1, passing through a device which can either change or retain that symbol. Such a machine can solve any problem which can be clearly stated (Alan Turing).

Turing Test   You are sitting at a terminal linked to another terminal which you can't see. If, by interacting with that other terminal, you can't tell whether it is operated by a person or a machine, then the machine has passed the Turing Test (Alan Turing).

Uncertainty   see **bit**

Unconditioned stimulus   see **Classical Conditioning**

Unconditioned reflex   see **Classical Conditioning**

User interface   The relationship between a person and a machine. Early computers were characterized by a **MACHO interface**, since they were used largely by engineers who were comfortable with technology and technological language. As the use of computers spread beyond this select group, it was necessary for the computer to present a more friendly interface. The **WIMP** (window-icon-mouse-pulldownmenu) **interface** wiped out the MACHO interface. It is based on the user illusion that the person is working on documents stored in folders sitting on a desktop.

Utopia   see **Dystopia**

Vampire Effect   The fact that we tend to remember video information more than audio information when presented by both simultaneously, as in television.

Variable schedule   see **Total reinforcement**

Verbal behavior   Behavior rewarded through the mediation of other people (B. F. Skinner). There are three mechanisms for the acquisition of verbal behavior:
- **Echoic response**   The child is rewarded for imitating an adult,
- **Tact**   The child names an object in the presence of that object and is given the object (con**tact**),
- **Mand**   The child names the satisfier of a need when experiencing the need and is given the satisfier of the need (de**mand**).

Videotext   A hybrid telephone-television system proposed in the 1980s. Every industrialized country was championing its version - Canada the Telidon system, France the Minitel system, and so on. An early precursor of the internet, it was rendered redundant when the internet emerged.

Virtual Village   A virtual version of a village containing information about the village as an integrated and interactive database. Users will learn about the real village by exploring the virtual village. It is a prototype of the major tools used in an inside-out educational system.

Visual cliff   An apparatus designed to study depth perception in young organisms. It consisted of a glass-topped table with a wooden plank across the middle. One side was designed to look deep (hence "visual" cliff). Young organisms invariably chose the shallow side, demonstrating that they could perceive depth.

Visual field   The snapshot of the world seen by a person at any moment. It could be considered as the "*still*" in the **mind movie**.

Wallace Paradox   The fact that the theory of evolution can explain only how we got to a hunter-gatherer society. It can't explain how we managed the transitions from hunter-gatherer to agricultural, industrial, and now information societies over historical time. Evolution moves too slowly to explain such "sudden" changes (Alfred Russel Wallace).

Wearcomp   Computing technology which is worn rather than simply carried.

WIMP interface   see **User interface**

Xanadu Project   One vision of the future of the internet in which the money which users pay for information is distributed to the creators of this information (Ted Nelson).

Zeitgeist   German for the spirit of the times. The times seem to be ripe for a particular invention, as evidenced by the fact that inventions are often invented simultaneously by two or more people.

Zoopraxiscope   A device consisting of a wheel containing 24 images which when spun presented those images in turn through a gap, creating an illusion of motion. This was the precursor of the movie camera (Edward Muybridge).

REFERENCES

AMOS

William Amos
The Originals: Who's Really Who in Fiction
London: Jonathan Cape, 1985

ANDERSON

Martin Anderson
Impostors in the Temple
New York: Simon & Schuster, 1992

AUEL

Jean Auel
The Clan of the Cave Bear
New York: Crown, 1980

AUF DER
MAUR

Nick Auf der Maur (Edited by David Bist)
Nick: A Montreal Life
Montreal: Véhicule Press, 1998

BARDINI

Thierry Bardini
Bootstrapping:
Douglas Engelbart, Coevolution, and the
Origins of Personal Computing
Stanford, California: Stanford University Press,
2000

BARKOW
ET AL

Jerome H. Barkow, Leda Cosmides & John
Tooby (Editors)
The Adapted Mind: Evolutionary Psychology
and the Generation of Culture
New York: Oxford University Press, 1992

BARTHES

Roland Barthes
Mythologies
London: Paladin, 1973

BAYERS

Chip Bayers
The inner Bazos
Wired, March 1998, Volume 7.03,
Pages 114-121, 172-175, 186-187

BECKER

Ernest Becker
The Denial of Death
New York: Free Press, 1973

BENYUS

Janine Benyus
Biomimicry: Innovation Inspired by Nature
New York: William Morrow, 1998

BERELSON &
STEINER

Bernard Berelson & Gary Steiner
Human Behavior:
An Inventory of Scientific Findings
New York: Harcourt, Brace & World, 1964

BLOOM A

Allan Bloom
The Closing of the American Mind
New York: Simon & Schuster, 1987

BLOOM H

Harold Bloom
Global Brain: The Evolution of Mass Mind
from the Big Bang to the 21st Century
New York: John Wiley, 2003

BOLTER

Jay David Bolter
Writing Space: The Computer, Hypertext, and
the History of Writing
Hillsdale, New Jersey: Lawrence Erlbaum,
1991

BOYLE

T. C. Boyle
Drop City
New York: Penguin, 2004

BRAND

Stewart Brand
The Media Lab: Inventing the Future at MIT
New York: Viking, 1987

BRANDT

Willy Brandt
North-South: A Programme for Survival
Saint-Amand, France: Editions Gaillimard, 1980

BRANTLINGER   Patrick Bratlinger
Bread and Circuses:
Theories of Mass Culture as Social Decay
Ithaca: Cornell University Press, 1983

BRANWYN   Gareth Branwyn
The desire to be wired
Wired, September/October 1993, Pages 62-65,
113

BROCKMAN   John Brockman (Editor)
Digerati: Encounters with the Cyber Elite
San Francisco: HardWired, 1996

BRUNER   Jerome T. Bruner
Child's Talk
New York: W. W. Norton, 1988

BRYSON   Bill Bryson
Made in America: An Informal History of the
English Language in the United States
New York: William Morrow, 1994

BUCKE   Richard Maurice Bucke
Cosmic Consciousness
New York: W. P. Dutton, 1991

BUSH   Vannevar Bush
As we may think
Atlantic Monthly, 176 (1), Pages 641-649

CAHILL   Thomas Cahill
How the Irish Saved Civilization: The Untold
Story of Ireland's Heroic Role from the Fall
of Rome to the Rise of Medieval Europe
New York: Doubleday, 1995

CALVIN

William H. Calvin
A Brief History of the Mind:
From Apes to Intellect and Beyond
Oxford: Oxford University Press, 2004

CANADIAN
TRANSPORT-
ATION

Canadian Transportation
C. P. R. machine processes paper work
Canadian Transportation, September 1955,
Pages 475-476

CHATWIN

Bruce Chatwin
The Songlines
New York: Viking Penguin, 1987

CHIN-CHUAN

Lee Chin-Chuan
Media Imperialism Reconsidered:
The Homogenization of Television Culture
Beverly Hills, California: Sage, 1981

CHOMSKY 1959

Noam Chomsky
Review of B. F. Skinner "Verbal Behavior"
Language, 1959, 35, Pages 26-58

CHOMSKY 1966

Noam Chomsky
Cartesian Linguistics
New York: Harper & Row, 1966

CLARK

Andy Clark
Natural-born Cyborgs: Why Minds and
Technologies are Made to Merge
Oxford: Oxford University Press, 2003

CLARKE

Arthur C. Clarke
How the World was One:
Beyond the Global Village
New York: Bantam, 1992

COHEN

Adam Cohen
The Perfect Store: Inside eBay
San Francisco: Back Bay Books, 2003

CRICHTON

Michael Crichton
Prey
New York: HarperCollins, 2002

CROSARIOL

Beppi Crosariol
Killer App is e-mail
The Globe & Mail, 28 June 1997, Pages C1, C8

CROWLEY &
HEYER

David Crowley & Paul Heyer (Editors)
Communication in History: Technology,
Culture, Society (Third Edition)
New York: Longman, 1999

DAMER

Bruce Damer
Avatars!: Exploring and Building Virtual
Worlds on the Internet
Berkeley, California: Peachpit Press, 1998

DARWIN

Charles Darwin
On the Origin of Species
London: John Murray, 1859

DE CHARDIN

Pierre Teilhard de Chardin
The Phenomenon of Man
New York: Perennial, 1976

DE KERCK-
HOVE 1995

Derrick de Kerckhove
The Skin of Culture:
Investigating the New Electronic Reality
Toronto: Somerville House, 1995

DE KERCK-
HOVE 1997

Derrick de Kerckhove
Connected Intelligence:
The Arrival of the Web Society
Toronto: Somerville House, 1997

DE SOTO

Hernando De Soto
The Mystery of Capital:
Why Capitalism Triumphs in the West and
Fails Everywhere Else
New York: Basic Books, 2003

DEACON

Terrence W. Deacon
The Symbolic Species:
The Co-evolution of Language and the Brain
New York: W. W. Norton, 1997

DEGLER

Carl N. Degler
In Search of Human Nature:
The Decline and Revival of Darwinism in
American Social Thought
New York: Oxford University Press, 1991

DENNETT 1987

Daniel C. Dennett
Consciousness
in GREGORY, Pages 160-164

DESMOND &
MOORE

Adrian Desmond & James Moore
Darwin: The Life of a Tormented Evolutionist
New York: W. W. Norton, 1991

DEWDNEY

Christopher Dewdney
Last Flesh: Life in the Transhuman Era
Toronto: HarperCollins, 1998

DIAMOND

Jared Diamond
Guns, Germs, and Steel: The Fates of Human
Societies
New York: W. W. Norton, 1999

DIXON

N. F. Dixon
Subliminal perception
in GREGORY, Pages 752-755

DONALD

Merlin Donald
A Mind So Rare:
The Evolution of Human Consciousness
New York: W. W. Norton, 2001

DREXLER

K. Eric Drexler
Engines of Creation
New York: Doubleday, 1986

DUKE

Alex Duke
Importing Oxbridge:
English Residential Colleges and American
Universities
New Haven: Yale University Press, 1996

DUNBAR

Robin Dunbar
Grooming, Gossip, and the Evolution of
Language
London: Faber & Faber, 1996

EHRENREICH

Barbara Ehrenreich
Nickel and Dimed:
On (Not) Getting By in America
New York: Henry Holt, 2001

ELLUL

Jacques Ellul
The Technological Society
New York: Knopf, 1964

FERRARINI

Elizabeth Ferrarini
Confessions of an Infomaniac
Berkeley: Sybex, 1984

FERRAROTTI

Franco Ferrarotti
The End of Conversation: The Impact of Mass
Media on Modern Society
New York: Greenwood Press, 1988

FESTINGER   Leon Festinger, H. W. Reicken & Stanley
ET AL   Schachter
                   When Prophecy Fails
                   Minneapolis: Minnesota University Press, 1956

FEYNMAN   Richard P. Feynman
                   There's plenty of room at the bottom
                   Engineering and Science, Volume 23 (1960), Page 22

FISHER &   David E. Fisher & Marshall Jon Fisher
FISHER   **Tube: The Invention of Television**
                   San Diego: Harcourt, Brace, 1997

FJERMEDAL   Grant Fjermedal
                   **The Tomorrow-Makers: A Brave New
                   World of Living-Brain Machines**
                   New York: Macmillan, 1986

FLANAGAN   Owen J. Flanagan
                   The Science of the Mind (Second Edition)
                   Cambridge, Massachusetts: MIT Press, 1991

FORSTER   E. M. Forster
                   (Edited by David Leavitt & Mark Mitchell)
                   The Machine Stops
                   in **Selected Stories of E. M. Forster**
                   New York: Penguin, 2001, Pages 91-123

FUKUYAMA   Francis Fukuyama
1992   **The End of History and the Last Man**
                   New York: Free Press, 1992

FUKUYAMA   Francis Fukuyama
2003   **Our Posthuman Future: Consequences of
                   the Biotechnology Revolution**
                   New York: Picador, 2003

FULLER   R. Buckminster Fuller
                   Utopia or Oblivion
                   New York: Bantam, 1969

GALTUNG

Johan Galtung
Towards Self-reliance and Global Interdependence
Ottawa: Department of Environment, 1978

GARDINER 1970

W. Lambert Gardiner
Psychology: A Story of a Search
Monterey, California: Brooks/Cole, 1970, 1973

GARDINER 1973

W. Lambert Gardiner
An Invitation to Cognitive Psychology
Monterey, California: Brooks/Cole, 1973

GARDINER 1980

W. Lambert Gardiner
The Psychology of Teaching
Monterey, California: Brooks/Cole, 1980

GARDINER 1987

W. Lambert Gardiner
The Ubiquitous Chip:
The Human Impact of Electronic Technology
Hudson Heights, Quebec: Scot & Siliclone, 1987

GARDINER 1997

W. Lambert Gardiner
What kind of cyborg do you plan to be?
in George E. Lasker (Editor).
Advances in Sociocybernetics and Human Development
Volume IV. Proceedings of the Ninth International Conference on Systems Research, Informatics and Cybernetics, in Baden Baden, Germany on 18-23 August, 1997, Pages 108-115

GARDINER 2002

W. Lambert Gardiner
A History of Media
Victoria, B. C.: Trafford, 2002

GARDINER 2005

W. Lambert Gardiner
Turning Teaching Inside-Out
(in preparation)

GATES

Bill Gates
(with Nathan Myhrvold & Peter Rinearson)
The Road Ahead
New York: Penguin, 1995

GIBSON E &
WALK R

E. J. Gibson & R. D. Walk
The "Visual Cliff"
Scientific American, 1960, 202(4), Pages 64-71

GIBSON W
1984

William Gibson
Neuromancer
New York: Ace, 1984

GIBSON W
1987

William Gibson
Count Zero
New York: Ace, 1987

GIBSON W
1988

William Gibson
Mona Lisa Overdrive
New York: Bantam, 1988

GIBSON W
2003

William Gibson
Pattern Recognition
New York: Berkley Books, 2003

GIBSON W &
STERLING B

William Gibson & Bruce Sterling
The Difference Engine
London: Victor Gollancz, 1990

GIGANTES

Philippe Gigantes
Power and Greed:
A Short History of the World
New York: Carroll & Graf, 2002

GLEICK

James Gleick
Faster:
The Acceleration of Just About Everything
New York: Vintage, 2000

GLOVER

Jonathan Glover
Humanity:
A Moral History of the Twentieth Century
London: Random House, 2001

GODFREY &
PARKHILL

David Godfrey & Douglas Parkhill (Editors)
Gutenberg Two:
The New Electronics and Social Change
(Second Edition, Revised)
Victoria, B. C.: Press Porcépic, 1980

GOLDSTEIN

Tom Goldstein (Editor)
Killing the Messenger:
100 Years of Media Criticism
New York: Columbia University Press, 1989

GRAY

Chris Hables Gray (Editor)
The Cyborg Handbook
London: Routledge, 1995

GREGORY

Richard Gregory (Editor)
The Oxford Companion to the Mind
Oxford: Oxford University Press, 1987

GROSSMAN

Lev Grossman
Meet the Chipsons
Time, 11 March 2002, Pages 44-45

HARAWAY

Donna J. Haraway
Simians, Cyborgs, and Women:
The Reinvention of Nature
London: Routledge, 1991

HARPERS

Harper's Magazine
Camille Paglia & Neil Postman: She wants her TV!
He wants his book!
Harper's Magazine, March 1991, Pages 44-55
(reprinted in CROWLEY & HEYER, Pages 288-
300)

HAWKING   Stephen W. Hawking
                   A Brief History of Time
                   New York: Bantam, 1998

HAYLES   Katherine N. Hayles
                   **How We Became Post-human: Virtual Bodies
                   in Cybernetics, Literature, and Informatics**
                   Chicago: University of Chicago Press, 1999

HELSEL &   Sandra K. Helsel & Judith Paris Roth (Editors)
ROTH   **Virtual Reality: Theory, Practice, and Promise**
                   Westport, Connecticut: Meckler, 1991

HOCKETT   Charles F. Hockett
                   Animal "languages" and human language
                   Human Biology, 1959, 31, Pages 32-39

HOMER-DIXON   Thomas Homer-Dixon
                   The Ingenuity Gap
                   Toronto: Random House of Canada, 2001

HONORE   Carl Honore
1992   *The man behind the smile*
                   The Globe & Mail, 28 December 1992, Page
                   A13

HONORE   Carl Honore
2004   **In Praise of Slow: How a Worldwide
                   Movement is Challenging the Cult of Speed**
                   Toronto: Knopf Canada, 2004

HORN   Stacey Horn
                   **Cyberville: Clicks, Culture and the Creation
                   of an Online Town**
                   New York: Warner, 1998

HUXLEY 1932   Aldous Huxley
                   Brave New World
                   New York: Perennial, 1998 (1932)

HUXLEY 1962

Aldous Huxley
Island
New York: Perrenial, 2002 (1962)

ILLICH

Ivan Illich
De-Schooling Society
New York: Harper & Row, 1971

IMMEN

Wallace Immen
Morse tapped out
The Globe and Mail, 2 February 1999, Page
A9

INGRAM 1992

Jay Ingram
**Talk, Talk, Talk: An Investigation into the
Mystery of Speech**
Toronto: Viking, 1992

INGRAM 1998

Jay Ingram
**The Barmaid's Brain: and Other Strange Tales
from Science**
Toronto: Viking, 1998

INNIS 1950

Harold A. Innis
Empire and Communication
Oxford: Oxford University Press, 1950

INNIS 1951

Harold A. Innis
The Bias of Communication
Toronto: University of Toronto Press, 1951

IRVING

John Irving
My Movie Business: A Memoir
Toronto: Alfred A Knopf, 1999

IRWIN

William Irwin (Editor)
**The Matrix and Philosophy:
Welcome to the Desert of the Real**
Chicago: Open Court, 2002

JOURNAL OF
COMMUNIC-
ATION

Journal of Communication
Ferment in the Field
Journal of Communication, 33 (3), Summer
1983

JUNG

Carl Gustav Jung
Memories, Dreams, Reflections
New York: Vintage, 1989

JUSTER

Robert Juster
The virtual hereafter
VIA Magazine, November 1999, Pages 43-44

KANE

Margaret Kane
The next portal killer app
ZDNet Tech News, 7 September 1999

KAPLAN

Robert Kaplan
The Nothing That Is:
A Natural History of Zero
New York: Oxford University Press, 1999

KELLY

Kevin Kelly
Out of Control: The New Biology of Mach-
ines, Social Systems, and the Economic World
Reading, Massachusetts: Addison-Wesley, 1994

KIMBALL

Roger Kimball
Tenured Radicals: How Politics Has
Corrupted Our Higher Education
New York: Harper & Row, 1990

KINGSBURY

Donald Kingsbury
Psychohistorical Crisis
New York: Tom Doherty Associates, 2001

KLEIN

Naomi Klein
No Logo: Taking Aim at the Brand Bullies
New York: Picador, 2000

KOESTLER

Arthur Koestler
The Act of Creation
London: Hutchinson, 1964

KROKER 1984

Arthur Kroker
Technology and the Canadian Mind:
Innis, McLuhan, Grant
Montreal: New World Perspectives, 1984

KROKER 1993

Arthur Kroker
Spasm: Virtual Reality, Android Music,
Electric Flesh
New York: St. Martin's Press, 1993

KROKER &
WEINSTEIN

Arthur Kroker & Michael A. Weinstein
Data Trash: The Theory of the Virtual Class
Montreal: New World Perspectives, 1994

KRUEGER

Myron W. Krueger
Artificial Reality 2 (Second Edition)
New York: Addison-Wesley, 1998

KURZWEIL

Ray Kurzweil
The Age of Spiritual Machines: When
Computers Exceed Human Intelligence
New York: Penguin, 1999

LAMBERT

Wallace E. Lambert
Bilingualism and language acquisition
Annals of the New York Academy of Sciences,
December 1981, 379, Pages 9-22

LASHLEY

Kurt S. Lashley
Mass action in cerebral function
Science, 1931, 73, Pages 245-254

LASN

Kalle Lasn
Culture Jam: The Uncooling of America [tm]
Vancouver: Eagle Brook, 1999

LAUREL

Brenda Laurel
Computers as Theater
New York: Addison-Wesley, 1993

LEVINSON 1997

Paul Levinson
The Soft Edge: A Natural History and Future of the Information Revolution
London: Routledge, 1997

LEVINSON 1999

Paul Levinson
Digital McLuhan:
A Guide to the Information Millennium
London: Routledge, 1999

LEVY

Steven Levy
Hackers: Heroes of the Computer Revolution
New York: Dell, 1984

LOGAN 1986

Robert K. Logan
The Alphabet Effect: The Impact of the Phonetic Alphabet on the Development of Western Civilization
New York: St. Martin's Press, 1986

LOGAN 1995

Robert K. Logan
The Fifth Language:
Learning a Living in the Computer Age
Toronto: Stoddart, 1995

LOGAN 2000

Robert K. Logan
The Sixth Language:
Learning a Living in the Internet Age
Toronto: Stoddart, 2000

LORENZ

Konrad Lorenz
On Aggression
New York: Harcourt Brace Jovanovitch, 1966

LOVELOCK

James Lovelock
Gaia: A New Look at Life on Earth
(Third Edition)
Oxford: Oxford University Press, 2000

MADDI & COSTI

S. R. Maddi & P. T. Costi
Humanism in Personology:
Allport, Maslow, and Murphy
Chicago: Aldine, 1972

MADDOX

Brenda Maddox
Rosalind Franklin: The Dark Lady of DNA
New York: HarperCollins, 2002

MANGUEL

Alberto Manguel
A History of Reading
Toronto: Alfred A. Knopf Canada, 1996

MANN &
NIEDZVIECKI

Steve Mann & Hal Niedzviecki
Cyborg: Digital Destiny and Human Possib-
ilities in the Age of the Wearable Computer
Toronto: Doubleday Canada, 2001

MARCHAND M

Michel Marchand
The Minitel Saga: A French Success Story
Paris: Larousse, 1988

MARCHAND P

Philip Marchand
Marshall McLuhan:
The Medium and the Messenger
Toronto: Random House, 1989

MARCUS

Gary Marcus
The Birth of the Mind:
How a Tiny Number of Genes Creates the
Complexities of Human Thought
New York: Basic Books, 2003

MASLOW

Abraham H. Maslow
Toward a Psychology of Being
(Second Edition)
Princeton, New Jersey: Van Nostrand, 1968

MAYR

Ernst Mayr
Toward a New Philosophy of Biology:
Observations of an Evolutionist
Cambridge, Massachusetts: Harvard
University Press, 1988

MAZLICH

Bruce Mazlich
The Fourth Discontinuity:
The Co-evolution of Humans and Machines
New Haven, Connecticut: Yale University
Press, 1993

MCCLOUD
1993

Scott McCloud
Understanding Comics: The Invisible Art
New York: HarperCollins, 1993

MCCLOUD
2000

Scott McCloud
Reinventing Comics
New York: HarperCollins, 2000

MCCONNELL

James V. McConnell
Memory transfer through cannibalism in
planarians
Journal of Neuropsychiatry, 3, Supplement 1 -
August 1962, Pages 42-48

MCLUHAN E

Eric McLuhan
Electric Language:
Understanding the Message
Toronto: Buzz Books, 1998

MCLUHAN M

Marshall McLuhan
Understanding Media: The Extensions of Man
New York: McGraw-Hill, 1964

MCLUHAN M & MCLUHAN E	Marshall McLuhan & Eric McLuhan **Laws of Media: The New Science** Toronto: University of Toronto Press, 1988
MCLUHAN & NEVITT	Marshall McLuhan & Barrington Nevitt Meaning medium message **Communication** 1(1974), Pages 27-33
MCPHAIL	Thomas L., McPhail **Electronic Colonialism: The Future of Inter- national Broadcasting and Communication** Beverly Hills, California: Sage Library of Social Research 126, 1981
MEAD	Margaret Mead **Culture and Commitment: The New Relationships Between the Generations in the 1970s** (Revised and Updated) New York: Columbia University Press, 1978
MEADOWS ET AL	Donella H. Meadows, Dennis L. Meadows, Jorgen Randers & William W. Behrens 111 **The Limits to Growth** New York: New American Library, 1972
MILES	Rosalind Miles **The Women's History of the World** London: HarperCollins, 1993
MILLER	George A. Miller *The magical number seven, plus or minus two: Some limits on our capacity for processing information* **Psychological Review**, 1956, 63, Pages 81-97
MILLER ET AL	George Miller, Eugene Galanter & Karl Pribram **Plans and the Structure of Behavior** New York: Holt, Rinehart & Winston, 1960

MITHEN

Steven Mithen
The Pre-History of the Mind: The Cognitive Origins of Art, Religion, and Science
London: Thames & Hudson, 1996

MOLINARO
ET AL

Matie Molinaro, Corinne McLuhan and William Toye (Editors)
Letters of Marshall McLuhan
Toronto: Oxford University Press, 1987

MOORE

Lynn Moore
Caught in a Web of online betting
Montreal Gazette, 10 June 2001, Pages A1, A6

MOTAVALLI

John Motavalli
Bamboozled at the Revolution: How Big Media Lost Billions in the Battle for the Internet
New York: Viking, 2002

MURRAY

Janet Horowitz Murray
**Hamlet on the Holodeck:
The Future of Narrative in Cyberspace**
Cambridge, Mass.: MIT Press, 1997

MUYBRIDGE

Eadweard Muybridge
(Lewis L. Brown, Editor)
Animals in Motion
New York: Dover, 1957

NEGROPONTE

Nicholas Negroponte
Being Digital
New York: Random House, 1995

NELSON
1974

Ted Nelson
Dream Machines/Computer Lib
Self-published, 1974

NELSON
1983

Ted Nelson
Literary Machines
Self-published, 1983

NEWMAN

John Henry Newman
The Idea of the University
(Rethinking the Western Tradition)
New Haven, Connecticut:
Yale University Press, 1996

NIELSEN

Jakob Nielsen
Hypertext & Hypermedia
San Diego, California: Academic Press, 1990

NORRE-
TRANDERS

Tor Norretranders
The User Illusion: Cutting Consciousness
Down to Size
New York: Viking, 1998

ORWELL

George Orwell (afterword by Erich Fromm)
1984
New York: Signet, 1990 (1949)

PARKER

Barbara Parker
Aha!
Victoria, B. C.: Trafford, 2001

PASK &
CURRAN

Gordon Pask & Susan Curran
Microman: Computers and the Evolution of
Consciousness
New York: Macmillan, 1982

PAVLOV

Ivan Petravich Pavlov
(Edited & translated by G. V. Anrep)
Conditioned Reflexes: An Investigation of
the Physiological Activity of the Cerebral
Cortex
London: Oxford University Press, 1927

PENFIELD   W. Penfield & L. Roberts
& ROBERTS   **Speech and Brain Mechanisms**
                  Princeton: Princeton University Press, 1959

PERCY   Walker Percy
                  The Message in the Bottle
                  New York: Farrar, Strauss & Giroux, 1982

PHILLIPS   Kevin Phillips
                  Wealth and Democracy:
                  A Political History of the American Rich
                  New York: Random House, 2003

PIAGET   Jean Piaget
                  The Child and Reality:
                  Problems of Genetic Psychology
                  New York: Grossman, 1973

PICKNETT &   Lynn Picknett & Clive Prince
PRINCE   **Turin Shroud: In Whose Image? The Truth**
                   Behind the Centuries-Old Conspiracy of
                   Silence
                   Toronto: Stoddart, 1980

PILLER   Charles Piller
                  Dreamnet
                  Macworld, October 1994

PINKER 1997   Steven Pinker
                  How the Mind Works
                  New York: W. W. Norton, 1997

PINKER 1999   Steven Pinker
                  Words and Rules:
                  The Ingredients of Language
                  New York: Basic Books, 1999

PINKER 2002   Steven Pinker
                  The Blank Slate:
                  The Modern Denial of Human Nature
                  New York: Viking, 2002

PITTS

Gordon Pitts
Kings of Convergence
Toronto: Random House of Canada, 2002

POLLAN

Michael Pollan
The Botany of Desire:
A Plant's-eye View of the World
New York: Random House, 2001

POOLE

Ithiel de Sola Poole (Editor)
The Social Impact of the Telephone
Cambridge, Massachusetts: MIT Press, 1977

POSTMAN 1986

Neil Postman
Amusing Ourselves to Death: Public
Discourse in the Age of Show Business
New York: Viking, 1986

POSTMAN 1993

Neil Postman
Technopoly:
The Surrender of Culture to Technology
New York: Viking, 1993

POWE 1987

Bruce W. Powe
The Solitary Outlaw:
Trudeau, Lewis, Gould, Canelli, McLuhan
Toronto: Lester & Orpen Dennys, 1987

POWE 1993

Bruce W. Powe
A Tremendous Canada of Light
Toronto: Coach House, Press, 1993

POWE 1995

Bruce W. Powe
Outage: A Journey into Electric City
Toronto: Random House of Canada, 1995

PRIBRAM

Karl H. Pribram
Languages of the Brain: Experimental Para-
doxes and Principles in Neuropsychology
Monterey, California: Brooks/Cole, 1971

PRITCHARD
ET AL

R. M. Pritchard, W. Heron & D. O. Hebb
Vision with a stabilized retinal image
Canadian Journal of Psychology, 1960, 14,
Page 67

RASKIN

Jef Raskin
**The Humane Interface: New Directions for
Designing Interactive Systems**
Reading, Massachusetts: Addison-Wesley,
2000

READINGS

Bill Readings
The University in Ruins
Cambridge, Mass.: Harvard University Press,
1996

RHEINGOLD
1985

Howard Rheingold
**Tools for Thought: The People and Ideas
Behind the Next Computer Revolution.**
New York: Simon & Schuster, 1985

RHEINGOLD
1993

Howard Rheingold
**The Virtual Community:
Homesteading on the Electronic Frontier**
Reading, Massachusetts: Addison-Wesley,1993

RHEINGOLD
2003

Howard Rheingold
Smart Mobs: The Next Social Revolution
New York: Basic Books, 2003

RIDLEY

Matt Ridley
**Genome: The Autobiography of a Species in
23 Chapters**
New York: HarperCollins, 2000

ROBERTS

Monty Roberts
The Man Who Listens to Horses
Toronto: Alfred A. Knopf Canada, 1996

ROBINSON

Andrew Robinson
**The Story of Writing: Alphabets,
Hieroglyphs and Pictograms**
London: Thames & Hudson, 1995

ROGERS

Everett M. Rogers
**A History of Communication Theory:
A Biographical Approach**
New York: Free Press, 1994

RUCKER
ET AL

Rudy Rucker, R. U. Sirius & Queen Mu
Mondo 2000: A User's Guide to the New Edge
New York: HarperCollins, 1992

SAGAN

Carl Sagan
**The Dragons of Eden: Speculations on the
Evolution of Human Intelligence**
New York: Ballantine, 1977

SAYRE

Anne Sayre
Rosalind Franklin and DNA
New York: W. W. Norton, 2000 (1975)

SCHMANDT-
BESSERAT

Denise Schmandt-Besserat
Before Writing (Two Volumes)
Austin: University of Texas Press, 1992

SCHWARTZ J

Jeffrey H. Schwartz
**Sudden Origins: Fossils, Genes, and the
Emergence of Species**
New York: John Wiley and Sons, 1999

SCHWARTZ T

Tony Schwartz
The Responsive Chord
Garden City, New York: Doubleday, 1972

SERVAN-
SCHREIBER

Jean-Jacques Servan-Schreiber
The World Challenge
New York: Simon & Schuster, 1981

SHANNON & WEAVER	Claude Shannon & Warren Weaver **The Mathematical Theory of Communication** Urbana, Illinois: University of Illinois Press, 1949
SHELDRAKE	Rupert Sheldrake **The Sense of Being Stared At:** **And Other Aspects of the Extended Mind** New York: Crown, 2003
SHELLEY	Mary Shelley **Frankenstein or The Modern Prometheus** Oxford: Oxford University Press, 1969
SHENK	David Shenk **Data Smog: Surviving the Information Glut** New York: HarperCollins, 1997
SHLAIN	Leonard Shlain **The Alphabet versus the Goddess:** **The Conflict Between Word and Image** New York: Viking, 1999
SIEFE	Charles Siefe **Zero: The Biography of a Dangerous Idea** New York: Viking, 2000
SILVERMAN & EALS	Irwin Silverman and Marion Eals *Sex differences in spatial abilities: Evolutionary theory and data* in BARKOW ET AL, Pages 533-549
SIMON	Herbert A. Simon **The Sciences of the Artificial** Cambridge, Massachusetts: MIT Press, 1969
SKINNER	B. F. Skinner **Verbal Behavior** New York: Appleton-Century-Crofts, 1957

SMITH

Page Smith
Killing the Spirit
Viking Penguin, 1990

SNOW

C. P. Snow
The Two Cultures
Cambridge, England: Cambridge University
Press, 1993

SOMERVILLE

Margaret Somerville
The Ethical Canary:
Science, Society, and the Human Spirit
Toronto: Penguin Canada, 2003

SPANNER

Spanner
Integrated data processing officially opened
Spanner, April 1957, Pages 4-8, 18-20

STEPHENSON
1992

Neal Stephenson
Snow Crash
New York: Bantam, 1992

STEPHENSON
1999

Neal Stephenson
Cryptonomicon
New York: Avon, 1999

STOCK

Gregory Stock
Metaman: The Merging of Humans and
Machines into a Global Superorganism
New York: Doubleday, 1993

STONE

Alluquère Rosanne (Sandy) Stone
The War of Desire and Technology at the
Close of the Mechanical Age
Cambridge, Massachusetts: The MIT Press,
1995

TAPSCOTT

Don Tapscott
Growing Up Digital:
The Rise of the Net Generation
New York: McGraw-Hill, 1998

THOMPSON

William Irwin Thompson
At The Edge of History
New York: Harper & Row, 1971

THORNDIKE

Edward L. Thorndike
Animal Intelligence
New York: Macmillan, 1911

TOFFLER 1971

Alvin Toffler
Future Shock
New York: Bantam, 1971

TOFFLER 1990

Alvin Toffler
Power Shift: Knowledge, Wealth, and
Violence at the Edge of the 21st Century
New York: Bantam, 1990

TOOBY &
DE VORE

John Tooby & James de Vore
The reconstruction of hominid behavioral
evolution through strategic modeling.
in KINZEY, Pages 183 - 237

TOSCHES

Nick Tosches
In the Hand of Dante
Boston: Little, Brown, 2002

TOYNBEE

Arnold Joseph Toynbee
A Study of History (12 Volumes)
London: Oxford University Press, 1934-1954

TURING

Alan M. Turing
Computing machinery and intelligence
Mind, 1950, Volume 59, Pages 285-310

TURKLE 1984   Sherry Turkle
                       The Second Self:
                       Computers and the Human Spirit
                       New York: Simon & Schuster, 1984

TURKLE 1995   Sherry Turkle
                       Life on the Screen:
                       Identity in the Age of the Internet
                       New York: Simon & Schuster, 1995

VALASKAKIS G   Gail Valaskakis
                       Being Native in North America
                       New York: Harper Collins, 2004

VALASKAKIS K   Kimon Valaskakis
1979   *The information society: The issue and the choices*
                       Information Society Program
                       (Integrating Volume)
                       Montreal: GAMMA, 1979

VALASKAKIS K   Kimon Valaskakis
2001   *It's about world governance*
                       Globe and Mail, 19 April 2001, Page A13

VALASKAKIS K   Kimon Valaskakis, Peter S. Sindell, J. Graham
ET AL   Smith & Iris Fitzpatrick-Martin
                       The Conserver Society:
                       A Workable Alternative for the Future
                       New York: Harper & Row, 1979

VAN DOREN   Charles Van Doren
                       A History of Knowledge:
                       Past, Present, and Future
                       New York: Ballantine Books, 1991

VEBLEN   Thorstein Veblen
                       The Theory of the Leisure Class
                       New York: Penguin, 1994 (1899)

VON FRISCH
1950

Karl von Frisch
Bees: Their Vision, Chemical Senses, and Language
New York: Cornell University Press, 1950

VON FRISCH
1967

Karl von Frisch
The Dance Language and Orientation of Bees
Cambridge, Massachusetts: Harvard University Press, 1967

WALEY

Arthur Waley
Three Ways of Thought in Ancient China
Palo Alto, California: Stanford University Press, 1983

WARWICK

Kevin Warwick
I, Cyborg
London: Century, 2002

WATSON JA

James B. Watson
The Double Helix: A Personal Account of the Discovery of the Structure of DNA
New York: Touchstone, 2001

WATSON JO

John B. Watson
Behaviorism
Chicago: University of Chicago Press, 1924

WEISKRANTZ

Larry Weiskrantz
Consciousness Lost and Found
New York: Oxford University Press, 1997

WELLS

H. G. Wells
Outline of History (2 Volumes)
New York: Scholarly Press, 1974 (1920)

WHITE

Keith White
The Killer App
Utne Reader, September-October 1991, Pages 77-81

WILSON

Edward O. Wilson
Consilience: The Unity of Knowledge
New York: Knopf, 1998

WHOLE
EARTH
REVIEW

Is the body obsolete?
(Poll conducted by Mark O'Brien)
Whole Earth Review, 6 (1989), Page 36

WOLFRAM

Stephen Wolfram
A New Kind of Science
Champlain, Illinois: Wolfram Media, 2002

YEFFETH

Glenn Yeffeth (Editor)
Taking the Red Pill: Science, Philosophy, and Religion in The Matrix
Dallas, Texas: Ben Bella Books, 2003

YOUNG

J. Z. Young
Visual response of octopus to crabs and other figures before and after training
Journal of Experimental Biology, 1956, 33, Pages 709-729

INDEX